CW00927216

NEW PERSPECTIVES ON WELSH INDUSTRIAL HISTORY

NEW PERSPECTIVES ON WELSH INDUSTRIAL HISTORY

EDITED BY LOUISE MISKELL

UNIVERSITY OF WALES PRESS

© The Contributors, 2020

All rights reserved. No part of this book may be reproduced in any material form (including photocopying or storing it in any medium by electronic means and whether or not transiently or incidentally to some other use of this publication) without the written permission of the copyright owner except in accordance with the provisions of the Copyright, Designs and Patents Act 1988. Applications for the copyright owner's written permission to reproduce any part of this publication should be addressed to The University of Wales Press, University Registry, King Edward VII Avenue, Cardiff CF10 3NS

www.uwp.co.uk

British Library Cataloguing-in-Publication Data
A catalogue record for this book is available from the British Library.

ISBN 978-1-78683-500-0
e-ISBN 978-1-78683-501-7

The rights of The Contributors to be identified as authors of this work have been asserted in accordance with sections 77 and 79 of the Copyright, Designs and Patents Act 1988.

FSC www.fsc.org MIX Paper from responsible sources FSC® C013604

Typeset by Chris Bell, cb design
Printed and bound by CPI Group (UK) Ltd, Croydon, CR0 4YY

CONTENTS

ACKNOWLEDGEMENTS

THIS BOOK started its life at a workshop event held at the National Waterfront Museum in Swansea in June 2015. Participants ranged from senior academics to the authors of recently completed PhD theses. All shared a sense of commitment to the task of bringing together a volume that would reflect some of the recent directions in the historical study of industrial Wales. Papers delivered at the workshop, all based on new research, covered more than two centuries of Welsh history. A number of recurring themes emerged, including the global interconnectedness of Welsh industry; the complexity of identities and relations in the workplace; the need for a better understanding of the products and markets for Welsh goods; the relative absence of the employer and the company from the historical literature; and the important role of the State in the economic life of Wales, especially since 1945. While attempting to address some of these themes, part of the intention of this volume is to highlight these as areas ripe for further historical scholarship.

A number of debts have been incurred in the preparation of this book. The original workshop event was co-organised by Dr Steven Gray and was generously sponsored by the Economic History Society. In addition to the contributors to this volume, scholarly presentations and contributions to discussions on that day were also made by David Selway, Adam Godfrey and Daryl Leeworthy. Dr Steven Gray read and commented on drafts of all of the chapters, while Martin Johnes and

Sam Blaxland offered helpful comments on the volume introduction. Ongoing support and interest in this venture has also been forthcoming from Professor Huw Bowen and Professor Pat Hudson, whose work on copper and on the woollen industry, respectively, has helped open up new perspectives on industrial Wales.

LIST OF ABBREVIATIONS

AEU	Amalgamated Engineering Union
BA	Birmingham Archives
BISF	British Iron and Steel Federation
BNS	British Nylon Spinners
BOS	basic oxygen steelmaking
BoT	Board of Trade
BSC	British Steel Corporation
CCL	Cardiff Central Library
EEC	European Economic Community
FDI	foreign direct investment
GFS	Girls Friendly Society
GA	Gwent Archives
ICI	Imperial Chemical Industries
IDC	industrial development certificate
ISTC	Iron and Steel Trades Confederation (formerly BISAKTA: British Iron, Steel and Kindred Trades Association)
LG	Lucky Goldstar
LSE	London School of Economics
MIFERMA	*Société Anonyme des Mines de Fer de Mauritanie*
PP	Parliamentary Papers
RBA	Richard Burton Archives
SCOW	Steel Company of Wales

SRC	Shotton Record Centre
SWCA	*South Wales Coal Annual*
SWCC	South Wales Coalfield Collection
TNA	The National Archives
WDA	Welsh Development Agency
WET	*Welsh Economic Trends*
WINtech	Wales investment and technology
WINvest	Wales investment location
WMIE	Wales and Monmouthshire Industrial Estate Corporation
WMR	Warwick Modern Records

LIST OF TABLES AND FIGURES

TABLES

FIGURES

NOTES ON CONTRIBUTORS

Trevor Boyns is Professor of Accounting and Business history at Cardiff University. He has a long-standing interest in the history of the south Wales coalfield and has written a number of articles relating to various aspects thereof, most recently focused on the pre-First World War export trade. He has also published widely on the history of cost accounting and is the joint author of *A History of Management Accounting: The British Experience* (Routledge, 2013).

Ben Curtis is a historian of modern south Wales, the coal industry, industrial disability, and de/industrialisation. He is currently a research fellow at the University of Wolverhampton, working on the '"On Behalf of the People": Work, Community and Class in the British Coal Industry 1947–1994' project. He is the author of *The South Wales Miners, 1964–1985* (University of Wales Press, 2013), as well as numerous other academic journal articles and book chapters.

Chris Evans teaches history at the University of South Wales. Recent publications include '"Voyage iron": an Atlantic slave trade currency, its European origins, and West African impact', *Past & Present* (2018) (co-authored with Göran Rydén), and 'The plantation hoe: the rise and fall of an Atlantic commodity', *The William and Mary Quarterly* (2012).

Leon Gooberman is a lecturer in employment relations at Cardiff Business School, Cardiff University. His research interests include government intervention in the economy, the evolution of employer collective organisations, and deindustrialisation. His recent publications include *From Depression to Devolution: Economy and Government in Wales, 1934–2006* (University of Wales Press, 2017) and journal articles in *Business History*, *Contemporary British History* and *Urban History*.

Carys Howells is a teaching fellow in modern British history at the University of Warwick. She completed a PhD at Swansea University in 2015, her thesis focusing on the domestic service industry in south Wales between 1871 and 1921. Her research interests currently centre on the development of the domestic service and retail sectors in Britain.

Louise Miskell teaches history at Swansea University. She has researched and published widely on industrial towns in Victorian Britain and on the history of the copper and steel industries in Wales. She is currently researching the impact of the steel industry on urban Wales in the twentieth century.

Bleddyn Penny is a teacher at Fitzalan High School in Cardiff. He researches the history of working-class leisure, communities, politics and industrial relations in twentieth-century Britain. He completed his PhD thesis at Swansea University in 2016 on the social history of Port Talbot's steelworkers since the Second World War and has also published on industrial paternalism and employee leisure in postwar Ebbw Vale.

Steven Thompson is an historian of nineteenth- and twentieth-century Wales and Britain. His research interests include the history of health, social welfare and the labour movement. He was a co-investigator on the Wellcome Trust research project, 'Disability and Industrial Society: a Comparative History of British Coalfields, 1780–1948', and is editor of *Llafur*, the journal of the Welsh People's History Society.

INTRODUCTION

INDUSTRIAL WALES: HISTORICAL TRADITIONS AND APPROACHES

LOUISE MISKELL

In 1983 a colloquium on 'The Economic Development of South Wales 1780–1945', was held at Gregynog Hall in Montgomeryshire. The aim was to liberate economic history in Wales from 'an academic no man's land' and to provide 'an opportunity for economic historians rather than their social or political counterparts' to offer their interpretations of the industrial region of south Wales. Participants included scholars from departments of economics and history in the University of Wales and beyond. Their papers subsequently formed a volume of essays published in 1986.[1] It featured chapters on subjects familiar to readers of Welsh history, including the iron and coal industries, railways, shipping and canals, but with a focus on issues of capital formation, raw material supply and new technology, rather than with questions of worker-employer relations, social conditions and industrial disputes that were the more familiar stock of Welsh history by the early 1980s. It was a welcome endeavour, but a fleeting one. *Modern South Wales* was the last multi-authored collection of economic history essays on Wales to appear in print.[2]

The mid-1980s was a difficult period for economic history in Britain. Economic recession had hit heavy industry and manufacturing hard. Job losses and closures of coal mines, steelworks and car manufacturing plants across the country caused uncertainty about what future direction the UK economy would take. Meanwhile, higher education funding cuts saw falling numbers of students and degree schemes in the subject. Many of the departments of economic history that had been established in British universities in the 1960s were closed or merged and when occupants of economic history chairs retired, they were not replaced.[3] *History Today* ran an extended feature in February 1985 entitled 'What is Economic History?' in which seven eminent economic historians gave their assessments of the state of the discipline and its future.[4] Some blamed the rise of econometrics for making the subject less accessible to prospective students and the public at large. For others, however, economic history was fundamental to understanding human survival, and too important to be confined to the work of specialist departments. Its absorption into history departments simply demonstrated that it was now an accepted part of mainstream historical enquiry.

In Wales the discussion was different. Economic history had never occupied the status of a clear sub-field of Welsh history, with a dedicated journal or a regular forum for scholarly exchange. Reasons for this are not difficult to find. For some, the whole concept of Welsh economic history was problematic: industrialisation was a decidedly non-Welsh process, reliant on outside capital and responsible for the Anglicisation of large parts of Wales.[5] For others, there was neither the available data nor the evidence of a diversity of economic development throughout the whole of Wales to support the notion of a distinctive Welsh economy,[6] and, to some extent, research on different sectors of economic life, such as agriculture, business and finance or maritime trade, has been too sparse to suggest otherwise.[7] As one influential economic historian pointed out, the existence of primary industries alone was not enough to justify writing about a Welsh economy, separate from that of Britain as a whole.[8] This has had far-reaching implications for the kinds of questions and analyses historians of modern Wales have undertaken. As the editors of the *Modern South Wales* volume acknowledged: 'Much of the story of south Wales's economic past is to be found implicitly in studies and research that are essentially social or political history.'[9] County histories, general texts on the history of Wales and books on the politics and society of the south Wales coalfield often included analysis of aspects of Wales's economic past,[10] but this was usually subordinate to the examination of social questions, especially the study of industrial communities, their institutions and their traditions of protest. The growth of labour history, in particular, fostered this approach. It offered a way for Welsh historians to examine their industrial history by focusing on the distinctive social characteristics and traditions of industrial communities. It required little engagement with wider economic questions or with tricky debates over whether there was any such thing as a 'Welsh economy'. The dominance of labour history in Welsh historical writing in the postwar period has helped create a distinctive brand of 'industrial history' in Wales, in which economic questions have been of secondary importance to the study of social life. Yet it would be wrong to assume that Welsh economic history has no real history of its own. For some historians of Wales, economic questions have provided much more than just background noise. Before introducing the eight new essays offered in this volume, this introduction traces some of the traditions and influences that have shaped the history of industrial Wales. In doing so it aims to make the background noise of Welsh economic life a little more discernible.

The historical study of industrial Wales gained much of its early stimulus from developments in the discipline of economic history in England. The London School of Economics (LSE), founded in 1895, had a formative role to play in the careers of some of Wales's most influential scholars in the first half of the twentieth century. For medievalist William Rees (1887–1978), his period of study for a doctorate in social science there during the First World War was 'a turning point' in his academic career.[11] He conducted new archival research, bibliographic work and historical mapping at a time when few other historians of Wales were acquainted with such techniques, immersing himself in archival research at the Public Record Office. Rees had returned to take up a post in the Department of History in Cardiff by the time some of his contemporaries from the LSE were founding the Economic History Society and its journal, the *Economic History Review* in 1926.[12] His departure also predated the arrival of Brinley Thomas as lecturer there in 1931, fresh from his MA in economics at Aberystwyth and the publication in 1930 of his work on labour migration into the Glamorgan coalfield.[13] Rees's own most significant contribution to the economic history of Wales, *Industry Before the Industrial Revolution*, appeared much later, but raised some key questions about the timing and chronology of industrial development. Looking not just at Wales but at 'the western half of southern Britain', he argued that mining and metal smelting underwent technical advancement for at least two centuries earlier than the more readily acknowledged industrial revolution of the late eighteenth and early nineteenth century.[14]

William Rees and Brinley Thomas were two early pioneers in an otherwise sparsely populated field. Rees and his namesake, J. F. Rees (1883–1967), historian and newly appointed principal at Cardiff,[15] supplied the *Economic History Review* with a six-page bibliography of Welsh economic history for its second volume in 1930.[16] Compared to similar surveys of French and German economic history that had appeared in the first two issues of the new journal, the bibliography on Wales was thin and its authors were frank about the infancy of their subject. They acknowledged a clutch of new studies published in the 1920s by J. F. Rees himself, Ness Edwards and Evan J. Jones, but concluded that these were 'preliminary'.[17] Contemporary reviewers seemed to agree. The work by Bangor University economist Evan Jones, for example, was a volume of essays including chapters on woollens, non-ferrous metals, the iron industry, coal and shipping.[18] A critical review in *The Economic Journal* the following year highlighted its lack of engagement with theory and its too-ready acceptance of the conclusions of other writers.[19]

More innovative was the volume by A. H. Dodd, published in 1933, on *The Industrial Revolution in North Wales*.[20] By the time of the book's publication, Dodd was Professor of History at Bangor and part of a department that had the lion's share of Welsh history's 'energy, passion and discourse' in the decade and a half before 1945.[21] His interest in economic history had been piqued at the tutorial classes run by R. H. Tawney in Wrexham before the First World War as part of the collaborative venture between the University of Oxford and the Workers' Educational Association.[22] Dodd's work was a reaction to recent interpretations of the industrial revolution that were based on the study of the English textile industries.[23] These, Dodd insisted, were 'highly unrepresentative' and encouraged too narrow a chronological and geographical understanding of 'the wide diffusion of industrial enterprise'.[24] Like William Rees, he was an early example of a scholar of the economic history of Wales struggling to relate the Welsh experience to interpretations of the industrial revolution in Britain. His response was a wide-ranging survey of economic activity in north Wales from the seventeenth century onwards, which examined the social impact of economic change as well as patterns of industrial development. It was envisaged as a contribution to modern Welsh history as well as to debates on the industrial revolution.

It was not until 1950 that a counterpart volume of similar importance appeared on industrialisation in south Wales.[25] Its author, A. H. John, had completed much of the research for the book in the mid-1930s when he held the Rhondda Research Studentship at Cambridge, but the outbreak of war delayed publication.[26] John's study covered a narrower chronology than that of Dodd, but he adopted an outward-looking and innovative approach to his subject. In particular, the inclusion of a chapter on 'The markets of the coalfield' was a rare attempt by a historian of Wales to consider the reach and significance of the products of Welsh mines, ironworks and tinplate mills in a global economy. The inclusion of a set of statistical appendices along with population maps of the region also brought some much-needed quantitative data on Welsh economic development into the public domain. Significantly, an updated version of the volume by Dodd was reprinted the following year, and the two books were reviewed together in 1953 by a Canadian reviewer who concluded that they did not tell a happy story of Welsh economic life: 'Practically every chapter in Professor Dodd's book ends on a note of decline', he observed, while John's study revealed that south Wales, with its over-reliance on producer-goods industries, was 'subject to the vagaries of international markets' and 'constantly in danger of becoming a depressed area.'[27]

While the works of John and Dodd succeeded in putting Welsh economic history on the map, other historians of Wales were slow to follow in their footsteps. Two further publications to appear in the 1950s, both of which explored economic aspects of the south Wales coalfield, were Morris's and Williams's study of *The South Wales Coal Industry* and E. D. Lewis's *The Rhondda Valleys*, which appeared in print a year later.[28] Elsewhere, new research by R. O. Roberts on the early copper industry in the Swansea region was beginning to appear in local history journals and edited collections.[29] It meticulously pieced together the patterns of business partnership and capital underpinning Swansea's success as a non-ferrous smelting centre in the decades after 1720, but was probably less well known beyond Wales than it deserved to be. The same could not be said of Brinley Thomas's 1959 article, 'Wales and the Atlantic economy',[30] which was based on a detailed statistical analysis of the movement of people into the coalfield as well as emigration from Wales in the late nineteenth and early twentieth centuries. Thomas's contention that Wales experienced unusually low levels of rural emigration because the industrialisation of south Wales allowed it to absorb much of the migrant exodus from rural counties, and that this in turn strengthened Welsh cultural and linguistic traditions that were transplanted to the coalfield, caused much debate among both historians of migration and of Welsh identity.[31]

By the late 1950s, however, the study of industrial Wales extended well beyond the range of the few scholars who might have considered themselves economic historians. This widening scholarly engagement stemmed from the flowering of the social sciences in the postwar period. Newly established university departments such as the Department of Industrial Relations at Cardiff became the focus of ambitious research projects on industrialisation and its impact on contemporary society. There, in the late 1950s, an entire research team dedicated itself to examining the impact of the expansion of the steel industry on class and identity in the town of Port Talbot.[32] The early work of the Cardiff-based research team predated the better-known 'affluent worker' studies by Goldthorpe et. al. who attempted to understand the implications of rising worker affluence for class identity among car workers in Luton.[33] Principal researcher George F. Thomason went on to become professor and to develop the department as a key part of Cardiff's growing Faculty of Economic and Social Science.[34] Other groundbreaking research using survey and interviewing techniques was eliciting evidence of changing attitudes towards neighbourhood and community in Britain's postwar towns.[35] In the new Department of Sociology and Anthropology at Swansea, Chris Harris and Colin Rosser led a study of kinship and social change in Swansea.[36] Their colleagues in Geography, including Graham Humphrys and Rosemary Bromley, made a major physical as well as scholarly impact on the industrial region in the widely acclaimed Lower Swansea Valley Project, which mobilised town councillors, community groups and academics in a collaborative assault on the sites of contamination and dereliction left behind after the decline of metal smelting on the banks of the Tawe river.[37]

The rise of social sciences gave significant momentum to the growth of economic history as an independent discipline in British universities. The study of human economic development over time became a core part of the new 'science of society' pursued by anthropologists, sociologists and political economists as well as economic historians.[38] It was a boom time for economic history in Britain, with the number of chairs in the subject in British universities doubling as separate departments of Economic History were established across the country.[39] A. H. John was awarded a personal chair at LSE in 1965. At Swansea, William Alan (Max) Cole was appointed to the first chair of Economic History in the University of Wales, in 1966. Although the chair was established in a large faculty of Economic and Social Science that originally offered BSc Econ. degrees, Cole succeeded in establishing separate degree courses in both single- and joint-honours Economic History in response to high student demand. He later said of his early years at Swansea: 'we were soon bursting at the seams and new members of staff had to be appointed who provided a wider range of courses which in turn promoted a demand for opportunities for a greater degree of specialization in the subject.'[40]

There were some marked differences of scholarly outlook between economic historians and their counterparts in the history departments in Welsh universities. Max Cole, having made his name as co-author of an influential work on British economic growth,[41] was sceptical of recent trends in historical writing that emphasised the subjectivity of the historian and the slippery concept of historical fact.[42] His inaugural lecture at Swansea, entitled 'Economic History as a Social Science', identified attitudes towards objective knowledge as the key issue on which economic historians shared more with social science than other branches of historical study. He speculated that

> it may well be that one reason why economic history, alone among the different branches of historical study, is today establishing its position in the social science faculties of British universities, is that economic historians have been rather less inclined than some of their colleagues to indulge in the pessimism of the 'history teaches us nothing' school.[43]

In these circumstances, it would not have been surprising had a significant gulf opened up between economic history and history in Wales, but conflict of this kind never materialised.[44] Instead, the emerging landscape of historical scholarship provided fertile territory for alliances between the economic historians and an emerging generation of new 'Welsh historians'.

By the 1960s Welsh history was enjoying a boom of its own. The publication, in 1950, of David Williams's *A History of Modern Wales*, 'the first synthesis of modern Welsh history written by a professional historian on the basis of substantial archival research',[45] had set the bar for a new generation of historians. Its chapters on agrarian discontent and the social consequences of industrialisation, along with Williams's other studies of Chartist leader John Frost and of the Rebecca Riots[46] inspired a new generation of historians of modern Wales like Gwyn Williams and David J. V. Jones to investigate traditions of social protest in the rural and industrial communities of the nineteenth and twentieth centuries.[47] At the time of his death, one of David Williams's appreciative successors hailed him as 'quite literally a pioneer [after whom] the history of Wales could never be the same.'[48] Important as David Williams undoubtedly was, he did not shift the direction of Welsh history single-handedly. The growing influence of Marxist perspectives in the social sciences in Britain and the publication of compelling new works of socioeconomic history by E. P. Thompson, Eric Hobsbawm and others also struck a chord with historians of modern Wales.[49] The emergence of labour history as a sub-discipline in the early 1960s added further momentum. The contemporaneous launch of new, flagship journals in Welsh history and labour history in the same year seemed to symbolise the extent of their common endeavours.[50] Wales's industrial past, and the coalfield in particular, was ripe territory for the practice of 'history from below'. Questions of industrial output, capital and markets, of the kind that A. H. Dodd and Arthur John had begun to explore, were set aside in favour of inquiries about the working-class experience and the social lives of ordinary people. It seemed that the territory of industrial history in Wales had been claimed, decisively, by a new generation of labour historians.

In one sense, developments in Wales simply mirrored what was happening elsewhere in Britain. In the two decades after 1960, the rapidly expanding fields of social history and the social sciences encouraged greater specialisation by historians in sub-fields such as labour history, urban history, medical history and business history.[51] But given the relatively small pool of academic historians actively engaged in research on the Welsh past, estimated by one of their number to amount to 'a few dozen at most',[52] the dominance of labour history in Wales was more complete. It is not far-fetched to say that for a period from the late 1960s to the early 1980s, modern Welsh history was almost synonymous with labour history,[53] and practitioners generated a critical mass of studies about the industrial communities of Wales and their battles for decent wages and conditions of work.[54] The personnel of Llafur, the Welsh People's History Society, established in 1970, illustrated as much. Formed against a backdrop of pit closures and fears over the loss of the historical records of the coalfield, it drew on the full spectrum of Welsh historical talent, with David Williams as its first president, up-and-coming labour historians like Hywel Francis and Dai Smith on its committee, and an editorial panel that included economic historian L. J. Williams, and social historian Ieuan Gwynedd Jones.[55] Its journal, *Llafur*, became an important vehicle for research articles on the south Wales coalfield, its communities and institutions. Early issues of the journal marked anniversaries of the South Wales Miners' Federation and the General Strike.[56]

The emergence of a confident new, labour history-dominated, Welsh History 'brand' helped set the tone for relations between historical scholars and their social science-leaning counterparts in economic history. Individuals forged collaborations that bridged the dividing lines between departments, faculties and even institutions. At Aberystwyth it was historian David Williams who led a study group on 'the industrial revolution in Wales' in 1961, which highlighted the need for a publication bringing together various contributions on Welsh industrial history. But it was the chair of Economic History at Exeter, W. E. Minchinton, whose research interests ranged widely across the economic history and industrial archaeology of south Wales and the south-west of England, who edited the resulting volume of essays.[57] At Swansea there were similar collaborations between the department of History and the department of Economic History. There, a group of historians led by Glanmor Williams drew on the support of W. A. Cole to make a successful application for funding from the Social Science Research Council for a south Wales coalfield history project that aimed to preserve a written, audio and visual record of the coalfield and its communities.[58]

The South Wales Coalfield History Project exemplified the blurred boundaries between labour history and economic history in Wales in this period. The project threw much light on the Welsh economic experience, but did not identify itself as economic history. In its research methodologies, however, it owed much to the social sciences. The use of oral interviewing as an evidence-gathering technique, common in social science research but novel in a historical context, was used as a method of capturing the lived experiences of residents of the coalfield. One of the most important outcomes of the project was the development of a collection of audio recordings with some 176 subjects and running to 330 hours of taped conversations.[59] Later, the importance of the South Wales Miners' Library in Swansea, founded in 1973 to house the archival records of the coalfield, identified and collected as a result of the coalfield history project, was vigorously defended by Cole during the period of higher education funding cuts in the 1980s.[60]

Although in its day, the strength of the labour history tradition in Wales was broadly viewed as something to be celebrated and protected, its deep imprint on the kinds of historical questions being posed by Welsh historians and the type of history being written have given rise to more recent criticism. The *modus operandi* of both the coalfield history project and the Lower Swansea Valley Project before it, relied on close engagement with members of the public to deliver their respective agendas, and a similar 'beyond the academy' mission was also deeply embedded in the ethos of Llafur, whose intention was, 'to forge links between historians and the wider public.'[61] It was an approach that helped foster popular participation but which also, in the views of some, mitigated against engagement with some of the more challenging concepts and theories being debated in historical sub-disciplines elsewhere in Britain. For labour historians in Wales, this meant almost a complete disengagement with the postmodernist debates that dominated the discipline in the late twentieth century, but which represented 'a turn away from the popular.'[62]

The same concern for public accessibility may well have accounted for what L. J. Williams termed the 'anti-numerical' tradition of modern Welsh history 'which privileged the charting of human experience, social life and national identity in qualitative form'.[63] While the 'cliometrics revolution', 'i.e. research that combines economic theory, quantitative methods, hypothesis testing, counterfactual alternatives and traditional techniques of economic history',[64] was gaining ground elsewhere in Britain, Welsh scholars kept their distance. One author playfully suggested that Welsh history's avoidance of 'the "advanced technology" of the "new economic history" might be considered 'a blessing in disguise',[65] but there were far-reaching repercussions for economic history in Wales, not least in the lack of reliable quantitative data on Welsh industry. The main journals of Welsh history, L. J. Williams noted, 'contain only rare excursions into quantification', and as a whole the discipline was deprived of significant quantitative data for analysis, which was a major hindrance to the historical analysis of Welsh industrialisation.

Earlier attempts had been made by Williams's fellow economists in the University of Wales to supply statistical sources on the Welsh economy. In Cardiff, Anne Martin and J. Parry Lewis's statistical handbook, with a preface by Brinley Thomas, was published in 1953, while Williams's predecessor as Professor of Economics at Aberystwyth, E. T. Nevin, produced a volume of *The Social Accounts of the Welsh Economy* four years later.[66] But there remained a dearth of easily accessible historical statistics for Wales. Williams's contribution, the *Digest of Welsh Historical Statistics*, appeared in two volumes in 1985.[67] It was modelled on two earlier volumes of British historical statistics,[68] and it provided a comprehensive reference point for statistical data relating to Wales's industries as well as its people and places. A further volume of statistical data relating to the period from 1974 to 1996 appeared a decade later and was published online and in print form.[69] Most of the work for this project was undertaken while Williams was Professor of Economics at Aberystwyth, but as he made clear in his collection of reflective essays, published after his retirement, it was a mission that he considered to be unfinished. Colleagues elsewhere in the university at Aberystwyth took up the challenge. In 1996 Dennis Thomas, in the Business School, along with Dot Jones, produced an innovative data package and handbook on the post-1945 Welsh economy that included sixty-one statistical tables of socioeconomic indicators.[70] Although innovative in its time, the production of the work in the now obsolete 3.5 inch-disk format ironically ensured that its shelf-life was shorter than that of a conventional print publication.

Since the turn of the millennium, academic scholars have continued to probe new areas of analysis. In the late twentieth century, a number of historians embraced comparative approaches to bring new perspectives to Welsh economic development.[71] As was the case in the 1960s and 1970s, collaborative projects have continued to produce some of the best academic scholarship and the widest public engagement. The Disability and Industrial Society project, funded by the Wellcome Trust, investigated the impact of industrial society on the physically impaired. A core group of Welsh historians, together with academic colleagues in other former coalfield regions, used comparative, statistical and qualitative methods to uncover the experiences of the disabled in industrial communities and workplaces.[72] Elsewhere, funding from the Leverhulme Trust helped initiate a new international research network to investigate the global connections of the Swansea copper industry,[73] while support from the Economic and Social Research Council and Welsh Government enabled Swansea historians to build on the work of their Lower Swansea Valley Project predecessors, with a heritage-led regeneration project aimed at improving the visibility and interpretation of historic sites of copper smelting in the lower Swansea valley.[74] Developments at other heritage sites has helped to foster public interest in Wales's industrial past. The opening of a new museum to house the industrial and maritime collections of Amgueddfa Cymru/National Museum Wales in Swansea in 2004 and the ongoing popularity of Amgueddfa Cymru/National Museum Wales's other industrial museums at Big Pit and, to a lesser extent, the National Slate Museum and the National Wool Museum attests to the ongoing public appetite for industrial history.[75]

Interest in comparative history, the role of international academic collaborations, as well as the challenges of interpreting industrial heritage for new generations with little direct connection to the industries of Wales's past, have contributed to a shift away from labour history narratives of the Welsh industrial past. Recent research on industrial Wales has aimed to look beyond the working-class experience and the twin economic pillars of coal and iron, to uncover a more diverse picture of the Welsh industrial past, and one which connects what was happening in Wales more closely with the global economy.[76] The essays in this volume offer a snapshot of these new directions. Few, if any, of their authors could be categorised straightforwardly as either 'economic historians' or 'labour historians'. Instead their scholarship owes as much to the influences of business history, global history and gender history as it does to the labour history tradition. Their essays, collectively, offer some new perspectives on industrial Wales.

The first two essays in the collection, by Chris Evans on the copper industry and Trevor Boyns on the coal trade, adopt an outward-looking view of their subjects as they strive to situate the south Wales centres of these industries in an international framework of market demand, technological development and global economic conditions. The Welsh tradition of industrial history, much like that of Britain as a whole, has been better at documenting the supply side rather than the demand side, as studies have focused on charting the internal dynamics of industrial communities and workplaces, but, as Evans notes, a more 'panoramic' view can pay dividends. In the case of the copper industry, he reveals how embedded 'Swansea Copper' was in global economic developments from the late eighteenth century, such as the slaving economy of West Africa, the sugar refining industry in the Caribbean and in the building and fitting of naval and merchant fleets in Europe and America. In Trevor Boyns's chapter, the fundamental importance of Welsh coal to French industrialisation is revealed through a careful quantitative analysis of export destinations in the nineteenth and early twentieth centuries. These chapters begin to open a window on the economic impact of Welsh industry well beyond Wales.

In previous collections of essays on Welsh economic history, there has been a conspicuous absence of research by women scholars.[77] Moreover, despite the pioneering efforts of Dot Jones and Mari Williams, among others, to point out their vital contribution to Welsh industrial life, the economic activity of women in Wales remains underrepresented in the published literature.[78] Some of the best recent research on the economic activity of women in Wales is to be found in postgraduate theses, exploring a variety of economic sectors including the iron industry, retail and the service sector.[79] This volume brings some of this material into print for the first time with the inclusion of a chapter by Carys Howells on the domestic service sector in Wales. Howells offers a compelling case for viewing domestic service as an industry in its own right, with distinctive internal hierarchies, recruitment practices and patterns of supply and demand. Her observation that, in Wales, servants were almost as numerous as those employed in mining and quarrying in the last quarter of the nineteenth century underscores the point that this needs to be viewed as a mainstream, not a marginal part of Welsh economic life.

Another contribution based on research conducted for a PhD thesis[80] is Bleddyn Penny's examination of some three decades of industrial disputes in Port Talbot steelworks after 1945. On the face of it, of all of the chapters in the volume, Penny's contribution is the most closely aligned to the traditional interests of Welsh labour historians in the protest patterns of the industrial working classes, but it offers some direct challenges to that narrative. Penny shows that the frequent steelworker disputes in Wales's premier postwar steelworks were not, primarily, worker-versus-employer confrontations, but rather the product of deep divisions and rivalries between different groups of workers, raising fundamental questions about ideas of class identity and worker solidarity in the industrial workplace in postwar Wales. His chapter demonstrates the potential for research on the steelworker experience to change the way we view the industrial worker in Wales.

The absence of a comprehensive study of steel in Wales has been identified as a significant gap in our knowledge of Welsh industrial history,[81] and although this has yet to be filled, recent studies of Port Talbot and other Welsh steelworks offer some promising beginnings.[82] No apology is made, then, for the inclusion of two chapters on the Port Talbot steel industry in this volume. The chapter by Louise Miskell takes a very different perspective to that of Penny's study of industrial disputes, focusing instead on the challenges faced by the Steel Company of Wales to the globalisation of the industry after the Second World War. The company, formed in 1947, was one of the key success stories of the postwar economy in Wales, presiding over the construction of Europe's largest steelworks and expanding its production and labour force to meet the demands of the consumer boom of the 1950s. Yet, as output increased and competition from new steel-producing nations intensified, the need to source new supplies of iron ore tested the expertise and resources of SCOW and required the company to make significant investments in new facilities to remain competitive.

The approach adopted in the chapter by Miskell and its use of company records enables an employer-eye view of industrial development to emerge, of a kind that has featured little in in the analysis of Welsh industrial history.[83] It is a theme pursued further in this volume by Steven Thompson in his chapter on industrial welfare capitalism. Thompson offers an analysis of changing employer approaches to worker welfare over the course of the century before the Second World

War. Using the activities of G. T. Clark, manager of Dowlais Ironworks, W. T. Lewis, coalowner and prime mover in the Monmouthshire and South Wales Coalowners' Association, and Alfred Mond, proprietor of the eponymous nickelworks in Clydach in the Swansea valley, Thompson shows how approaches to worker welfare evolved from the paternalism of the mid-nineteenth century towards ideas of partnership and participation by the interwar years. His chapter uncovers some of the complex motives and ideals shaping employer attitudes towards their workers in industrial Wales, and cautions against any simple polarisation of employer/employee interests.

As well as playing its part in putting the employer and the company back into the history of industrial Wales, a key aim of this volume is to extend the chronology of that history in the postwar period. With a few notable exceptions, relatively little historical analysis of the Welsh industrial economy has extended to the period after the First World War, let alone the post-1945 era.[84] Minchinton, in the introduction to his 1969 edited collection, *Industrial South Wales*, divided the history of industrialisation in Wales into three phases: the first based on investment in the iron industry in the second half of the eighteenth century; the second focused on developments in the coal industry from 1850; and the third, a phase of economic diversification in the twentieth century with major developments on the south Wales coast. Crucially, the third of these phases was deemed to be 'beyond the scope' of the volume.[85] Williams and Baber, in their 1986 collection, adopted broadly the same chronology, with the bulk of chapters in their volume focused on the period from 1840 to1914. A section on 'The twentieth century' extended the analysis further, but not beyond 1945.

Until very recently, students and scholars of industrial Wales had precious few resources on which to base their interpretations of the Welsh economy in the postwar era. As the coal industry declined and employment levels in the steel sector contracted sharply, charting the impact of the erosion of Wales's traditional industries was left primarily to the social scientists,[86] while historians were, in the main, content to keep their gaze focused on the earlier era. Since 2010, the publication of new studies by Martin Johnes, Ben Curtis and Leon Gooberman has helped to change this.[87] The chapters in this volume by Gooberman and Curtis, and by Gooberman and Boyns, provide some important new insights into the place of manufacturing in the Welsh economy after the Second World War and the role of the state and its appointed agencies in attempting to steer the Welsh economy in new directions following the demise of its staple industries. In their analysis of Wales's short-lived 'age of the factories', Gooberman and Curtis trace the successes and failures of government-supported manufacturing ventures in south Wales through the life cycles of the Dunlop factory in Brynmawr and the British Nylon Spinners factory in Pontypool. As two of Wales's most iconic postwar factory premises, the rise and decline of these businesses epitomised both the ambition and the economic realities of the era. In the final chapter of the volume, Gooberman and Boyns offer an evaluation of the impact of the high level of state intervention in the Welsh economy through an analysis of the work of the Welsh Development Agency. They acknowledge some notable successes, especially in the agency's early years, but note the inability of the WDA to have much impact as the economy began to shift towards the service sector from the 1990s onwards.

A collection of essays on Welsh industrial history featuring just one chapter on coal might be viewed by some as an oddity. But it was the aim of the volume to offer a picture of Welsh industrial history that is less coal-dominated and less focused on the nineteenth and early twentieth centuries than has typically been the case in earlier studies. In doing so it is acknowledged that, from the vantage point of the early twenty-first century, several decades removed from the era when the coal industry dominated the Welsh economy, it is much easier to see beyond coal at what was happening elsewhere in industrial Wales; likewise, it is only now possible to stand back from the latter decades of the twentieth century, just far enough to be able to see them in the rear-view mirror. The essays in this volume do not offer a complete picture of the industrial past. There are important sections of the Welsh economy not represented in these pages, such as the production of woollen textiles, the slate industry, the retail and public sectors. The intention here was never to attempt an all-encompassing survey, but to reflect, instead, the direction of travel in the discipline, and to acknowledge how, after more than a century of writing about our industrial history, there is so much still to know.

NOTES

1 Colin Baber and L. J. Williams (eds), *Modern South Wales: Essays in Economic History* (Cardiff: University of Wales Press, 1986). The quotations in the first sentence of this paragraph are from the introductory chapter.

2 A number of important single-authored volumes on aspects of Wales's economic past have appeared since then, including L. J. Williams, *Was Wales Industrialised? Essays in Modern Welsh History* (Llandysul: Gomer, 1995); and L. Gooberman, *From Depression to Devolution: Economy and Government in Wales, 1934–2006* (Cardiff: University of Wales Press, 2017). See also the collection of essays published by Cardiff and Swansea economists that deals with the period from the 1960s to the mid-1980s: K. D. George and L. Mainwaring (eds), *The Welsh Economy* (Cardiff: University of Wales Press, 1988).

3 For a brief summary of the major developments in the discipline of economic history in Britain, see N. Harte, 'The Economic History Society, 1926–2001', *http://www.history.ac.uk/makinghistory/resources/articles/EHS.html* (accessed 13 August 2018).

4 'What is economic history?', *History Today*, 35/2 (February 1985), 35–43. The seven contributors were: Martin Daunton, Roderick Floud, N. F. R. Crafts, T. C. Barker, A. W. Coats, A. G. Hopkins and D. C. Coleman.

5 See D. Williams, *A History of Modern Wales* (London: John Murray, 1950), p. 269.

6 For further details of this discussion see T. Boyns, 'The Welsh economy – historical myth or modern reality?', *Llafur*, 9/2 (2005), 84–94.

7 Exceptions to this include, R. J. Moore-Colyer, 'Horse and equine improvement in the economy of modern Wales', *Agricultural History Review*, 39/2 (1991), 122–42; M. D. Matthews, 'Coal communities: aspects of the economic and social impact of coastal shipping in south-west Wales, *c.*1700–1820', *Maritime Wales*, 25 (2004), 56–71; R. O. Roberts, 'Financial crisis and the Swansea "branch bank" of England, 1826', National Library of Wales Journal, 11/1 (1959), 76–85.

8 Williams, *Was Wales Industrialised?*, p. 33.

9 Baber and Williams (eds), *Modern South Wales*, p. 1.

10 Examples include chapters on non-ferrous metal smelting, iron, steel and tinplate, the coal industry, agriculture, banking and on the twentieth-century economy, in G. Williams and A. H. John (eds), *Glamorgan County History. Volume V: Industrial Glamorgan* (Cardiff: Glamorgan County History Trust, 1980). For Gwent, see chapters on 'The Rural Economy', 'Communications and Commerce', 'The Iron and Steel Industry' and 'The Coal Industry', in C. Williams and S. R. Williams (eds), *Gwent County History Volume IV: Industrial Monmouthshire, 1780–1914* (Cardiff: University of Wales Press, 2011). See P. Jenkins, *A History of Modern Wales, 1536–1990*

(London: Longman, 1992), for the chapter 'The Coming of Industry and Economy and Society, 1920–1990'; and G. H. Jenkins, *A Concise History of Wales* (Cambridge: Cambridge University Press, 2007), for the chapter 'The crucible of the modern world'.

11 R. A. Griffiths, 'William Rees and the Modern Study of Medieval Wales', in R. A. Griffiths and P. R. Schofield (eds), *Wales and the Welsh in the Middle Ages* (Cardiff: University of Wales Press, 2011), p. 206.

12 For details see Harte, 'The Economic History Society, 1926–2001', *www.history.ac.uk/makinghistory/resources/articles/EHS.html* (accessed 13 August 2018).

13 B. Thomas, 'The migration of labour into the Glamorganshire coalfield (1861–1911)', *Economica*, 30 (November 1930), 275–94. See also R. Thomas, 'Obituary: Professor Brinley Thomas, economist (1906–1994)', *The Independent*, 8 September 1994.

14 'Foreword', in W. Rees, *Industry before the Industrial Revolution, Volume 1* (Cardiff: University of Wales Press, 1968).

15 E. D. Jones, 'Rees, Sir James Frederick (1883–1967), Principal of the University College at Cardiff', *Dictionary of Welsh Biography, http://yba.llgc.org.uk/en/s2-REES-FRE-1883.html* (accessed 2 August 2018).

16 J. F. Rees and W. Rees, 'A select bibliography of the economic history of Wales', *Economic History Review*, 2/2 (1930), 320–6.

17 Rees and Rees, 'Bibliography', 324.

18 Evan J. Jones, *Some Contributions to the Economic History of Wales* (London: P. S. King and Son Ltd, 1928).

19 W. J. Roberts, 'Review of E. J. Evans, *Some Contributions to the Economic History of Wales*', *The Economic Journal*, 39/154 (1929), 284–6.

20 A. H. Dodd, *The Industrial Revolution in North Wales* (Cardiff: University of Wales Press Board, 1933).

21 G. H. Jenkins, 'Clio and Wales: Welsh remembrancers and historical writing, 1751–2001', *Transactions of the Honourable Society of Cymmrodorion*, 8 (2001), 127.

22 See 'Preface' in Dodd, *The Industrial Revolution in North Wales*; and L. Goldman, 'The first students in the Workers' Educational Association: individual enlightenment and collective advance', in S. K. Roberts (ed.), *A Ministry of Enthusiasm: Centenary Essays on the Workers' Educational Association* (London: Pluto Press, 2003), pp. 42–3.

23 In particular, Paul Mantoux, *The Industrial Revolution in the Eighteenth Century: an Outline of the Beginnings of the Modern Factory System in England* (New York: Harcourt, Brace & Co., 1928).

24 Dodd, 'Preface', p. v.

25 Although note the earlier work of trade unionist and later Labour MP, Ness Edwards, *The Industrial Revolution in South Wales* (London: Labour Publishing company, 1924).

26 A. H. John, *The Industrial Development of South Wales, 1750–1850: An Essay* (Cardiff: University of Wales Press, 1950).

27 J. H. Dales, 'Review of *The Industrial Revolution in North Wales* by A. H. Dodd, and *The Industrial Development of South Wales, 1750–1859: An Essay* by A. H. John', in *The Canadian Journal of Economics and Political Science*, 19/1 (February 1953), 111–13.

28 J. H. Morris and L. J. Williams, *The South Wales Coal Industry, 1841–1875* (Cardiff: University of Wales Press, 1958); E. D. Lewis, *The Rhondda Valleys: A Study in Industrial Development, 1800 to the Present Day* (London: Phoenix House, 1959).

29 See, for example, R. O. Roberts, 'Copper and economic growth in Britain, 1729–84', *National Library of Wales Journal*, 10/1 (1957), 65–74; R. O. Roberts, 'Enterprise and capital for non-ferrous metal smelting in Glamorgan, 1694–1924', *Morgannwg*, 23 (1979), 48–82.

30 B. Thomas, 'Wales and the Atlantic economy', *Scottish Journal of Political Economy*, VI (November 1959), 169–92.

31 His later reflections on some of this reaction can be found in B. Thomas, 'A cauldron of rebirth: population and the Welsh language in the nineteenth century', *Welsh History Review*, 13/4 (1987), 418–37.

32 George F. Thomason, 'An analysis of the effects of industrial changes upon selected communities in south Wales' (unpublished PhD thesis, University College of Wales, Cardiff, 1963), see the preface, p. 3.

33 J. H. Goldthorpe, D. Lockwood, F. Bechhofer and J. Platt, *The Affluent Worker in the Class Structure* (Cambridge: Cambridge University Press, 1969).

34 David Simpson, 'Obituary: George F. Thomason (1927–2017)', *The Guardian*, 26 February 2017.

35 The pioneering study was M. D. Young and P. Willmott, *Family and Kinship in East London* (London: Routledge and Kegan Paul, 1957).

36 C. Rosser and C. C. Harris, *The Family and Social Change: A Study of Family and Kinship in a South Wales Town* (London: Routledge and Kegan Paul, 1965).

37 The project generated a series of reports on geology, soil, housing, and human ecology. See also K. J. Hilton, *The Lower Swansea Valley Project* (London: Longmans, 1967); R. Bromley and G. Humphrys (eds), *Dealing with Dereliction: The Redevelopment of the Lower Swansea Valley* (Swansea: University College Swansea, 1979).

38 S. Pollard, 'Economic history: a science of society', *Past & Present*, 30 (April 1965), 3–22.

39 See Harte, 'The Economic History Society, 1926–2001', *www.history.ac.uk/makinghistory/resources/articles/EHS.html* (accessed 13 August 2018).

40 W. A. Cole, interviewed by A. J. H. Latham, in J. S. Lyons, L. P. Cain and S. H. Williamson (eds), *Reflections on the Cliometrics Revolution: Conversations with Economic Historians* (Oxford: Routledge, 2008), p. 152.

41 P. Deane and W. A. Cole, *British Economic Growth, 1688–1959: Trends and Structure* (Cambridge: Cambridge University Press, 1962).

42 E. H. Carr, *What is History?* (Harmondsworth: Penguin, 1964).

43 W. A. Cole, 'Economic history as a social science', inaugural lecture, University College of Swansea, 24 October 1967, p. 10.

44 The more obvious tensions were between nationalist and working-class schools of historians in Wales. See G. H. Jenkins, 'Reading history: modern Wales', *History Today*, 37/2 (1987), 49–53.

45 N. Evans, 'Writing the social history of modern Wales: approaches, achievements and problems', *Social History*, 17/3 (1992), 480.

46 Williams, *A History of Modern Wales*; D. Williams, *John Frost: A Study in Chartism* (Cardiff: University of Wales Press, 1939); D. Williams, *The Rebecca Riots: A Study in Agrarian Discontent* (Cardiff: University of Wales Press, 1955).

47 See, for example, G. A. Williams, Merthyr Politics: *The Making of a Working-class Tradition* (Cardiff: University of Wales Press, 1966); G. A. Williams, *Artisans and Sans-culottes: Popular Movements in France and Britain during the French Revolution* (London: Edward Arnold, 1968); D. J. V. Jones, *Before Rebecca: Popular Protests in Wales, 1793–1835* (London: Allen Lane, 1973); D. J. V. Jones, *The Last Rising: The Newport Insurrection of 1839* (Oxford: Clarendon, 1985).

48 G. A. Williams, 'David Williams', *Llafur*, 2/3 (1978), 7–9.

49 Although Neil Evans is careful to point out that Gwyn Williams and David Jones were not imitators of the English Marxist historians. See Evans, 'Writing the social history of modern Wales', 480.

50 The Society for the Study of Labour History launched its journal, *Labour History Review*, in 1960. In the same year, the first issue of *Welsh History Review* was published.

51 For details see P. Hudson, 'Economic History in Britain. The "first industrial nation" ', in F. Boldizzoni and P. Hudson (eds), *Routledge Handbook of Global Economic History* (Routledge: New York, 2016), p. 29.

52 K. O. Morgan, 'Consensus and Conflict in Welsh History', in D. W. Howell and K. O. Morgan (eds), *Crime, Protest and Police in Modern British Society* (Cardiff: University of Wales Press, 1999), p. 18.

53 Perhaps the most notable exception to this is the work of K. O. Morgan on Welsh political history. See, for example, *Wales in British Politics 1868–1922* (Cardiff: University of Wales Press, 1963); *Rebirth of a Nation: Wales 1880–1980* (Oxford: Oxford University Press; Cardiff: University of Wales Press, 1981); *Modern Wales: Politics, Places and People* (Cardiff: University of Wales Press, 1995).

54 See, for example, David J. V. Jones, 'The Scotch Cattle and their black domain', *Welsh History Review*, 5/3 (1971), 220–49; G. A. Williams, *The Merthyr Rising* (London: Croom Helm, 1978); H. Francis and D. Smith, *The Fed: A History of the South Wales Miners in the Twentieth Century* (London:

Lawrence and Wishart, 1980); R. Merfyn Jones, *The North Wales Quarrymen, 1874–1922* (Cardiff: University of Wales Press, 1981); D. Egan, Pobl, *Protest a Gwleidyddiaeth: Mudiadau Poblogaidd yng Nghymru'r Bedwaredd Ganrif ar Bymtheg* (Llandysul: Gomer, 1988).

55 See *Llafur*, 1/1 (May 1972), 1.

56 See *Llafur*, 1/2 (May 1973), Special Number: 75th Anniversary of the South Wales Miners' Federation, and *Llafur*, 2/2 (Spring 1977), 1,926.

57 W. E. Minchinton (ed.), *Industrial South Wales, 1750–1914. Essays in Welsh Economic History* (London: Frank Cass, 1969).

58 The South Wales Coalfield History Project researchers were R. Merfyn Jones, Hywel Francis, Alun Morgan and David Egan. See 'South Wales Coalfield History Project. Final Report' (July 1974), p. viii.

59 'South Wales Coalfield History Project. Final Report', p. v.

60 Information supplied by Hywel Francis to L. Miskell, email correspondence, 8 August 2018. See also H. Francis and S. F. Williams, *Do Miners Read Dickens? Origins and Progress of the South Wales Miners Library, 1973–2013* (Cardigan: Parthian, 2013).

61 See *Llafur*, 1/2 (May 1973), Special Number: 75th. Anniversary of the South Wales Miners' Federation, 2.

62 A. Croll, 'People's remembrancers in a post-modern age: contemplating the non-crisis of Welsh labour history', *Llafur*, 8/1 (2000), 12.

63 Williams, 'Figures in Welsh History', in *Was Wales Industrialised?*, pp. 80–1.

64 Quoted in 'Preface', Lyons, Cain and Williamson (eds), *Reflections on the Cliometrics Revolution*, p. xii.

65 Chris Williams, *Capitalism, Community and Conflict: The South Wales Coalfield, 1898–1947* (Cardiff: University of Wales Press, 1998), p. 2.

66 A. Martin and J. Parry Lewis, *Welsh Economic Statistics: A Handbook of Sources* (Cardiff: University College of South Wales and Monmouthshire, 1953); E. T. Nevin, *The Social Accounts of the Welsh Economy* (Aberystwyth: University of Wales Press, 1957).

67 L. J. Williams, *Digest of Welsh Historical Statistics*, vols 1 and 2 (Cardiff: Welsh Office, 1985).

68 B. R. Mitchell and P. Deane, *Abstract of British Historical Statistics* (Cambridge: Cambridge University Press, 1962), and B. R. Mitchell and H. G. Jones, *Second Abstract of British Historical Statistics* (Cambridge: Cambridge University Press, 1971). See also, *https://discover.ukdataservice.ac.uk/Catalogue/?sn=4097&type=Data%20catalogue* (accessed 29 August 2018).

69 L. J. Williams, *Digest of Welsh Historical Statistics, 1974–1996* (Cardiff: Welsh Office, 1998); See also, *https://gov.wales/statistics-and-research/digest-welsh-historical-statistics/?lang=en* (accessed 27 July 2018).

70 D. Thomas and D. Jones, *Welsh Economy and Society Post-1945: A Database of Statistical and Documentary Material* (Cardiff: University of Wales Press, 1996).

71 N. Evans, 'Two Paths to Economic Development: Wales and the North-east of England', in P. Hudson (ed.), *Regions and Industries: A Perspective on the Industrial Revolution in Britain* (Cambridge, 1989), pp. 201–27; L. James, 'War and industry: a study of the industrial relations in the mining regions of south Wales and the Ruhr during the Great War, 1914–1918', *Labour History Review*, 68/2 (2003), 195–215; S. Berger, A. Croll and N. LaPorte (eds), *Towards a Comparative History of Coalfield Societies* (Aldershot: Ashgate, 2005).

72 D. M. Turner and D. Blackie, *Disability in the Industrial Revolution: Physical Impairment in British Coalmining, 1780–1880* (Manchester: Manchester University Press, 2018); D. M. Turner et. al., 'Disability and industrial society 1780–1948: a comparative cultural history of British coalfields: statistical compendium' (data set), Zenodo: *http://doi.org/10.5281/zenodo.183686* (accessed 30 August 2018).

73 See C. Evans and O. Saunders, 'A world of copper: globalizing the industrial revolution, 1830–70', *Journal of Global History*, 10/1 (2015), 3–26. See also articles by C. Evans, L. Miskell and W. D. Jones in *Welsh History Review*, 27/1 (2014).

74 For details see *www.welshcopper.org.uk* (accessed 30 August 2018).

75 It should be noted that although visitors rate their experiences highly, these sites do not attract the visitor numbers of comparable museums in English industrial regions. See S. Thurley, 'Review of Amgueddfa Cymu', June 2017 *https://gov.wales/docs/drah/publications/180109-amgueddfa-cymru-review-en.pdf* (accessed 12 September 2018).

76 See, for example, C. Evans, 'Global commerce and industrial organization in an eighteenth-century Welsh enterprise: the Melingriffith Company', *Welsh History Review*, 20/3 (2001), 413–34; T. Boyns and S. Gray, 'Welsh coal and the informal empire in South America, 1850–1913', *Atlantic Studies: Literary, Cultural and Historical Perspectives*, 13/1 (2016), 53–77; and the chapters by Huw Bowen, Chris Evans and Trevor Burnard, in H. V. Bowen (ed.), *Wales and the British Overseas Empire: Interactions and Influences, 1650–1830* (Manchester: Manchester University Press, 2011).

77 There were no female chapter contributors in Minchinton (ed.), *Industrial South Wales, 1750–1914*, in Baber and Williams (eds), *Modern South Wales*, or in Williams and John (eds), *Glamorgan County History Volume V: Industrial Glamorgan*. However, a chapter on 'Agriculture' by Anne Martin appeared in B. Thomas (ed.), *The Welsh Economy: Studies in Expansion* (Cardiff: University of Wales Press, 1962). Sian Rhiannon Williams and Margaret Escott both contributed chapters to Williams and Williams (eds), *Gwent County History Volume IV: Industrial Monmouthshire, 1780–1914*.

78 D. Jones, 'Counting the Cost of Coal: Women's Lives in the Rhondda, 1881–1911', in A. V. John (ed.), *Our Mother's Land: Chapters in Welsh Women's History, 1830–1839* (Cardiff: University of Wales Press, 1991), pp. 109–33;

M. A. Williams, *A Forgotten Army: Female Munitions Workers of South Wales, 1939–1945* (Cardiff: University of Wales Press, 2002). Other studies include M. F. Stevens, 'Women brewers in fourteenth century Ruthin', *Transactions of the Denbighshire Historical Society*, 54 (2005/6), 15–31; B. Jenkins, 'Women's professional employment in Wales during the First World War', *Welsh History Review*, 28/4 (2017), 646–75; S. Howard, 'Servants in early modern Wales: co-operation, conflict and survival', *Llafur*, 9/1 (2004), 33–43; E. Richardson, 'Women farmers of Snowdonia, 1750–1900', *Rural History*, 25/2 (2014), 161–81.

79 See, for example, A. Milburn, 'Female employment in nineteenth-century ironworking districts: Merthyr Tydfil and the Shropshire coalfield, 1841–1881' (unpublished PhD thesis, Swansea University, 2013); C. Howells, 'Sales assistants, shops and the development of Cardiff's retail sector, 1850–1920' (unpublished MA thesis, Swansea University, 2010); C. Howells, 'Wales's hidden industry: domestic service in south Wales, 1871–1921' (unpublished PhD thesis, Swansea University, 2014).

80 B. Penny, 'Class, work and community: Port Talbot's steelworkers, 1951–1988' (unpublished PhD thesis, Swansea University, 2016).

81 See Williams, *Capitalism, Community and Conflict*, p. 2.

82 See also S. Parry, 'History of the steel industry in the Port Talbot area, 1900–1988' (unpublished PhD thesis, University of Leeds, 2011); Andrew Morel du Boil, 'The closure of East Moors steelworks: a 1970s of decline and calamity, possibility and calm' (unpublished MA dissertation, Swansea University, 2015); L. Miskell, 'Doing it for themselves: the Steel Company of Wales and the study of American industrial productivity, *c.*1945–1955', *Enterprise and Society*, 18/1 (2017), 184–213.

83 Exceptions to this include M. J. Daunton, 'The Dowlais Iron Company in the iron industry, 1800–1850', *Welsh History Review*, 6/1 (January 1972), 16–45.

84 See, for example, C. Baber and J. Dessant, 'Modern Glamorgan: Economic Development after 1945', in G. Williams and A. H. John (eds), *Glamorgan County History Volume V: Industrial Glamorgan* (Cardiff: Glamorgan County History Trust, 1980), pp. 581–658; Thomas (ed.), *The Welsh Economy: Studies in Expansion*; and the final chapter in Lewis, *The Rhondda Valleys*.

85 Minchinton (ed.), *Industrial South Wales*, p. xi.

86 See, for example, R. Fevre, *Wales is Closed: The Quiet Privatisation of British Steel* (Nottingham: Spokesman, 1989); H. N. Lins, 'Changes in production and employment decline in the south Wales steel industry' (unpublished MSc Econ. thesis, University College of Swansea, 1982).

87 M. Johnes, *Wales Since 1939* (Manchester: Manchester University Press, 2012); B. Curtis, *The South Wales Miners, 1964–1985* (Cardiff: University of Wales Press, 2013); Gooberman, *From Depression to Devolution: Economy and Government in Wales, 1934–2006.*

WELSH COPPER: WHAT, WHEN AND WHERE?

CHRIS EVANS

COPPER was one of the great success stories of industrial Wales – perhaps the greatest. Coal looms far larger in the popular imagination and iron smelting has proved more enduring (the blast furnaces that still loom over Port Talbot stand testimony to that), but neither coal nor iron achieved quite the global eminence of Welsh copper. In the early decades of the nineteenth century Wales may have turned out half the world's smelted copper. To be more precise, the best part of the world's copper was produced within a ten-mile radius of 'Copperopolis', the town of Swansea. That, at least, is the story told in popular accounts of the Swansea district, in which high, sometimes extravagant, proportions of world output are attributed to south-west Wales.[1] In actual fact, Swansea's dominance was not quite as pronounced as is sometimes thought. Even so, between the 1770s and the 1850s Welsh copper was a genuine global hegemon.

The story of Welsh copper rings with superlatives. Yet it is also a story that is difficult to grapple with. There is no authoritative history of Welsh copper nor, indeed, of British non-ferrous metals more generally. Henry Hamilton's *The British Brass and Copper Industry to 1800* (1926) appeared in a golden age for British economic history, one that saw the publication of classic works on Yorkshire woollens and worsteds, iron and steel, and Lancashire cotton.[2] Yet its achievement was not built upon in subsequent decades. Besides, Hamilton's *Brass and Copper* was a history that ended somewhat arbitrarily in 1800, at a moment when the history of Welsh copper was but half done. That is not to say that work on Swansea lapsed. On the contrary, Swansea's industrial history found its doyen in R. O. Roberts, whose work, published between the 1950s and 1980s, remains a key resource for understanding Welsh copper. Roberts had an unrivalled knowledge of the locality and he is still an indispensable guide to the labyrinthine partnerships that governed Swansea's copper sector, but he was not given to bold overarching statements, still less to construing the place of Welsh copper within a wider landscape of economic change.[3]

It is time, perhaps, to take a more panoramic view. This essay endeavours to do so, synthesising our existing knowledge and drawing upon the new wave of research on Swansea copper that has emerged in the last decade.[4] It asks some very simple definitional questions: *what* was Welsh copper? *When* was Welsh copper? And *where* was Welsh copper?

WHAT WAS WELSH COPPER?

The answer to the 'what' question may seem obvious. Welsh copper had a distinguishing feature – it was smelted using mineral coal at a time when copper smelters everywhere else, from Chile to China, relied on vegetable fuel, whether firewood or charcoal, as they had for long centuries. The use of reverberatory furnaces in which the fuel and the ore on which it acted were kept separate was transformational. Smelters had always spurned the use of coal because of the sulphurous impurities it tended to contain. In standard furnaces, in which fuel and ore were intermingled, those impurities would impair the final product. The adoption of the reverberatory furnace resolved that problem: a low brick partition divided the grate in which the coal was burnt from the furnace bowl containing the ore. A fierce draught generated by the tall chimney that rose from the furthest end of the furnace bowl drew flames across the partition, while the low, downward-sloping roof of the furnace reflected ('reverberated') heat onto the charge of ore.[5]

The coal-fuelled reverberatory became Wales's signature technology. It paved the way for a major expansion of production, expansion that was historically unexampled. It could only have been achieved on the basis of fossil fuel. Vegetable fuel was finite, in the sense that the acreage given over to woodland was necessarily limited. Land that was devoted to coppice woods, after all, was land that could not be used to grow food crops or to pasture animals. Nor could vegetable energy reserves be easily renewed. Coppices would re-sprout after felling but regrowth took fifteen to twenty years. Tapping subterranean energy reserves evaded those difficulties. Coal reserves, to the eighteenth-century eye, seemed inexhaustible. From the vantage point of the twenty-first century, of course, humankind's resort to fossil fuels appears a fateful bargain, one that brought environmental squalor and anthropogenic climate change in its wake. But for early modern people the use of coal was liberating; it brought release from cramping energy shortages.[6]

Welsh copper represented then a radical technological departure, but there was more at stake than the substitution of one source of heat energy for another. The use of mineral coal brought about new organisational and spatial arrangements as well. Firstly, there was a concentration of production in larger and larger units. Copper smelting that was reliant on vegetable fuel was necessarily dispersed for fear of overstraining local woodlands. Coal-fired furnaces could be multiplied and massed on a single site, giving rise to the long arcade-like smelting halls that were a feature of Welsh copper. Each of these could house dozens of reverberatories. By 1780, there were sixty furnaces at Freeman & Co.'s White Rock works in the Swansea valley, a further fifty at Lockwood & Morris's Llangyfelach works, and forty more at the Middle Bank works of George Pengree & Co. In all, there were 310 reverberatories at work in the Swansea district.[7] These works were clustered near the southern edge of the coal seams that cut across the Swansea and Neath valleys.

There were no local ore bodies to exploit, however. That absence was one of the most singular features of Welsh copper. Since prehistory, the smelting of ores had always taken place in close proximity to the mines from which they were raised, drawing upon forest resources that were immediately circumjacent. The production of fuel, the mining of ore and its smelting coincided in space. The Welsh model of copper smelting was revolutionary because the extraction of ore and its reduction were spatially distinct. Instead of fuel being carried a relatively short distance to the ore, the ore was brought to the fuel – and brought over a substantial distance because the major source of copper ore in eighteenth-century Britain was Cornwall. It was economically viable to do so because Cornish mines were located within striking distance of the coast, enabling ore to be shipped across the Bristol channel to Swansea bay with the bare minimum of land carriage. The ore was brought to Wales rather than Welsh coal being taken to Cornwall because the reverberatory was so voracious a consumer of coal: 18 tons of coal, so Matthew Boulton reckoned, were required to produce a single ton of copper.[8] It was an arrangement that made Swansea – the smelting centre without any ore of its own to smelt – an industrial town that broke with every precedent.

WHERE WAS WELSH COPPER?

So close was the association between Swansea and coal-fired technologies that copper smelting using the reverberatory furnace became known as the 'Welsh' process. The Welsh process was not Welsh in origin, however. It was pioneered elsewhere and was slow to be domesticated in south Wales. The reverberatory furnace seems to have evolved out of the melting furnaces used by late medieval bell and cannon founders in central Europe. It is spoken of in the British Isles by the early seventeenth century but its actual use in industrial production is hard to document before the 1670s. Even then, the reverberatory was applied to the smelting of lead ores, not copper, and the earliest experimental furnaces had no particular Welsh associations. Indeed, the first generation of reverberatories was scattered far and wide. Examples could be found at: 'White-Haven in Cumberland: near Ashburton, in the Peak [District]: near Auderly Edge, Cheshire: near Dizart in Flintshire: at Neath in Glamorganshire: near St Austils, in Cornwall: near the Saw-Mill, in Southwark: [and] at Fox-Hall [i.e. Vauxhall]'.[9] Moreover, when the smelting of copper with reverberatories began to coalesce around a single centre in the late seventeenth century, it was Bristol, not Swansea, that came to the fore.

The advantages of Bristol were plain enough to the early copper masters. It was England's second city, with a rich merchant class and a burgeoning international trade. Bristol could therefore furnish both capital and markets for the nascent industry. Critically, the city could also offer coal: the Kingswood coalfield lay just to the east, while the Forest of Dean coal measures were close by on the other side of the Severn. Bristol's centrality for the new copper industry began to flag as the eighteenth century wore on, however. Cornish ore had a long way to come, and when the ore barques arrived they had to contend with a harbour that was crowded and subject to heavy charges. The Swansea district offered abundant coal at a cheaper rate and – decisively – a much shorter passage from Cornish ports. Because of that, the Swansea and Neath valleys began to exert a gravitational pull. Copper production continued in the Bristol region but it was no longer the locus of dynamic growth. That was now found much further to the west.

The first copper works in the Swansea valley was opened at Llangyfelach in 1717. Dedicated copper making in the Neath valley began in 1732, when the Costers, a Bristol-based family with established interests in smelting and Cornish mining, took over the Melincryddan works, previously used for lead production. Within five years the Costers had moved to a new, purpose-built plant in the Swansea valley at White Rock. The age of Welsh copper was under way. Welsh smelting did not yet loom large on the national landscape, however. The locational logic that underwrote growth in the Swansea district took time to unfold. The long-established works of the Bristol region were substantial and represented a massive quantity of sunk capital; they were also, as we shall see, well integrated with local brass making. There was little to be gained and much to be lost by writing them off. In the 1740s, Bristol was still the single largest centre of copper production in the British Isles. From the 1750s, though, investment surged into the Swansea district. At mid-century there were only three operational copper works in the Swansea and Neath valleys. By 1800 there were fourteen.[10]

The uplift began in the early 1750s and accelerated over the course of the Seven Years' War. Copper output in Britain fluctuated around the 1,000-ton mark in the 1740s; in 1760 it breached 2,000 tons annually for the first time. Further growth led to the 3,000-ton mark being passed in 1768. The 1770s and 1780s saw output lurch upwards again and with tectonic violence: 4,000 tons of metal was turned out in 1775, well over 5,000 tons in 1779, and 7,000 tons in 1783. This is as dramatic a story as the Industrial Revolution has to tell. The Swansea district was not unique, though, in exhibiting rapid growth. Indeed, the eighteenth century was a time of expanding production globally, especially on the frontiers of the great Eurasian empires. Growth in the Russian empire, which had no copper industry to speak of at the start of the eighteenth century, was stupendous. A series of huge smelting works were created from 1720s, firstly in the Urals and then the Altai mountains (where the modern republics of Russia, Kazakhstan, China and Mongolia meet); by the 1760s they were capable of producing 3,500 tons of smelted copper annually, a volume in excess of contemporary British production.[11] There were even more dramatic developments on the south-west border of the Chinese empire, with the imperial authorities ploughing resources into remote but copper-rich Yunnan province.[12] The results were startling: close on 9,000 tons of copper was shipped out of Yunnan annually in the 1770s.[13] There were, however, two vital points of difference between Wales and the new spaces of mineral exploitation in Russia and China. First, timber-dependent Chinese and Russian producers could not sustain such vertiginous growth over the long term in the way that coal-fuelled Swansea could. Secondly, there is the question of the uses to which all this additional copper was put. Most Russian and Chinese copper was struck into coin and put into domestic circulation. The fate of Welsh copper was quite different: much of it was destined for external markets.

One answer to the question 'Where was Welsh Copper?' might be the West Indies, for colonial consumption played a vital role. The Caribbean sugar sector absorbed very large amounts of copper. It was embodied in the suite of boiling pans – 'coppers' – which every plantation required to process the freshly harvested cane. Nuala Zahedieh has estimated that the 115,000 captive labourers on the English islands in 1700 'would have needed around 8,517 copper boilers, weighing an estimated 1,123 tons, almost twice the weight of England's copper coinage at the time'.[14] And as sugar production in the islands grew, so did the volume of copper consumed. By 1770, when there were 434,000 enslaved workers in the British Caribbean, the total weight of embodied copper – taking in boilers, coolers and boiling house implements – would have come to over 4,240 tons.[15]

Copper and cupreous goods also played a major role in the procurement of enslaved labour in Africa. Lengths of copper ('Guinea Rods') acted as a currency in many slave marts, as did manillas (bracelets formed from brass or a copper-lead alloy). These were churned out in large quantities from the very early days of Welsh copper. The pioneering works at White Rock, Swansea, featured a 'manilla house', while the processing mill at Holywell in Flintshire was dedicated almost entirely to 'drawing down copper to rods for the Guinea trade', turning out 40 tons a year. The manufacturing process was specially designed to impart extra ductility to the metal because Africans 'use the rods as ornaments and wind them around arms and legs'.[16] The rods were forwarded to Liverpool for loading onto ships like the *Quixote*, which sailed for the Bight of Biafra in 1783 with 5,000 copper rods, twenty boxes of brass rods and 800 manillas in its hold.[17] In all, the *Quixote* carried trade goods that embodied 2.4 tons of copper. There was nothing unusual in this. The invoice of the *Africa*, which cleared Bristol for the Bight in 1774, told the same story: its cargo included 4,000 copper rods, 200 'Neptunes' (shallow brass bowls over a metre across), and sixteen casks of manillas. There was well over 4 tons of copper here, either in pure or alloyed form.[18]

The African market was fundamental, or so the Anglesey copper magnate Thomas Williams claimed in 1788. Without it, he and his associates would never have been persuaded to lay out money at the Parys mountain mine, on works in the Swansea district, or at Holywell. The articles he manufactured were 'entirely for the African market and not saleable for any other'.[19] This was a considerable exaggeration, made for political purposes (Williams was railing against the proposed abolition of the slave trade). The world of Atlantic slavery absorbed a good portion of British copper output – well over half of total copper/brass exports at mid-century – but from the 1760s the most important overseas market was to be found in the east, not the west. When the East India Company exported copper to Indian Ocean markets in the 1730s and 1740s, it usually sent out modest quantities. On those occasions when the company felt the need to export very large quantities, as it did in the early 1740s, it must surely have relied on continental suppliers. From the 1760s, however, with the company established as a territorial power in Bengal, its exports picked up sharply and the contract to supply it with copper became a matter of obsessive interest to Welsh smelters. It is not hard to see why. Between 1760 and 1799 annual exports by the East India Company averaged 26.6 per cent of smelted copper production in the British Isles – an astonishing proportion.[20]

Few British industries were as export-orientated, but the volume of copper consumed within the metropolitan economy should not be overlooked. Much, it seems certain, was devoted to traditional products sold on traditional markets, but there were also new applications for copper. Some were related to the success of the Atlantic plantation system. Distilling, which made use of enormous copper vessels, boomed, as did sugar refining.[21] London became a major centre for both over the course of the eighteenth century. The city reportedly had eighty sugar refineries in the 1750s, with twenty more in Bristol.[22] Other new uses of copper were related to the navigation of colonial waters. The sheathing of ships' hulls stands out in this respect. Wood-boring marine organisms represented a major problem for ship owners. *Teredo navalis*, the 'ship worm', was a particular nuisance. Left unchecked, *teredo navalis* could dramatically curtail a ship's operational life. Its depredations meant that ocean-going vessels had to be regularly scraped clean in dock, a laborious and expensive exercise. The idea of fixing thin metal sheets to fend off these pestiferous molluscs was an old one, but it was not until the 1770s that the technical difficulties in attaching the sheets were overcome. Once they were, the 'copper-bottoming' of ships became a boom area.[23] The numbers are eye-opening. In the mid-1780s, Matthew Boulton reckoned that 1,000 tons of copper was consumed in the 'Sheathing of Shipping' at British shipyards, with a further 1,500 tons absorbed by 'Navy Bolts, Nails & other Naval Uses'. This was *one quarter* of the copper then traded by British merchants. Boulton also assumed that a significant proportion of the 2,000 tons of copper exported to France was consumed by the French Navy, so it may be that the naval market accounted for as much as a third of the copper produced in Britain at that time.[24]

The production of copper sheets required rolling mills. These were part of the Swansea district's industrial landscape from an early date, but Wales never dominated rolling as it did smelting. Throughout the eighteenth century and far into the nineteenth the processing of copper was centred on the Thames valley to the west of London. The reasons are clear enough. In the seventeenth century, when Britain was dependent on Swedish imports, there was an obvious logic to locating copper mills in the vicinity of London, the great centre for trade with the Baltic, harnessing the Thames and its many tributaries to power battery hammers and rolls. The processing of copper remained a matter for the south-east of England long after Britain had ended its reliance on Baltic imports. After all, London was the largest single market for the finished metal. It was thronged with coppersmiths and braziers, while the Thames gave ready access to the royal dockyards at Deptford and Chatham.

Another answer, then, to the question 'Where was Welsh Copper?' would be the Home Counties. In fact, it might be more useful to think of an M4 copper trade than a Welsh copper industry in the eighteenth century, for the constituent parts of the copper and brass-making sector were distributed along the modern arterial route that stretches from London to south Wales. Smelting was focused on coal-rich Swansea; brass making was the preserve of the Bristol region because calamine, the zinc-bearing mineral that was an indispensable input, was mined in the nearby Mendip Hills; and copper processing was concentrated in Middlesex and Surrey. Very often, these different elements were controlled by a single partnership or a set of overlapping partnerships. The English Copper Company, for example, smelted Cornish ores in south Wales at Melincryddan (between the 1740s and 1760s) and Taibach (from the 1770s), but it also had a rolling mill on the river Wandle at Wimbledon and maintained a riverfront depot at Vauxhall.[25] As the industry's capacity grew in the second half of the eighteenth century, these mills began to assume a new scale. The rolling mill at Wraysbury in Buckinghamshire, near the confluence of the River Colne and the Thames, employed forty-four workers in 1803.[26] The mill at Harefield in Middlesex, further up the Colne valley, was still more formidable. The pioneer American industrialist Joseph Warren Revere, who visited in 1804, was hugely impressed:

> This works all the time imploys 150 workmen night & day, before I saw these I thought the works for Iron extremely well fitted but this is beyond description altho so many wheels & all of Iron there is no noise no chattering but all goes like Clock work & you can talk & be heard the same as in open air these works have been newly Built within fourteen years & should suppose from the immense Stock not less than a million Sterling Capitall.[27]

Interestingly, Revere subsequently travelled to Swansea but found the smelting works there less remarkable.

WHEN WAS WELSH COPPER?

Copper smelting in south-west Wales began in the 1710s, as we have seen; it developed rapidly from the 1750s, with profound effects further up the supply chain. The proliferation of works in the Swansea district required Cornish producers to greatly increase the volume of ore they raised. For the most part, Cornish mine adventurers did so. The headlong expansion of copper smelting in the age of the American Revolution did not just rely upon Cornish production, however. A completely new resource, the ore lode discovered at Parys mountain, Anglesey, came into play. Opencast working began here in the 1760s, although it was not until the late 1770s that Anglesey ores took on importance. From then until the end of the century, material from Parys mountain represented a major addition to the feedstock of Welsh smelters. At its peak in the 1780s and early 1790s, Anglesey regularly accounted for over a third of British copper ore production.

The output of British copper mines, measured in terms of metallic content rather than weight, quadrupled in the thirty years between 1760 and 1790. In the thirty years that followed, 1791–1820, it remained stable. Production at Parys mountain, which had contributed so much to the phase of explosive growth, stalled at the end of the 1790s and fell away rapidly in the early 1800s. There was continued growth in the south-west of England, however, which counterbalanced Anglesey's collapse. Productivity gains played a critical role. Most notably, improvements in steam technology allowed Cornish mines to be better drained and driven deeper. New areas of mineral exploitation also began to be opened up, especially in the south and east of the county. Despite these developments, the demand for furnace stuff clearly outstripped supply. The Welsh copper sector continued to grow: the foundation of the Llanelly Copperworks Co. in 1805 and Spitty Bank Copper Co. in 1809 marked the incorporation of Llanelli and its environs into the Swansea district, while the opening of the Hafod works, also in 1809, added greatly to the crush of smelting works in the lower Swansea valley.[28] One solution was to draw upon Irish resources. Ireland had contributed ores to the British smelting industry in the eighteenth century, but intermittently and in small quantities. In the post-Napoleonic years there were new and important developments in the far west of Cork at Allihies and around Bunmahon on the Waterford coast, inaugurating a regular traffic between Munster and Swansea bay.[29] Until the 1830s, that was as far as ore barques went. Welsh smelters were unable to access minerals from further afield because of tariff restrictions, but once significant alterations were made to the customs regime, as happened in the late 1820s, foreign ores could enter the British market on a competitive basis.[30] With this, Welsh copper went global. The Swansea district, with its dependence on seaborne ore, had always been anomalous but it was an anomaly confined to British and Irish waters. After 1830 that was no longer so. All of a sudden, the French metallurgist Frédéric Le Play exclaimed, that the Welsh copper sector seemed to know 'no limits other than those of the globe itself'. Swansea received ores 'from the island of Cuba, from Mexico, from Colombia, from Peru, from Chile, from Australia and from New Zealand'.[31] South Wales was now the 'central smelter for minerals from East and West'.[32]

The first phase of Welsh copper's global age, from *c.*1830 to the mid-1840s, was dominated by Latin American ores, those of Gran Colombia, Chile and Cuba. Of these, the Cuban contribution was the most important; it outgrew the trade in Chilean ores and outlasted mining at Aroa in modern Venezuela, which was abandoned in 1844. The Cuban mining sector was revolutionised when two British-owned companies, the Cobre Company and the Royal Santiago Mining Company, began to exploit the deposits at El Cobre in the east of the island. Old workings that had been derelict for more than a century were rejuvenated by British capital and Cornish deep-mining methods, and with great success. Shipped to Swansea from the deep-water anchorage at Santiago de Cuba, El Cobre's ores would account for more than half of the foreign ores entering Britain *c.*1840.[33] Over the course of the 1840s, however, Welsh copper's global connections were reshaped as the exploitation of Australasian ore deposits began. The new colony of South Australia played a central role. As pastoralists advanced north from Adelaide they hit upon mineral outcrops, first at Kapunda in 1842 and then at Burra Burra in 1844. The discoveries at 'the Burra' were transformative. The South Australian Mining Association, established there in 1845, enjoyed dizzying success. It paid out fifteen dividends, each of 200 per cent, in the first five years of its existence.[34] It was more than enough to spark a prospecting frenzy. Copper may have been overshadowed by the gold rush of the early 1850s, but beyond the attention-grabbing developments on the Victorian goldfields there was a steady spread of copper mining: Western Australia in 1851, New South Wales in 1858 and Queensland in 1862.

The consolidation of Australian mining coincided with a further extension of Swansea's reach. By the end of the 1850s, Welsh copper's supply lines stretched out to Namaqualand in southern Africa, to Algeria, to the Iberian peninsula, to the United States, and to Newfoundland.[35] As a result, the mix of ores used in the Swansea district became increasingly multinational. The mix smelted at the Hafod works in 1848 included the local (ores from the Fowey Consols in Cornwall and Wheal Friendship in Devon), the distant (Cuban ores), and the super-distant (ores from Burra).[36] There was no disadvantage in such a miscellany. On the contrary, it worked very much to the benefit of Swansea's smelters. Smelting by blast furnace, still the norm in continental Europe, was a single-stage process well suited to a homogeneous mineral charge. The Welsh process, by contrast, was a multistage operation involving several different reverberatories, each one housing a different stage in the reduction process. Here, heterogeneity was a positive advantage; each part of the mineral charge played its own role in an elaborate sequence of chemical reactions that eventually yielded fine copper. Supply chains that snaked around the world actually complemented the Welsh process.

The hold that Welsh smelters had over this global supply network was never completely secure. Only in the Cuban case were the mines actually owned by British companies. Both the Cobre Company and the Royal Santiago Mining Company had their headquarters in the City and both raised prodigious sums on the London money markets. At its flotation in 1835, the Cobre Company was valued at £480,000. Both companies, London corporate addresses notwithstanding, were closely aligned with the Welsh smelting sector. The Cobre Company was associated with the Grenfell family, proprietors of the Middle Bank works, Swansea, while the Royal Santiago Mining Company was linked to Michael Williams of the Morfa works, which sat directly opposite the Middle Bank on the west bank of the Tawe. British industrialists were not able to exert a similarly direct influence over Chilean mining. The mines there remained under the control of *mineros*, traditional mine adventurers who put indigenous labourers to work. The mines remained on a modest scale too. The technologically advanced, heavily capitalised form of mining that the British implanted in Cuba was slow to take root in Chile. British capital rarely made an appearance in the mining sector; it went instead to the merchant houses in Valparaíso that assembled cargoes for the 'Swansea-fitted' barques that braved Cape Horn. Australian mines, unlike those of Chile, did make ready use of Cornish miners and mining practices, using capital raised locally to do so. The South Australian Mining Association was the child of Adelaide's nascent business community, not City financiers. These local capitalists saw no reason why they should dance to Swansea's tune. Almost from the outset, they sought to establish a smelting works in South Australia. The result was a Welsh-style works at Kooringa, adjacent to the Burra mine, where six reverberatories were lit in 1849. Everything necessary, down to bricks with which to build the furnaces, was shipped from south Wales. That included the workforce, recruited in the Llanelli area and from Cwmavon on the Swansea district's eastern edge.

The migrants who left Wales for South Australia were not unique. The 1840s saw a wave of out-migration from the Swansea district. These were hard times in early industrial Britain and the copper sector was not exempted from the downturns that punctuated the 1830s and 1840s. The history of labour in the copper industry has yet to be written but there were clearly bitter workplace tensions. The sector-wide strike in 1843 is evidence of that.[37] It ended on the masters' terms, not the workers'. In its aftermath, many furnace men must have decided to take up opportunities abroad rather than endure poor living at home. And opportunities there were. 'English' [*sic*] works were opened at Lirquén and Herradura in Chile's Norte Chico in the mid-1840s.[38] In the United States, the first Welsh-style smelting plant was built at Baltimore. It was staffed by Welsh migrants, many of them former employees of the Llanelly Copperworks Co.[39] A second works, once again staffed by men from the Swansea district, opened on the other side of Baltimore harbour in 1850.[40]

The world of Welsh copper had begun to break up. South Wales was the 'central smelter for minerals from East and West' no longer. There was a growing tendency for smelting firms to build plant close to the ore (as the British-owned Mexican & South American Company did at Herradura), a tendency driven by improvements in fuel efficiency. New patent methods (John Napier's, for example, which was employed at Kooringa) abbreviated the multistage Welsh process; in doing so, they detached the Welsh process from its original geological moorings in coal-rich south Wales.[41] The 'central smelter' that had been the Swansea district was increasingly just one of many.

The decentralisation of the global copper industry was greatly accelerated by the American Civil War. Surging demand brought new ore fields in the American interior into play and had smelting capacity in the United States roaring upwards. The restoration of peace saw metal markets glutted and prices slump. The world's older mining districts were ill-prepared for this. Many of them collapsed. Mining ceased at El Cobre, for example, and work at Burra was suspended. Cornwall, which had been the world's most important centre of copper mining in the 1850s, went into steep decline. In 1861, as the American war began, 145,500 tons of ore were raised in the county; ten years later, Cornish output stood at just 47,500 tons.[42]

The Welsh copper industry was not yet moribund but it was no longer hegemonic. Copper production continued to climb through the 1870s and 1880s, but advances in Wales were dwarfed by those taking place at new mining centres such as Butte, Montana. When the Swansea industrialist Henry Hussey Vivian made a tour of inspection of industrial America in 1877, he marvelled at the country's mineral riches and the vim with which they were being exploited. That the United States was already in advance of Britain in some sectors was perfectly clear: 'That she will ever again depend on England for iron or steel seems to me impossible'.[43] Vivian could not quite bring himself to make the same stark admission with respect to copper, but he could not have been blind to the direction of travel. US production more than doubled in the 1870s. In the 1880s, American output jagged upwards once more, from 32,500 tons in 1881 to 128,900 tons in 1891. A decade after that, output stood at 273,100 tons.[44] American copper had become truly gargantuan, dominated by super-capitalised combines. Welsh copper had become superfluous to American needs.

Much of the growth achieved in the United States depended upon the use of Welsh methods, but Welsh methods that now took on a distended form. Writing in 1910, a US metallurgist compared 'the small Swansea type' of reverberatory that had been brought to the American West in the 1870s 'to the furnaces now in use'. There was no comparison. Those early furnaces appeared puny things, with a hearth area of just 105 sq ft. The typical American calciner hearth of 1910 extended across 1,967 sq ft.[45] The freewheeling US industry did not restrict itself to time-tested Welsh practices, however. It borrowed freely from other traditions, some coal-burning, some that dispensed with coal altogether: the Manhès converter, for example, a French twist on the Bessemer process used in steel production, or electrolytic refining. Swansea producers could not match the scale or ambition of their upstart American rivals, although not necessarily because of technological conservatism:

> It would be a mistake to think that the Swansea district sank into torpor. Leading firms like Vivians were well aware of what was globally current and were quick to install Manhes converters at their Hafod works. However, the huge amounts of capital sunk in still-effective 'Welsh' smelting works inhibited the take-up of new methods across the Swansea district as a whole. Indeed, there was little incentive to write off old plants when the new methods' principal savings lay in labour and coal, factors of production that were both relatively cheap in Swansea.[46]

Smelting continued in the Swansea district into the first decades of the twentieth century but at a growing competitive disadvantage. The end did not come until 1924, but by then Welsh-smelted copper had long ceased to be of global significance. Wales retained some residual importance as a centre for the refining and processing of metals smelted elsewhere, but this was a niche role, nothing more.

WHAT ABOUT WELSH COPPER?

Welsh copper had three distinguishing features. First, it was coal-fuelled. It exploited fossilised biomass at a time when every other copper production system in the world relied upon vegetable fuel. The same transition, when made in the iron industry, has garnered far more historiographical and popular attention; yet the breakthrough in copper was fully accomplished before Abraham Darby turned his mind to smelting iron with coke, and it came a century before Henry Cort experimented with refining iron in coal-fired reverberatory furnaces. The second distinctive feature of Welsh copper lay in the use of non-local ores, shipped in from distant mines. This was without real precedent. Metals had been traded over long distances for many centuries; ores never were. Coal and seaborne ore could be successfully combined because of the third distinguishing feature: the use of the reverberatory furnace.

The reverberatory allowed coal to be used as an energy source without adversely affecting the metal produced. Reverberatories could also be multiplied on a single site, allowing for the development of large-scale industry. This was the Welsh trinity: coal – seaborne ore – reverberatories. It was not a system native to Wales – it was first brought to perfection in the Bristol region – but in south-west Wales it found the optimal geological and geographical setting.

The Swansea and Neath valleys provided the ideal location for smelting Cornish ores. It did not follow that the Swansea district should host other links in the cuprous commodity chain. Brass making was centred on Bristol and the rolling of sheet copper in the Thames valley for very good reasons. There are grounds for arguing, in fact, that 'Welsh copper' was very often something that happened in England. Indeed, the reach of Welsh copper went much further. It was strikingly colonial; its eighteenth-century take-off was reliant upon imperial expansion in both the Atlantic and Indian oceans. There were other parts of the world (central Asia, south-west China) that witnessed a dramatic rise in copper production in the eighteenth century but they lacked the Swansea district's global reach. Welsh copper's globality took a different turn in the mid-nineteenth century when shipments of ore, hitherto restricted to home waters, began to arrive from places of antipodean remoteness. Material fetched from advancing imperial frontiers in Australasia and southern Africa made its way to Swansea bay, courtesy of Cornish miners, the pioneer corps of empire. So did furnace stuff sourced from Latin America, summoned up by Anglo merchant houses and mining companies that drew upon and ramified informal British power. And before long, migrants from the Swansea district did their bit to globalise Britain's Industrial Revolution, implanting Welsh 'best practice' at smelting sites on four different continents. Seen in this light, Welsh copper was not just an element of Welsh industrialisation, it was a vital material ingredient of the nineteenth-century 'British World'.

NOTES

1 Swansea Museum's website takes the palm for hyperbole: 'In the nineteenth century 90% of the world's copper was smelted in Swansea valley [*sic*]'. See *http://www.swanseamuseum.co.uk/whats-on/past-exhibitions/copperopolis/copperopolis-and-the-world* (accessed 23 February 2018).

2 H. Heaton, *The Yorkshire Woollen and Worsted Industries: From the Earliest Times up to the Industrial Revolution* (Oxford: Oxford University Press, 1920); T. S. Ashton, *Iron and Steel in the Industrial Revolution* (Manchester: Manchester University Press, 1924); A. P. Wadsworth and Julia de Lacy Mann, *The Cotton Trade and Industrial Lancashire, 1600–1780* (Manchester: Manchester University Press, 1931).

3 R. O. Roberts, 'The development and decline of copper and other non-ferrous metal industries in south Wales', *Transactions of the Honourable Society of Cymmrodorion* (1956), 78–115, and 'The smelting of non-ferrous metals since 1750', in G. Williams and A. H. John (eds), *Glamorgan County History. Volume V: Industrial Glamorgan from 1700 to 1970* (Cardiff: Glamorgan County History Trust, 1980), pp. 47–95. These works are rich in detail but anyone seeking a clearer interpretive line should consult J. R. Harris's biographical study *The Copper King: A Biography of Thomas Williams of Llanidan* (Liverpool: Liverpool University Press, 1964). Other valuable scholarship is to be found in unpublished doctoral theses or postgraduate research that has been only partially published: see J. Morton, 'The rise of the modern copper and brass industry in Britain 1690–1750' (unpublished PhD thesis, University of Birmingham, 1985), and E. Newell, 'The British copper ore trade in the nineteenth century, with particular reference to Cornwall and Swansea' (unpublished DPhil thesis, University of Oxford, 1988).

4 L. Miskell (ed.), *The Origins of an Industrial Region: Robert Morris and the First Swansea Copper Works* (Newport: South Wales Record Society, 2010); C. Evans and O. Saunders, 'A world of copper: globalizing the industrial revolution, 1830–1870', *Journal of Global History*, 10/1 (2015), 3–26, and the articles in a themed issue of *Welsh History Review* in 2014: Chris Evans, 'El Cobre: Cuban ore and the globalization of Swansea copper, 1830–1870', *Welsh History Review*, 27/1 (2014), 112–31; W. D. Jones, 'Labour migration and cross-cultural encounters: Welsh copper workers in Chile in the nineteenth century', *Welsh History Review*, 27/1 (2014), 132–54; L. Miskell, 'From Copperopolis to Coquimbo: international knowledge networks in the copper industry of the 1820s', *Welsh History Review*, 27/1 (2014), 92–111.

5 Morton, 'Rise of the modern copper and brass industry', pp. 50–86.

6 E. A. Wrigley, *Continuity, Chance and Change: The Character of the Industrial Revolution in England* (Cambridge: Cambridge University Press, 1990).

7 Birmingham Archives [hereafter BA], Matthew Boulton papers, MS 3782/12/108/27, p. 78.

8 BA, Matthew Boulton papers, MS 3782/12/108/27, p. 79.

9 British Library, Add. MS. 25095, 'Two Discourses on Metals by John Woodward, M.D.', fo. 98.

10 Roberts, 'The smelting of non-ferrous metals since 1750', table 4, pp. 86–91.

11 I. Blanchard, *Russia's 'Age of Silver': Precious Metal Production and Economic Growth in the Eighteenth Century* (London: Routledge, 1989).

12 T. Hirzel and N. Kim (eds), *Metals, Monies, and Markets in Early Modern Societies: East Asian and Global Perspectives* (Berlin: LIT Verlag, 2008).

13 H. Ulrich Vogel, 'Chinese central monetary policy, 1644–1800', *Late Imperial China*, 8/2 (1987), 1–52. The standard reference work, C. J. Schmitz's *World Non-Ferrous Metal Production and Prices, 1700–1976* (London: Frank Cass, 1979), does not cover China in the eighteenth century.

14 N. Zahedieh, 'Technique or demand? The revival of the English copper industry ca 1680–1730', in P. R. Rössner (ed.), *Cities-Coins-Commerce: Essays presented to Ian Blanchard on the Occasion of his Seventieth Birthday* (Stuttgart: Franz Steiner Verlag, 2012), pp. 167–73, at 169.

15 N. Zahedieh, 'Colonies, copper and the market for inventive activity in England and Wales, 1680–1730', *Economic History Review*, 66/3 (2013), 805–25, at 811, table 3. The figure for 1770 is likely to be an underestimate, probably a considerable underestimate, given that the dimensions of sugar boilers increased over the course of the eighteenth century.

16 S. Hughes, *Copperopolis: Landscapes of the Early Industrial Period in Swansea* (Aberystwyth: Royal Commission on the Ancient and Historical Monuments of Wales, 2000), p. 46; T. Berg and P. Berg (eds), *R. R. Angerstein's Illustrated Travel Diary, 1753–1755: Industry in England and Wales from a Swedish Perspective* (London: Science Museum, 2001), p. 324.

17 Keele University Library Special Collections and Archives, Raymond Richards Collection, William Davenport & Co. trading invoices and accounts, invoice of the *Quixote*, 1783.

18 Bristol Archives, 45039, accounts of the *Africa*, 1774–6.

19 Parliamentary Archives, 10/7/88, petition dated 9 July 1788.

20 Huw Bowen [2007], 'East India Company: Trade and Domestic Financial Statistics, 1755–1838', UK Data Service SN: 5690. The data presented here have been set against the production figures given in J. C. Symons, 'The mining and smelting of copper in England and Wales 1760–1820' (unpublished MPhil thesis, Coventry University, 2003), p. 173, table 2.5, which represent the assumed metallic content of ores raised in Cornwall, Anglesey and Staffordshire. Data for Irish ores are only intermittently available but the omissions do not significantly affect the overall conclusions because Irish copper ore usually represented less than 2 per cent and frequently less than 1 per cent of the total.

21 J. J. McCusker, 'The business of distilling in the Old World and the New World during the seventeenth and eighteenth centuries: the rise of a new enterprise

and its connection with colonial America', in J. J. McCusker and K. Morgan (eds), *The Early Modern Atlantic Economy* (Cambridge: Cambridge University Press, 2000), pp. 186–224.

22 *An Account of the Late Application to Parliament, from the Sugar Refiners, Grocers, &c. of the Cities of London and Westminster, the Borough of Southwark, and of the City of Bristol* (London: J. Brotherton, 1753), p. 42.

23 J. R. Harris, 'Copper and shipping in the eighteenth century', *Economic History Review*, 19/3 (1966), 550–68.

24 BA, Matthew Boulton papers, MS 3782/12/108/27, p. 70. Boulton estimated contemporary British production at 7,650 tons, with a further 2,000 tons of scrap copper in circulation.

25 Duchy of Cornwall Archive, DOC/S/108, survey of the manor of Kennington, 1786.

26 Buckinghamshire Archives, D G/R 6/19. Wraysbury was operated by Williams & Grenfell, the partnership that smelted copper at the Middle Bank works in the lower Swansea valley and traded the metal from its warehouse on Upper Thames Street in the City.

27 Massachusetts Historical Society, Revere Family Papers, Joseph W. Revere journal 1804–5, 22 December 1804. Joseph Warren was the son of the renowned Patriot Paul Revere, whose rolling mill at Canton outside Boston, Massachusetts, was to introduce British best practice to the United States: see R. Martello, *Midnight Ride, Industrial Dawn, Paul Revere and the Growth of Industrial Enterprise* (Baltimore: Johns Hopkins University Press, 2010), chapter 8.

28 R. S. Craig, R. Protheroe Jones and M. V. Symons, *The Industrial and Maritime History of Llanelli and Burry Port 1750–2000* (Carmarthen: Carmarthenshire County Council, 2002), pp. 108–42; R. R. Toomey, 'Vivian and Sons, 1809–1924: a study of the firm in the copper and related industries' (unpublished PhD thesis, University of Wales, 1979), pp. 10–14.

29 R. A. Williams, *The Berehaven Mines* (Kenmare: A. B. O'Connor, 1993); D. Cowman, *The Making and Breaking of a Mining Community: The Copper Coast, County Waterford 1825–1875* (Dublin: Mining History Trust of Ireland, 2006).

30 E. Newell, '"Copperopolis": the rise and fall of the copper industry in the Swansea district, 1826–1921', *Business History*, 32/3 (1990), 75–97.

31 Frédéric Le Play, *Description des procédés métallurgiques employés dans le Pays de Galles pour la fabrication du cuivre* (Paris: Carilian-Goeury et Von Dalmont, 1848), pp. 6–7.

32 Le Play, *Description des procédés*, p. 387. It is important to remember, though, that most of the ore smelted in south Wales continued to come from the south-west of England. Cornish production peaked in 1854 at 184,858 tons (metallic content = 11,979 tons). Devon's copper ore output peaked in 1856 at 42,219 tons (= 2,543 tons of copper). R. Burt et al., *Mining in*

Cornwall and Devon: Mines and Men (Exeter: University of Exeter Press, 2014), pp. 56, 80.

33 Evans, 'El Cobre'; I. Roldán de Montaud, 'El ciclo cubano del cobre en el siglo XIX, 1830–1868', *Bolétin Geolgico y Minero*, 119/3 (2008), 361–82.

34 J. Shute, *Henry Ayers: The Man who Became a Rock* (London: I. B. Tauris, 2010).

35 A. Snowden Piggot, *The Chemistry and Metallurgy of Copper, Including a Description of the Principal Copper Mines of the United States and other Countries* (Philadelphia: Lindsay & Blakiston, 1858), provides an inventory of production zones in the mid-nineteenth century, at pp. 193–285.

36 J. Percy, *Metallurgy: The Art of Extracting Metals from their Ores, and Adapting them to Various Purposes of Manufacture* (London: John Murray, 1861), p. 322.

37 A. Godfrey, '"We would rather starve idle than starve while working hard": the Swansea copperworkers' strike of 1843', *Llafur*, 11/4 (2015), 5–25.

38 L. Valenzuela, 'The Chilean copper-smelting industry in the mid-nineteenth century: phases of expansion and stagnation, 1834–1858', *Journal of Latin American Studies*, 24/3 (1992), 507–50.

39 See the letter of 20 November 1848 from David Keener of the Baltimore & Cuba Copper Co. to R. J. Nevill in Llanelli remitting the wages of Baltimore-based Welsh workers to their wives in Wales: National Library of Wales, Nevill 2357.

40 C. K. Hyde, *Copper for America: The United States Copper Industry from Colonial Times to the 1990s* (Tucson: University of Arizona Press, 1998), pp. 23–4.

41 M. Davies, 'Balanced costs: inland copper smelting location and fuel in South Australia 1848–76: were they so naive?', University of Western Australia, Department of Economics, working paper 05-25 (2005), pp. 1–17.

42 Burt et al., *Mining in Cornwall and Devon*, p. 56.

43 H. Hussey Vivian, *Notes of a Tour in America* (London: Edward Stanton, 1878), p. 250.

44 Schmitz, *World Non-Ferrous Metal Production and Prices*, pp. 64, 69.

45 E. D. Peters, *The Practice of Copper Smelting* (New York and London: McGraw-Hill Book Co., 1911), p. 326.

46 Evans and Saunders, 'A world of copper', 22.

ENUMERATING THE WELSH-FRENCH COAL TRADE c.1833–1913

OPENING PANDORA'S BOX

TREVOR BOYNS

INTRODUCTION

COAL was the key power source of the nineteenth century, fuelling the needs of industry, transportation and households, and the south Wales coalfield was a major supplier of such fuel throughout much of the industrialising world during the study period. In keeping with one of the main themes of this book, therefore, this chapter examines the customers and markets for south Wales coal in its major overseas destination, France. Coal exports were important to the coalfield's development but, beyond broad generalisations, little detailed analysis has been undertaken of this trade. One explanation for this is the lack of completeness, consistency and continuity of the British data, which makes answering key questions difficult, if not impossible. One stumbling block is that the most readily available data of the coal trade with France relate to Britain as a whole, and for this reason the first part of the chapter focuses on this. In the second part the focus is on Wales, although a lack of data means that the analysis is heavily oriented to the last twenty years of the study period. Despite being more readily available, even here the data can be frustrating, failing to provide answers to key questions such as how much coal of a specific type was shipped and/or what it was used for in France. In an attempt to overcome some of the deficiencies of the British data, the study also uses official French statistics, together with various secondary sources. However, trying to fuse together trade data from two countries is akin to opening Pandora's box; while such actions provide historians with the hope of better understanding the trade between the two countries, potentially providing new insights and opening up new research avenues, such an exercise is not without its pitfalls, releasing a whole plethora of new problems that add to the confusion and frustration of the historian. Nevertheless, as will be seen, such an exercise does enable us to conclude that Welsh coal played an important role in the industrialisation of France during the nineteenth century. In contrast to what appears to have been the case in many other destinations to which it was shipped before 1914, the use of Welsh coal as bunker fuel for shipping in French ports was of relatively minor importance. Of far greater significance was its use, alongside that from other British coalfields, to sustain the growing demand for power of both industry and the railways consequent on the industrialisation of France, a demand that could not be met from domestic sources.

COAL AND ITS USES

For many, coal is simply a black mineral that burns and provides heat. There are, however, different types of coal, each with its own specific characteristics (for example, percentages of carbon, hydrogen and volatile matter, calorific value, et cetera) and hence specific end uses. One classification[1] runs from bituminous coals at one end (high volatility and hydrogen, low carbon), encompassing house coals, gas coals and coking coals, through semi-bituminous (less volatile matter and hydrogen, but more carbon), including blending and caking steam coals, through sub-bituminous or dry steam coals to anthracite (low volatile matter and hydrogen, but high carbon content). The south Wales coalfield produced all of these, the more bituminous being found in the south and east, while the semi- and sub-bituminous were to be found in the central regions, such as the Aberdare, Taff and Rhondda valleys, with the more anthracitic coals being found in the north and west of the coalfield.

The varying characteristics of the different types of coal, including the amount of sulphur they contained and the amount of ash they created, influenced the uses for which they were appropriate. Thus, anthracite was especially useful where heat and slow-burning were beneficial, as in agricultural processes such as malting, or for burning in specially constructed heating stoves, while bituminous coals could be used for purposes of generating gas, manufacturing coke for use in iron works, and providing steam power generated from boilers. The dry, smokeless steam coals of the central coalfield region were especially beneficial for transport, for example shipping and railway locomotives. In addition to coal and coke, south Wales also produced patent or manufactured fuel, made from small coal and tar-pitch and shaped into briquettes or ovoids (*boulets* in French). In 1913, 87 per cent of British output of such fuel was produced in south Wales,[2] most of it exported for use by foreign railways and shipping.

DATA SOURCES AND ISSUES

Two official sources of data are used in this chapter: on the British side the main source is the *Trade and Navigation Accounts*, a series of annual returns submitted to parliament that, prior to 1854, were presented as part of the annual *Finance Accounts* but thereafter as separate parliamentary 'blue books';[3] on the French side, data published in a series of official publications from 1833, often referred to as simply *SIM*,[4] are used. The first problem encountered in attempting to combine information from these two sources is that they use different measurement units: the British data are in imperial tons, whereas the French data are in metric tons (or, in the early years, quintals).[5] In this chapter, all French data have been converted into imperial tons. Second, in theory, the amount of coal exported from one country to another should equal the amount imported by the latter from the former, but the trade statistics of two countries historically often show differences. In part, this reflects the definitions of exports and imports adopted.[6] A parliamentary paper in the early 1880s comparing the English export figures with the French import figures for the same product recognised this problem, but commented that, for coal, the discrepancy was much smaller than for most other articles, not least because all coal sent was domestically produced in the United Kingdom, and all that which 'goes to France is probably consumed there'.[7] Nevertheless, differences amounting to as much as 20 per cent are found in the early part of the study period when figures were relatively small and less reliable.

The annual sources cited above, and compilations based thereon, have been supplemented by information provided in secondary histories and related works, together with ad hoc parliamentary papers and reports from British consular and diplomatic staff based in France, although some care has to be taken when using the last of these sources. Nevertheless, in conjunction with other material, the consular reports can help to throw light on the Welsh coal trade with France. However, before considering this in detail, since the most readily available data relate to the coal trade of Britain, and to provide context, the development of British overseas coal exports between 1833 and 1913 will be examined briefly.

BRITISH OVERSEAS COAL EXPORTS, 1833–1913

Exports of British coal to overseas destinations, rather than coastwise to other parts of the country, were 629,000 tons in 1833, accounting for just 2 per cent of estimated British output. They exceeded 1 million tons for the first time in 1837 (2.6 per cent of output) and, by 1913, had reached a staggering 73.4 million tons (see Figure 2.1 – 25.5 per cent of output).

Figure 2.1: Coal exports, UK and south Wales, 1833–1913 (000 tons)

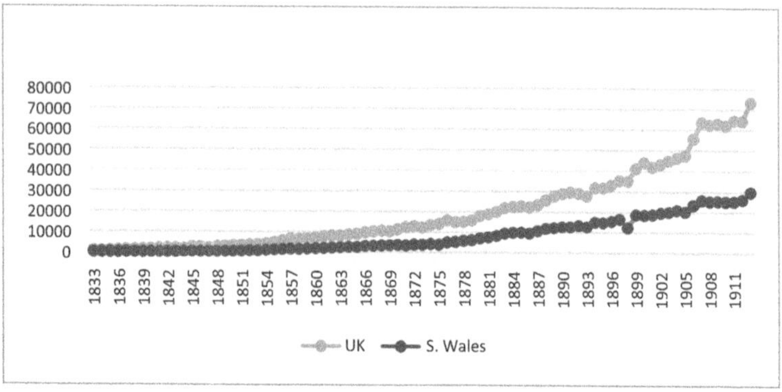

Source: Based on data presented in Mitchell and Deane, *Abstract of British Historical Statistics*, p. 121.

Different rates of industrialisation, the availability of domestic fuel supplies and their strategic importance in relation to major shipping routes led to a change in the relative importance of different geographical regions/countries as markets for British coal between 1830 and 1913 (see Table 2.1). By 1850, it is clear from British data that France had become the most significant market, retaining its position as the single most important country of destination through to 1913, although by 1890 the Mediterranean region as a whole had overtaken France as the largest market, reflecting the growth especially of the bunker trade in the region following the completion of the Suez canal in 1869.

Table 2.1: Destination of British coal exports, 1830–1913 (%)

	1830	1850	1870	1890	1913
Russia	5.3	7.0	7.2	5.0	8.0
Scandinavia	1.7	3.1	5.6	7.7	9.6
Denmark	19.8	8.8	6.1	4.5	4.3
Germany	18.7	17.1	13.9	11.1	11.7
Holland and Belgium	4.5	4.8	4.6	3.7	5.3
France	10.3	18.3	18.1	16.9	17.2
Iberia	2.8	7.7	6.8	10.0	7.4
Mediterranean	2.5	9.7	6.7	18.2	17.5
Africa	1.2	2.4	4.5	8.2	7.9
North America	22.0	10.3	7.4	2.1	0.3
South America	0.7	4.5	5.6	6.5	9.9
Asia/Australasia	0.5	4.5	5.8	5.7	1.1
Total exports (m. tons)	**0.5**	3.2	11.2	**28.7**	73.4

Source: R. A. Church, *The History of the British Coal Industry, Vol. 3: 1830–1913 Victorian Pre-eminence* (Oxford: Clarendon Press, 1986), pp. 32, 35.

THE ANGLO[8]-FRENCH COAL TRADE, 1833–1913

Although France has a number of coalfields of its own, throughout its history it relied on imports to supplement its domestic production. In 1833, for example, domestic output of 2.03 million tons was supplemented by imports of 0.69 million tons, of which only 0.04 million tons came from Britain. The proportion of French coal consumption taken by imports rose from 25 per cent in 1833 to a third in 1847, and remained at around this level throughout the study period: in 1913, out of a total consumption of 62.8 million tons, 22.43 million tons (35.7 per cent) was imported. The low level of British imports in 1833 reflected the negative impact of British coal export duties and French import taxes introduced as a result of the revolutionary and Napoleonic wars.[9] In 1834, however, Britain began to reduce its export duties, finally abolishing them completely in 1850, while around the same time France similarly began to reduce its import taxes. Furthermore, the discrimination against (British) seaborne coal compared to (Belgian) overland imports was reduced.[10] The Anglo-French trade treaty of 1860 'committed France to abolishing all forms of discrimination against English coal within four years'.[11] These tax and duty changes, together with industrialisation, caused a major spurt in British coal exports to France, British and French data indicating that the total exceeded 500,000 tons by 1845, 1 million tons by 1856 and 2 million tons in 1872 (see Figure 2.2). French data also show that, from being used in the more westerly parts of the country in the earlier part of the century, British coal became increasingly ubiquitous, at least in the coastal regions (*littoral*) of France. As a result, from 1894, Britain became France's largest external supplier of coal, with total British coal imports surpassing those of Belgium. By 1911 British coal was being consumed in sixty-two out of the then seventy existing *départements* of France, compared to just thirty-four for German coal and thirty-two for Belgian coal.[12] In 1913 British coal imports amounted to 11.26 million tons, accounting for half of all French coal imports, compared to the 30 per cent that they had represented in 1840.[13] With the exception of the rapidly growing Parisian market, in which they competed, the markets for British and Belgian coal were distinct.[14]

With sea transport much cheaper than overland transport, and the best-placed French coalfields located between 100 and 200 kilometres from the sea, British 'maritime' coalfields, including south Wales, found themselves geographically favoured to serve the coastal areas of west and south-west France, situated as they were far away from French coalfields.[15] Thus, in 1836, of the 216,813 tons of British coal imported into France, 182,129 tons (86 per cent) was consumed

Figure 2.2: British and Welsh exports to France, 1833–1913 (tons)

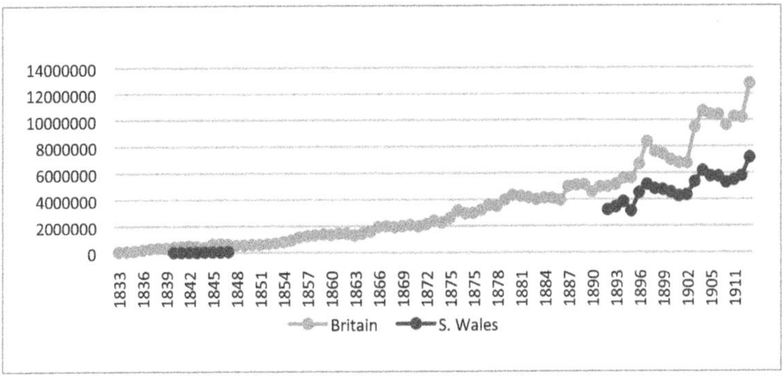

Sources: Britain: PP 'Annual Statement of Trade'
South Wales: 1840-7 – see sources to Table 2.4
1895-1909 – PP HC 'Coal exports &c'
1910-13 – PP Command Papers 'Coal shipments'.

Figure 2.3: Map of British coal consumption by *département*, 1879

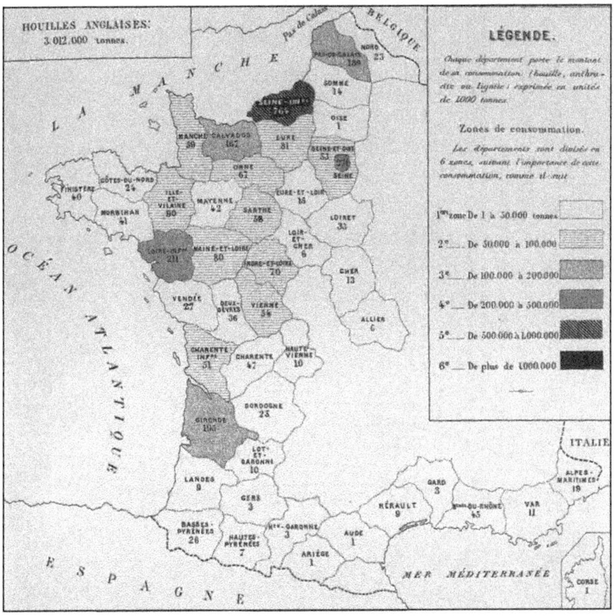

Source: SIM, 1879, between p. 22 and p. 23, taken from a digital copy available via the website of the Bibliothèque de l'École des mines de Paris – MINES ParisTech.

in those *départements* making up the French *littoral*, and this figure rarely, if ever, fell below 70 per cent before 1900 (see, for example, Figure 2.3).[16] Indeed, Crouzet has argued that 'English [*sic*] coal was a necessary condition for the industrial development which occurred during the nineteenth century along the estuaries of the Seine and the Loire, and, to a lesser extent, in the Gironde and Ardour'.[17] By 1911, despite a major increase in the amount of British coal imported to over 10 million tons, the proportion taken by the coastal *départements* had fallen to below two thirds, reflecting the major expansion of the market in Paris and its environs, which virtually trebled in size between 1900 and 1911.[18] In Figure 2.4, which shows the main importing *départements* between 1847 and 1911,[19] it can clearly be seen that, for most of the study period, the Seine-Inférieure département was the most important, before the growth of the Parisian market pushed Seine to the top. Most other *départements* depicted in Figure 2.4 showed a general rise throughout the period, although alongside Seine-Inférieure, two others showed a marked fall between 1903 and 1911: Gironde and Loire-Inférieure.

Since all of the British coal imported into France went by sea, it was the location of ports that heavily influenced which *départements* used British coal. In 1858, seven French ports received

Figure 2.4: Major importers of British coal, French *départements*, 1847–1911 (000 tons)

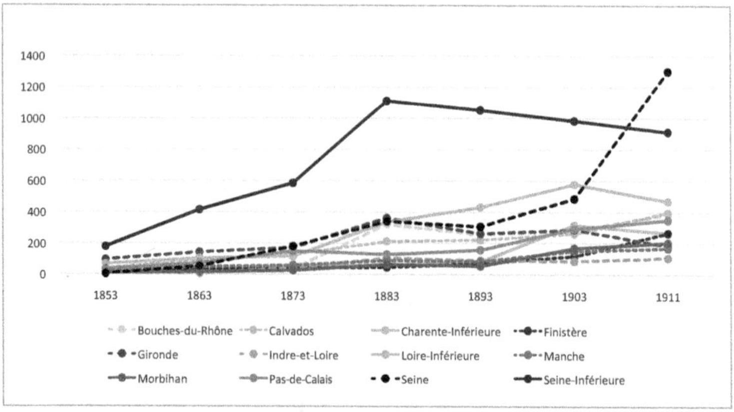

Source: Based on data in SIM for the years indicated.

more than 50,000 tons, namely Dieppe (240,000 tons), Le Havre (178,242 tons), Bordeaux (155,929 tons), Nantes (125,377 tons), Rouen (99,467 tons), Marseilles (87,270 tons) and Boulogne (64,879 tons).[20] By 1913, five of these remained in the top eight recipients of British coal (see Table 2.2): Rouen (the main port for the Seine-Inférieure and Seine *départements*), Bordeaux (Gironde), Nantes/Saint-Nazaire (Loire-Inférieure) and Marseilles (Bouches-du-Rhône), with Caen (Normandy), La Rochelle (Charente-Inférieure) and Le Havre (Seine-Inférieure). As Table 2.2 shows, by virtue both of its geographical proximity (and thereby lower transport costs) and its inherent qualities, British coal had a virtual monopoly of imports into many of these French ports.[21]

Table 2.2: Major ports for the importation of British coal into France, 1913 (tons)

	Total	**British**	**% British**
Rouen	2748983	2630658	95.7
Bordeaux	1559061	1502812	96.4
Saint-Nazaire	1010709	791813	78.3
Marseilles	946381	889309	94.0
Caen	787918	698635	88.7
La Rochelle	760208	723279	95.1
Nantes	650028	619014	95.2
Le Havre	517592	499951	96.6

Source: SIM, 1913, p. 98.

Within France, data on the consumption of coal, both domestically produced and imported, show that between 1847 and 1872 inclusive, when total French consumption rose from 7.53 million tons to 22.86 million tons, the main market was industry, around 70 per cent of all coal being consumed by 'factories', there being no more precise indication of its use within particular sectors.[22] Coal mines themselves used about 4 per cent of the total, transport 10 per cent, while the share consumed by households fell from more than 20 per cent in 1847 to around 13 per cent in the early 1870s. Within transport, the main share was taken by the railways, which consumed 2.07 million tons of coal or 8.5 per cent of total French consumption in 1873, compared to just 0.39 million tons (1.6 per cent) for shipping. By 1913 the main consumers were households and metallurgical works, both consuming *c.*12 million tons, or about one fifth each, while 'various industries' (i.e. non-specified) accounted for around 30 per cent, and mines and gas works each consumed 7–8 per cent. The share of transport, meanwhile, had nearly doubled: merchant shipping engaged in trade between French ports and territories consumed 1.69 million tons (2.5 per cent of total French consumption), while railways now consumed 8.93 million tons, or one in every 7 tons of coal consumed in France in 1913.

The first railway line completed in France, 23 kilometres long connecting Saint-Étienne to the Loire, commenced operation in 1828, with others following from 1830.[23] By 1840, 430 kilometres of line were being operated by 142 locomotives, and by 1872 the figures had reached 17,822 kilometres and 5,102 locomotives. By 1913 there were 16,962 locomotives in use in France.[24] As a result of such developments, total coal consumption by the French railways, comprising a mix of raw coal, coke and patent fuel briquettes, rose from 2.1 million tons in 1876 to 8.8 million tons in 1912. In 1876, the first year for which detailed figures are provided, of this total, coke, despite being the original fuel used in railway locomotives, was of negligible proportions, coal comprising 0.88 million tons (of which a third was imported) with briquettes accounting for 1.18 million tons (of which 40 per cent was of foreign origin); by 1912, coal consumption had reached 6.35 million tons (just under half being imported) and briquettes 2.21 million tons (more than 60 per cent imported). Most of the fuel was used on the railways of 'general interest', that is the main railway network (*grands reseaux*), and data in *SIM* reveal that, in 1897, 0.69 million tons of British coal[25] was used, representing just under 16 per cent of total railway consumption; by 1911 the figure had risen to 2.05 million tons, or 27 per cent of total consumption, although the proportion had been as high as 40.5 per cent in 1907.

Perhaps not surprisingly it was those companies operating lines in the west and north-west of the country that favoured British coal (for example, *Ouest/Etat* and *Orléans*), while those located in the north-east and east of the country (*Nord* and *Est*) used very little or none at all, favouring Belgian and German imports together with some local coal. The most significant consumers of British coal in 1911 were the state railway company (*Etat*),[26] which consumed over 1 million tons, the *Orléans* railway 0.6 million tons and the *Midi* railway just under 250,000 tons. However, some companies whose networks reached right across the country, such as *Paris-Lyon-Méditerrannée* (PLM), had more choice as to where to source their coal, and hence the amount of British coal used could fluctuate greatly from one year to the next, reflecting prices at the time contracts were effected. Thus, in some years, the PLM purchased more than 300,000 tons of British coal, while in other years it could be less than 100,000 tons.

The other element of transport on which the French statistics throw light is the demands of French merchant shipping, although this was much smaller than that of the railways, reflecting the relatively small size of the French fleet. The number of seagoing steamships, as opposed to steam vessels used for river transport, in service in France only rose slowly from 208 in 1860 to 510 in 1880 and 928 in 1906.[27] In 1897, when the registered tonnage of French steam shipping was just 499,230 tons, in marked contrast to the British figure of 6,663,601 tons,[28] just 750,000 tons of British coal were used as bunkers at French ports by French-registered vessels carrying out trade with other parts of France and French territories. This figure reached 1 million tons in 1909 and 1910, before falling back slightly in 1911, the last year for which data are presented.[29] Other data reveal that during the period 1906–11 the bulk (more than 85 per cent) of the British bunker coal so recorded was distributed via ports located in just five *départements* (listed in order of importance in 1911): Bouches-du-Rhône, Seine-Inférieure, Gironde, Loire-Inférieure and Charente-Inférieure.

THE SOURCE OF BRITISH COAL SENT TO FRANCE

It has been seen that between 1830 and 1913 British coal became ubiquitous within the coastal regions of France as well as reaching some inland areas, including Paris. With the ports of south Wales being closest to those of western France it is not surprising to find that the amount of coal shipped to France from the Bristol Channel ports[30] grew rapidly in the middle decades of the nineteenth century, overtaking that of any other major grouping of British ports, such as those of the north-east of England, the Humber or Scotland. Data deficiencies do not enable us to say precisely when this switchover occurred, but shipments to France from the Bristol Channel ports, which accounted for just 3 per cent in the early 1840s, had increased to 10.33 per cent by 1847. While the bulk of the coal shipped to France in the 1830s and 1840s came from ports serving the coalfields of the north-east and eastern England, the opening up of the central portions of the south Wales coalfield, and the development of the ports of Cardiff and Newport from the middle decades of the nineteenth century, meant that, by 1895, the Bristol Channel ports came to dominate the French market, accounting for nearly two thirds of British shipments, remaining at well above one half in 1913 (see Table 2.3).

Table 2.3: Exports of coal to France from different groups of British ports, 1895–1913 (%)

	1895	1900	1905	1910	1913
Bristol Channel ports	65	62	64	55	57
North-eastern ports	23	23	24	30	30
Humber ports	4	5	3	4	6
Scottish ports	7	10	8	9	7
Other ports	1	0	0	1	0

Source: Gibson, *A Compilation of Statistics*, p. 100.

THE WELSH COAL TRADE, 1833–1913

To provide context for the study of Welsh coal in France, the Welsh coal trade more generally is examined first. In 1833 exports of Welsh coal stood at just 17,030 tons and were still only 45,957 tons in 1841. However, in the 1840s they grew dramatically, exceeding 200,000 tons in 1844, reaching 500,000 tons in 1852 and 1 million tons by 1855. By 1913 they stood at 29.78 million tons (see Figure 2.1), making south Wales Britain's premier exporting coalfield, reflecting the high quality of Welsh steam coal and the location of its best coals close to the ports of shipment. These combined to provide overseas customers with a low unit cost per pound of evaporative power, resulting in south Wales coal being much in demand worldwide. Hence, in 1913, south Wales sent a much higher proportion (56.0 per cent) of its production overseas than any other British coalfield (the average for the British coal industry as a whole being just 26.9 per cent). Over the study period, the significance of the various south Wales ports shifted from Llanelli and Swansea in the west, the natural outlets for the semi-anthracitic coals, to Cardiff (including Barry and Penarth docks) and Newport serving the bituminous and smokeless steam coal regions of the central and eastern parts of the coalfield. However, in the early twentieth century an increasing demand for anthracite and the coming into operation of Port Talbot docks caused a slight shift back to the west.

Although Newport had surpassed Swansea by 1820 as the most important coal port in Wales, being considered ten years later as 'the largest coal supplying port in the Kingdom with the exception of the ports on the Wear and Tyne',[31] virtually all of the coal shipped from it at that time went coastwise to other parts of Britain and Ireland. Thus, foreign shipments from Swansea and Llanelli totalling 10,258 tons in 1830 still dwarfed those from Newport and Cardiff, which totalled just 2,641 tons.[32] Foreign shipments from Newport, however, grew rapidly in the first half of the 1840s, reaching almost 150,000 tons in both 1844 and 1845, before falling back as Cardiff began to play an increasingly dominant role, especially following the opening of the West Bute dock on 9 October 1839 and the first stretch of the Taff Vale Railway on 18 October 1840 (completed to Merthyr by April 1841).[33] These events enabled the opening up of the Aberdare valley and the steam coal areas of the central region of the coalfield, resulting in exports from Cardiff rising from 3,840 tons in 1837 to 45,102 tons in 1846, and to just over 1 million tons in 1860.[34]

As Figure 2.5 shows, Cardiff came to vastly outstrip the other south Wales ports not only due to the expansion of the town's Bute docks, but also the construction of new docks at neighbouring Barry and Penarth, which, for customs purposes, were included under the returns of the port of Cardiff. Indeed, without the addition of these dock facilities, coal shipments from Cardiff would have stagnated: exports from Barry docks first exceeded those of Cardiff docks in 1901 and with the sole exception of 1911 continued to do so up to the First World War.

Figure 2.5: The growth of coal exports from the main Welsh ports, 1833–1913 (tons)

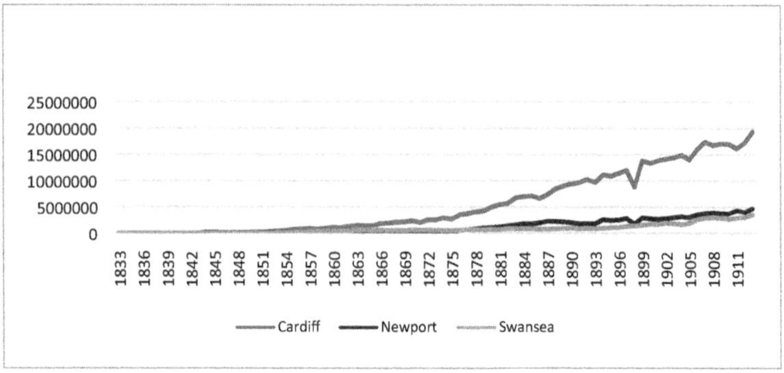

Source: Based on data in R. H. Walters, *The Economic and Business History of the South Wales Steam Coal Industry* (New York: Arno Press, 1977), appendix 12, pp. 365–6.

WELSH COAL IN FRANCE, 1833–1913

According to the Welsh economic historian Arthur John: 'Until the development of steamships, foreign trade in coal was mainly to the northern and western ports of France . . . In 1826–28, 80–85 ships sailed annually from Swansea, mostly with coal, of which 90 per cent went to France and Jersey'.[35] However, by the early 1830s steamships operating in the Mediterranean were using Llangennech coal[36] and while individuals such as R. J. Nevill, managing partner of the Llanelli copper works and owner of collieries in the Llanelli region, encouraged French steam packets to try Llanelli coals,[37] the predominance of the western ports faded as the geographical extent of the coal trade widened. Trade with France was encouraged following 'the reduction, in 1837, of French import duties on coal sent to ports lying between the Seine and Loire'.[38] John Nixon, a Durham mining engineer with experience of managing an ironworks and collieries in France, used the connections he had built up in Nantes to introduce Aberdare steam coal from Thomas Powell's collieries to the French market.[39] Having persuaded the sugar refiners of Nantes to try Welsh steam coal, through his contacts, he ultimately succeeded in getting it accepted by operators of river steamers, who found it to be of better quality and ultimately cheaper to use. This, in turn, led to 'orders for Welsh coal from the French government in preference to that of Newcastle'.[40]

Despite the rapid growth of exports from Cardiff in the 1840s, Swansea remained the largest source of coal shipped to France from Welsh ports in 1847 (see Table 2.4), though it seems likely that this position was rapidly overtaken as the smokeless steam coals of the central coalfield areas became ever more widely recognised for their superior qualities. A major factor in the ultimate success of such coals was the outcome of various trials, especially, but not only, those conducted by the British Admiralty between 1846 and 1875, which proved their superiority over Newcastle coal, and any admixture of the two for use in naval ships.[41]

Table 2.4: Shipments of coal, cinders and culm from Welsh ports to France, 1840–7 (tons)

	Cardiff	Llanelli	Milford	Newport	Swansea
1840	350	3019	-	780	7571
1841	90	2627	-	1819	5907
1842	30	4798	-	4518	8791
1843	611.5	1973.5	-	4598	6414
1844	7810	5441	-	13184	14426
1845	7726	6718	210	1831	18704
1846	8258.5	8131	-	-	19253
1847	18979	11228	275	1011	28139
Total					
1840–47	43855	43935.5	485	27741	109205
(% of total)	(19.47)	(19.51)	(0.22)	(12.32)	(48.49)

Sources: PP 1847, HC (520) 'Coals, cinders and culm'; PP 1847–8, HC (337) 'Coal-laden ships'.

Both Welsh and French businessmen were involved in developing the coal trade with France. By the end of 1848, George Insole & Son, colliery owners and shipping agents, had had their sales pamphlet translated into French and were shipping Aberaman coal to Nantes, Brest, Calais, Marseilles and Corsica.[42] In that same year the Frenchman, Hypolite Worms, whose 'main business was supplying plaster as an export cargo to English ships delivering coal to Rouen',[43] began to import coal from Cardiff and Newcastle to Rouen and Dieppe. By 1851 he was

> reputedly the largest French purchaser of English coal and amongst his chief customers were the steamship companies operating out of Le Havre and Marseille, and during the Crimean War he supplied coal to the French navy . . . By 1871, Worms et Cie. was handling 7 percent of all British coal exports and furnishing coal to all the navies of continental Europe.[44]

The Powell Duffryn Steam Coal Co. Ltd, formed in 1864, had a depot in Rouen from the earliest days,[45] and in February 1879 established a Paris committee based at its offices in the city to expand its business in France.[46] By 1880 promotional material produced by George Insole & Son indicated that the firm had agents at Rouen, Le Havre and Paris,[47] while L. Guéret Ltd[48] had established depots at Saint-Malo, Saint-Nazaire, Chantenay, Bordeaux, Marseilles and Tours by 1898. In that year, the company formed the Société Generale de Houilles et Agglomérés, with its headquarters in Paris, to take over these and its interests in patent fuel works, such as that established in the 1870s at Saint-Servan, just outside Saint-Malo.[49] On the eve of the First World War, Powell Duffryn operated a patent fuel manufacturing plant at Rouen capable of an annual production of 30,000 tons of *boulets*, and on 1 January 1914 established the Compagnie Française des Mines Powell Duffryn, headquartered in Rouen, to manage its French agencies and depots.[50]

Through the activities of these businesses and others, Welsh exports to France grew, though precise details are lacking for the period 1848–94. By 1895 Welsh exports had reached just over 3.2 million tons (accounting for 65.0 per cent of British coal shipped to the country) and rose to almost 7.25 million tons in 1913 (56.7 per cent of the British total) (see Figure 2.6), ensuring France remained the largest single market for south Wales coal exports before the First World War.[51] Over the period 1895–1913, shipments to France amounted to about 50 million tons, one eighth of south Wales coal exports over this period, but in 1913 alone they accounted for double this proportion (24.4 per cent), reflecting rapid growth in the immediate pre-First World War years, especially in shipments of gas and coking coals, and anthracite for the Paris/Seine market. These developments altered the relative importance of Welsh ports in the French coal trade, as indicated in Figure 2.5, which clearly shows a stagnation in exports from Cardiff after 1899, resulting in its share of the French coal trade falling from just under 70 per cent in 1895 to 40 per cent in 1913. In contrast, shipments from Swansea and Port Talbot grew: Swansea's shipments trebled from 0.62 million tons to 1.92 million tons between 1895 and 1913, its share of the French market thereby increasing from under 20 per cent to more than 30 per cent in 1911, before falling back slightly, while shipments from Port Talbot, which only commenced operations in 1904, had reached 1.1 million tons by 1913, when it accounted for 15.7 per cent of the French market.

Figure 2.6: Coal exports to France from various Welsh ports, 1895–1913

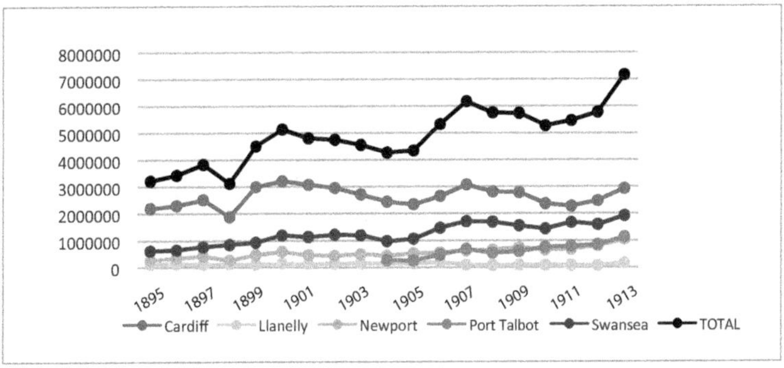

Sources: 1895-1909: PP HC 'Coal exports, &c.'; 1910-13: PP Cd 'Coal shipments'.

The total amount of coal sent to France from each Welsh port is known from 1895, and to each port from 1902. However, precise details as to the amount of each type of coal sent from each Welsh port to a specific French port is not known. For France as a whole, figures do exist for shipments of anthracite and 'steam', but since the latter encompasses all coal that was not anthracite, such data are of limited use. Nevertheless, the existing data do reveal some important shifts in emphasis, suggesting shifts in the nature of the local French coal markets. In 1902, Cardiff, on its own or in conjunction with Newport, dominated shipments of Welsh coal to the major French ports listed in Table 2.2, with the sole exception of Rouen, where Swansea and Llanelli dominated (and strengthened their hold to nearly three quarters in 1911). By 1911, however, there had been some significant changes (see Table 2.5): despite a stagnation in the aggregate amount of coal shipped to Le Havre, Nantes, La Pallice and Marseilles, at around 1.25 million tons, Cardiff and Newport retained their dominance at these ports, but at Caen, Saint-Nazaire, La Rochelle and Bordeaux, as combined shipments fell from 1.1 million tons in 1902 to 0.62 million tons in 1911, their dominance waned, with roughly equal amounts in the latter year coming from ports serving the eastern and western portions of the coalfield.[52]

While official data sources reveal little with respect to the type of coal shipped to individual French ports, consular reports can provide some insights into this and the uses to which it was put, as illustrated in the next section.

THE COAL TRADE OF KEY FRENCH PORTS

The location of Rouen on the River Seine, some 90 kilometres inland from its mouth at Le Havre, made it ideally situated for supplying not only local industries, among which were cotton spinning and weaving, engineering, chemicals and patent fuel manufacture,[53] but also Paris. This explains the dominance of anthracite and semi-anthracitic steam coals imported from Swansea and Llanelli. In 1909, aided by the growth of the capital's population,[54] the 'greater part' of the coal shipped to Rouen was 'transhipped into barges for Paris', including 101,730 tons of anthracite[55] destined for use in stoves that had become fashionable around the turn of the century.[56] By 1913 anthracite imports at Rouen amounted to 223,606 tons,[57] while Powell Duffryn coal shipped to the port was either converted into patent fuel at its own works situated there, or sent to Paris where it enjoyed a large market among electricity supply companies.[58]

In marked contrast to Rouen, three quarters of the shipments to Le Havre in 1911 originated from Cardiff. Some of this coal, together with that from Newport and Swansea, was probably used in local industries, the consul for Le Havre, reporting on the use of British coal in 1903, noting that: 'The local gas company imports about 60,000 tons, and about 400,000 tons are imported for manufacturing and domestic purposes'.[59] As a centre for the north Atlantic trade, undoubtedly some of the Cardiff coal sent to Le Havre would have been used for bunkering local French and oceangoing shipping. In 1903, for example, it was reported that

Table 2.5: Exports to France from various south Wales ports, 1911
Figures in tons (percentage of total Welsh shipments to French port given in parentheses)

	Cardiff	Newport	Port Talbot	Swansea	Total
Le Havre	355408 (76.3)	37113 (8.0)	1075 (0.2)	56958 (12.2)	465,532
Rouen	46777 (5.2)	157832 (17.5)	33578 (3.7)	618897 (68.7)	900,882
Caen	108487 (40.6)	5679 (2.1)	13233 (4.9)	124732 (46.6)	267,384
Saint-Nazaire	187089 (46.4)	27942 (6.9)	80352 (20.0)	107250 (26.6)	402,633
Nantes	132987 (50.2)	26698 (10.1)	63519 (24.0)	41595 (15.7)	264,799
La Rochelle	35769 (19.9)	160 (0.1)	72729 (40.5)	69016 (38.4)	179,645
La Pallice	109767 (68.6)	7988 (5.0)	9733 (6.1)	30241 (19.0)	159,917
Bordeaux	187449 (34.6)	63621 (11.7)	210300 (38.8)	80131 (14.8)	541,501
Marseilles	319557 (48.6)	264596 (40.2)	4105 (0.6)	68872 (10.5)	657,971

Source: Data from Browne's export list reproduced in *South Wales Coal Annual*, 1913, pp. 254–60. The 'total' figure also includes exports from Neath and Llanelli not separately listed.

'about 150,000 tons of Cardiff and Welsh steam coal [was unloaded at Le Havre] for the [use of] various lines of steamers'.[60] British data would suggest that this represented about 40 per cent of the Cardiff coal shipped to the port in that year. It was also noted, however, that the 'quantity of coal shipped to bunkers of British vessels is now exceedingly small, probably not more than 10,000 tons as shipowners find it more economical to proceed after discharging of cargo, to a British coaling port'.[61]

At Bordeaux, in the early years of the study, Welsh coal was destined for use by local industries and the railways. In 1838, for example, of the 20,630 tons of British coal imported, only 1,997 tons (or

9.7 per cent) was destined for use by steamships, the rest being consumed locally.[62] In his report for 1855, the British consul in Bordeaux noted that several coke works had been established there recently to supply the railways, with several 'high tonnage' steamers employed regularly between Cardiff and Bordeaux to provide them with coal.[63] However, the rapid rise in British coal imports at Bordeaux from 80,469 tons in 1858 to 400,000 tons in 1871 was not down to increasing railway demand but to the growth of new factories and the depletion of local supplies of wood.[64] Industrialisation in France during the middle decades of the nineteenth century was making wood fuel scarce and expensive, as forests were cleared, leading to even minor ports such as Charente, near Rochefort, importing sizeable amounts of British coal for 'local manufactories and distilleries'.[65]

At Nantes and neighbouring Saint-Nazaire, at the mouth of the Loire, coals from Cardiff and Port Talbot predominated in the early twentieth century. Having been a major port engaged in the slave trade, following the demise of this trade Nantes developed food processing (including the biscuit manufacturer LU) and shipbuilding industries. However, problems with the silting up of the Loire led in 1835 to the development of the port of Saint-Nazaire, where larger ships could unload their cargoes for transhipment to Nantes and further east along the Loire. More conveniently located, the trade of Saint-Nazaire eventually outstripped that of Nantes, and the town subsequently developed its own shipbuilding industry. On the eve of the First World War, Powell Duffryn noted that, in addition to Admiralty coals, its agency at Nantes supplied industrial and house coal.[66]

The pattern of shipments to La Rochelle and La Pallice echoes the contrast between those to Rouen and Le Havre. La Pallice, a new port facility located a few kilometres north-west of La Rochelle, was built to accommodate the largest vessels trading between Britain, South America and other parts of the world.[67] La Rochelle, with its small picturesque harbour on the edge of the town, could not cope with such vessels and so a new facility had to be developed if the town was not to lose its position as a trading port. While La Pallice focused on bunkering transatlantic shipping, obtaining 70 per cent of its imports in 1911 from Cardiff, the harbour of La Rochelle, where less than 20 per cent of imports comprised Cardiff coal, continued to accommodate smaller vessels bringing coal from other Welsh ports for the use of local industry.

Among the industries using coal imported through La Rochelle and neighbouring ports in the Charente-Martitime *département* were patent fuel plants, including La Grenouillère at Tonnay-Charente, and others at Rochefort and Marans.[68] Patent fuel plants had first been established in France in the 1840s and later included those established at or near ports such as Le Havre, Rouen, Saint-Malo, La Rochelle and Marseilles by Welsh companies such as L. Guéret Ltd and Powell Duffryn. These and other plants made use of Welsh small coals, the manufactured briquettes, along with those imported from Welsh patent fuel works[69] being used largely on the French railways. Thus, in 1904, the consul for La Rochelle and La Pallice noted: 'The State Railway authorities have [concluded] a [three-year] contract for 375,000 tons of Welsh small coal, the smallest to be made into briquettes in France and the larger to be burnt as coal in its natural state'.[70]

In the Mediterranean, the major French port, Marseilles, was an important industrial centre in its own right, refining mineral oil, sulphur and sugar, producing aluminium, soap, candles, glycerine, oils, tiles and chemicals, and milling flour.[71] In addition to being used in local industries, British coal was also imported for use by railways and for bunkering ships trading within and through the Mediterranean. In 1896 it was estimated that, out of British shipments of 572,847 tons, possibly 100,000 tons of small coal from Newcastle and Cardiff was for use in local industries, and about 90,000 tons comprised gas coal from the east coast of England.[72] Just before the First World War, it was noted that local factories were increasingly turning from the use of steam power to electricity, but this does not appear to have had much an impact on British coal shipments, which averaged around 1 million tons during the period 1910–12, the same level as in 1903. One possible explanation for the lack of decline is that, during the first decade of the twentieth century, the PLM railway company imported large amounts of British coal: the company contracted for 75,000 tons of Welsh coal for delivery during 1906,[73] while in 1907 it imported 320,000 tons of British coal and placed contracts for a further 500,000 tons.[74]

Another possible explanation is an increase in coal used for bunkering ships, although Marseilles faced competition from other southern European and north African ports, and suffered problems such as insufficient dock facilities and labour disputes. Gaining a clear picture is complicated since it is unclear if the terminology used in *SIM* and by British consular officials was the same, but figures presented by the latter suggest that there may have been a fall in the proportion of British shipments accounted for by bunkers from just over one half in 1903 to around 40 per cent in 1910 (411,117 tons of bunkers compared to 655,086 tons of imports).[75]

Whatever the precise size of the bunker trade at Marseilles, Cardiff coals predominated, it being recorded around the turn of the century that all of the bunker coal came from south Wales, 'Newcastle [coal] being unsuitable even at a reduced price'.[76] Although French steamship companies, as receivers of state subsidies, were under an obligation to purchase French coal, during the late 1880s many began to negotiate 'contracts for part-supplies of Welsh coal'.[77] In 1901 it was noted that French shipping companies 'cannot altogether do without the British article . . . All foreign shipping use British coal, and a number of French companies follow suit . . . even the French Navy has to look to the United Kingdom for its fuel'.[78] Thus, for example, it was reported in 1908 that three French shipping companies – Transports Maritimes, Compagnie Méditerranée and Compagnie de Navigation Mixte – had entered a joint arrangement to import coal directly from Britain through a common agent.[79]

THE MARKETS FOR SOUTH WALES COAL IN FRANCE – SOME CONCLUDING REMARKS

All that remained after the evils had been released from Pandora's box was hope. In embarking on this study it had been hoped that utilising French official data alongside British data and other sources, including British consular reports, would increase both knowledge and understanding of the Welsh coal trade with France, as well as enabling the emergence of a clear picture of the purposes for which Welsh coal was used and the amounts so used. Such hopes, however, proved somewhat optimistic. Nevertheless, it has been possible to gain some important insights. It is clear that Welsh coal played an important role in the industrialisation of France, something that was made possible through the removal of trade barriers on both sides of the English channel in the middle decades of the nineteenth century and ongoing improvements in steam shipping. Moreover, the evidence points to the French coal market before the First World War being a highly diversified one as far as south Wales colliery owners and shippers were concerned.

In contrast to the view that suggests that the bulk of Welsh coal exports in the long nineteenth century were destined for use as bunker fuel at their port of unloading,[80] our analysis has shown clearly that large amounts of Welsh coal and patent fuel were used widely across French industry and by French railways and French households. Yes, French ships trading within and between French territories, together with those of French international trading lines such as Messageries Maritimes and Compagnie Générale Transatlantique, and foreign ships calling at French ports such as Le Havre and Marseilles, filled their bunkers, at least in part, with Welsh coal, but this was not the major reason behind Welsh coal exports to France before 1914. The data unearthed in this study would suggest that, at a maximum, bunker coal accounted for no more than 24 per cent of Welsh coal exports to France.[81]

Despite the limitations exposed in this study, it is clear that, to develop a fuller understanding of Welsh coal exports and the uses to which they were put, more detailed studies of the Welsh coal trade with individual countries are clearly required, though finding relevant data may be problematic.

NOTES

1 *South Wales Coalfield (including Pembrokeshire) Regional Survey Report* (London: HMSO, 1946), p. 20.

2 F. A. Gibson, *A Compilation of Statistics (Technological, Commercial, and General) of the Coal Mining Industry of the United Kingdom, the Various Coalfields Thereof, and the Principal Foreign Countries of the World* (Cardiff: Western Mail Ltd, 1922), p. 125.

3 B. R. Mitchell and P. Deane, *Abstract of British Historical Statistics* (Cambridge: Cambridge University Press, 1962), p. 276, f.n.4. Data are taken both from the original source and various compilations thereof, including: Mitchell and Deane, *Abstract*; Gibson, *A Compilation of Statistics*; Mining Association of Great Britain, *Statistical Review of the Coal Industry – Supplement for 1937* (London: Mining Association of Great Britain, 1937); and *South Wales Coal Annual* (Cardiff: The Business Statistics Company Ltd, various years from 1903) [hereafter *SWCA*].

4 Under the law of 23 April 1833 (article 5), a statement of the metallurgical, mineralogical and geological works executed, organised or supervised by the corps of mining engineers was to be published and distributed to members of both Chambers of the French parliament at the opening of each session. Initially presented annually under the title *Compte rendu des travaux des*

ingénieurs des mines from 1833 to 1847, between 1847 and 1872 the data were published in a number of multi-year compilations, under the title *Résumé des Travaux Statistiques de l'Administration des Mines*. The multi-year returns for the years 1872–5 and 1876–8, and the annual returns thereafter, which also separately include data relating to Algeria, appeared under the title *Statistique de l'industrie minérale et des appareils à vapeur en France et en Algérie*. Following F. Crouzet, 'British coal in France in the nineteenth century', in F. Crouzet, *Britain Ascendant: Comparative Studies in France-British Economic History* (Cambridge: Cambridge University Press, 1990), all these sources will be referred to throughout as *SIM*. I would like to express my thanks to Marie-Noëlle Maisonneuve, *responsable des fonds patrimoniaux* at the *Bibliothèque MINES ParisTech*, for granting me access to online versions of *SIM* for the period 1833–1913. For access to this source, it is necessary to apply through the library's website: *https://patrimoine.mines-paristech.fr* (accessed 12 September 2018).

5 To convert imperial tons to metric tons it is necessary to multiply by 1.0161; conversely, multiply the number of metric tons by 0.9842 to convert to imperial tons. A quintal is one tenth of a metric ton.

6 The term 'exports' is used in the British statistics to refer to coal shipped as cargoes for discharging at a port of destination in another country. The term excludes bunker coal, that is fuel taken on board ships leaving British ports, whether British or foreign, for their own use. In the French data, imports exclude coal used to bunker foreign ships calling at French ports or French ships trading internationally and hence refer purely to coal retained within France for internal use, including the railways and as bunkers by French river transport and merchant ships trading between French ports and French territories.

7 Parliamentary Papers [hereafter PP] 1881, HC (405), 'Return of Trade between United Kingdom and France, 1861–79', p. 10.

8 Unless otherwise indicated, data in this section are taken from *SIM*. Although the data relate to imports from Britain, for the bulk of the period the French returns refer to shipments from *Angleterre* rather than *Grande Bretagne*, hence the use of the term 'Anglo-French' in the title of this section.

9 Crouzet, 'British coal', p. 414.

10 Crouzet, 'British coal', pp. 415–16.

11 Crouzet, 'British coal', p. 416.

12 *SIM*, 1911, p. 16.

13 The figure had been as high as 55.2 per cent in 1907.

14 Crouzet, 'British coal', pp. 420–1.

15 R. Radau, 'La Production houillère en Angleterre et en France', *Revue des Deux Mondes*, 17 (1876) (last accessed on 5 February 2013 at *http://fr.wikisource.org/wiki/La_Production_houillère_en_Angleterre_et_en_France*); Crouzet, 'British coal', p. 414.

16 Crouzet, 'British coal', p. 433.

17 Crouzet, 'British coal', p. 438.
18 Crouzet, 'British coal', pp. 433-4.
19 The last year in which the data appear in *SIM* is 1911, there being concerns expressed as to both their usefulness and their accuracy (*SIM*, 1912, p. 17).
20 'La commerce de la houille en 1858', *Annales des Mines Bulletin*, premier semester, XV (1859), p. 594.
21 British consular sources present a slightly different picture. Thus, for Rouen, the figure given for British coal is only 86.1 per cent in 1913 (PP Cd 7620-49, p. 5), though the lower percentage would seem to result from the inclusion of French coal brought in by canal and railway in the consul's figures for imports.
22 Industrialisation saw the number of industrial establishments in France using steam power rising from 6,543 in 1852 to more than 20,000 by 1868 and 30,000 in 1878 (*SIM*, 1900, Plate 19). By 1913 the figure had doubled again to in excess of 63,000 (*SIM*, 1913, p. 99).
23 *SIM*, 1900, Plate 19.
24 *SIM*, 1913, p. 100.
25 This figure includes the coal content of coke and briquettes, but the vast bulk comprised raw coal.
26 In 1909, *Etat* absorbed the *Chemin de fer de l'Ouest* concern, which had been a major user of British coal, regularly importing more than 400,000 tons and as much as 767,500 tons in 1907 and 688,300 tons in 1908.
27 *SIM*, 1906, p. 99.
28 PP 1901, HC (306), 'British ships', Part II, Tonnage of Merchant Navies (British and Foreign), p. 35.
29 *SIM*, 1911, *Tableaux, Première partie*, p. 118 – '*Tableau de la consummation des combustibles minéraux, 3 – Par les bateaux à vapeur de la marine merchande*'.
30 Technically, this term also covered the ports of Bristol, Bridgwater, Gloucester et cetera, but only small amounts were shipped from such ports, often comprising the transhipment of south Wales coal.
31 A. H. John, *The Industrial Development of South Wales 1750-1850: An Essay* (Cardiff: Merton Priory Press, 1995), pp. 116-17.
32 L. J. Williams, *Digest of Welsh Historical Statistics*, vol. 1 (Cardiff: Welsh Office, 1985), Coal Table 10, pp. 318-25.
33 J. H. Morris and L. J. Williams, *The South Wales Coal Industry, 1841-1875* (Cardiff: University of Wales Press, 1958), pp. 4, 20.
34 Williams, *Digest*, p. 318.
35 John, *Industrial Development*, p. 122.
36 John, *Industrial Development*, p. 120.
37 Morris and Williams, *The South Wales Coal Industry*, pp. 25-8.
38 Morris and Williams, *The South Wales Coal Industry*, p. 30.
39 For further details of Nixon's exploits in France, see J. E. Vincent, *John Nixon: Pioneer of the Steam Coal Trade in South Wales – A Memoir* (London: John Murray, 1900), especially chapters VI and VII. Nixon subsequently sank

collieries in south Wales, forming the basis of what later became Nixon's Navigation Co. Ltd.

40 Morris and Williams, *The South Wales Coal Industry*, p. 32.

41 Morris and Williams, *The South Wales Coal Industry*, pp. 33-40.

42 R. Watson, *Rhondda Coal, Cardiff Gold – The Insoles of Llandaff: Coal Owners and Shippers* (Cardiff: Merton Priory Press, 1997), p. 32.

43 M. S. Smith, *The Emergence of Modern Business Enterprise in France, 1800-1930* (Cambridge: Harvard University Press, 2006), p. 114.

44 Smith, *Emergence*, p. 115.

45 R. H. Walters, *The Economic and Business History of the South Wales Steam Coal Industry* (New York: Arno Press, 1977), p. 303.

46 Glamorgan Archives, DPD/2, Powell Duffryn Minute Book, entry for 18 February 1879.

47 Watson, *Rhondda Coal*, pp. 87-8.

48 L. Guerét Ltd was founded by a Frenchman, Louis Guérét, who came from Le Havre in 1868 to manage the Anchor patent fuel works of Tinel & Co. established at Maindy, Cardiff, two years earlier. He subsequently took over the Anchor works, developing his own business to encompass interests in shipping and colliery ownership (for further details, see *SWCA*, 1913, pp. 1-32).

49 Walters, *Economic and Business History*, p. 304; C. R. Muller, 'Saint-Malo – Saint-Servan: un port charbonnier', *Annales de Géographie*, 31 (1922), 456.

50 *The Powell Duffryn Steam Coal Company Limited, 1864–1914* (Cardiff: The Company, 1914), pp. 84, 90.

51 Gibson, *A Compilation of Statistics*, pp. 100-10.

52 *SWCA*, 1903, pp. 137-42; *SWCA*, 1913, pp. 254-60.

53 PP 1887, C. 4923-19, p. 16.

54 The population of Paris increased from under 800,000 in 1831 to over 2.2 million in 1881 and nearer 3 million by the eve of the First World War.

55 PP 1910, Cd 4962-86, p. 3.

56 PP 1898, C. 8648-49, p. 5.

57 In 1913 Swansea exported 1,009,360 tons of anthracite to France, while Llanelli exported 128,044 tons (*SWCA*, 1916, p. 169).

58 *The Powell Duffryn Steam Coal Company Limited*, pp. 84, 87.

59 PP 1904, Cd 1766-105, p. 21.

60 PP 1904, Cd 1766-105, p. 21.

61 PP 1904, Cd 1766-105, pp. 21-2.

62 *SIM*, 1838, p. 142.

63 PP 1857, Session I [C. 2201], p. 32. Following reports in the French literature of the successful experiments of the Taff Vale Railway in using steam coal in its natural state (see, for example, M. Couche, 'Sur l'emploi de la houille maigre du Pays de Galles dans les machines locomotives', *Annales des Mines*, 5th series, XV (1859)), French railway companies increasingly switched away from using coke to using Welsh steam coal.

64 PP 1872, C. 497, 'Reports relative to British Consular Establishments 1858 and 1871. Part I', p. 71.

65 PP 1857, Session I [C. 2201], p. 36.

66 *The Powell Duffryn Steam Coal Company Limited*, p. 92.

67 See entry in 11th edition of *Encyclopedia Britannica* (1911): *www.1911encyclopedia.org/La_Rochelle* (accessed 5 December 2012). For more details on the trade in Welsh coal to South America, see T. Boyns and S. Gray, 'Welsh coal and the informal empire in South America, 1850–1913', *Atlantic Studies: Literary, Cultural and Historical Perspectives*, 13/1 (2016), 53-77.

68 See *http://www.actuacity.com/usine-d-agglomeres-de-houille-charvet--puis-societe-charentaise-d-agglomeres_m24348/* (last accessed 4 April 2017).

69 A number of patent fuel works grew up at the main ports in south Wales during the study period, there being ten in operation at the outbreak of the First World War. In 1913 south Wales exported 2,031,148 tons of patent fuel, of which 12.4 per cent (250,974 tons) was shipped to France (*SWCA*, 1916, pp. 203-5).

70 PP 1906 (260), p. 19.

71 PP 1911, Cd 5465-120, p. 4.

72 PP 1897, C. 8277-106, p. 8.

73 PP 1906 (260), p. 31,

74 PP 1908, Cd 3727-112, p. 6.

75 PP 1904, Cd 1766-164, p. 6; PP 1911, Cd 5465-120, p. 6.

76 PP 1898, C. 8648-99, p. 8.

77 PP 1888, C. 5252-78, p. 4.

78 PP 1901, Cd 429-126, p. 14.

79 PP 1908, Cd 3727-112, p. 6.

80 D. A. Thomas (later Lord Rhondda) suggested that half of all British coal exported worldwide may have been used for navigation purposes, while Michael Asteris has suggested that, for south Wales, the proportion of exports used as ship's bunkers could be as high as 60 per cent. See D. A. Thomas, 'The growth and direction of our foreign trade in coal during the last half century', *Journal of the Royal Statistical Society*, 66 (1903), 469; M. Asteris, 'The rise and decline of south Wales coal exports, 1870–1930', *Welsh History Review*, 13/1 (1986), 31.

81 This figure is based on the assumption that all French imports of British coal used by French ships in 1910–11 recorded in *SIM* (an average of 0.97 million tons) came from south Wales, and that the discrepancy between the official British export data and French import data (averaging 0.33 million tons) represents coal used by non-French ships bunkering at French ports and, once again, comprised entirely Welsh coal. This maximum estimate falls within the range of 23 per cent to 29 per cent implied by the historian Brian Mitchell as the share of Welsh exports used as bunkers worldwide: B. R. Mitchell, *Economic Development of the British Coal Industry 1800–1914* (Cambridge: Cambridge University Press, 1984), p. 20.

HIDDEN LABOURS
THE DOMESTIC SERVICE INDUSTRY IN SOUTH WALES, 1871–1921

CARYS HOWELLS

INTRODUCTION

At the age of thirteen, Bessie Hopkins, a coal miner's daughter from Ystradgynlais, left her parents and seven siblings and travelled to Swansea to become a 'maid of all work' in the household of their landlord's daughter.[1] Her elder sister had previously held the position but had been sent home when her health had deteriorated to the extent that she could no longer carry out her domestic duties. As the second eldest daughter, Bessie inherited the position and in doing so retained the source of income for her family. Her first full-time position was to be a 'heartbreaking' experience, owing to the harsh treatment she received from her employers.[2] She was unable to communicate her unhappiness to her parents, as both incoming and outgoing letters were censored. It was only through the chance visit of an uncle, returning home on leave from the First World War, that a message was sent back to her mother who promptly removed her daughter from the household. This was to be the first of several service positions Bessie held before her eventual marriage. For another miner's daughter, Ada Carter, rather than an ordeal, entry into service was a much-welcomed lifeline. After receiving a beating from her father for missing a curfew, she 'went to bed with the *South Wales Echo* and read through the recruitment advertisements by candlelight'.[3] To escape her turbulent upbringing in Port Talbot, Ada accepted a position as scullery maid at Dynevor Castle in Llandeilo, where she remained for two years before leaving to fulfil her ambition of becoming a kitchen maid. It was the start of a career that would see her enter the employ of many wealthy households, most notably that of the Duke of Somerset. For Ada, service was not merely a source of income, it was also an arena in which personal aspirations could be formulated and realised.

Bessie and Ada were just two of thousands of people in Wales who entered domestic service in the late nineteenth and early twentieth century. In 1881 there were almost as many servants (98, 461) in Wales as there were mine and quarry workers combined (102, 995), and if the frequent under recording of women's work is taken into consideration, it may be claimed that up until the last decade of the nineteenth century the country possessed more maids than miners.[4] Yet, literature on the sector in Wales has remained sparse, with only a handful of studies having emerged in recent years. These have greatly enhanced our understanding of the lived experiences of maids and deepened our appreciation of domestic service as a vehicle for female migration to England.[5] This study, based on my doctoral research,[6] builds upon previous scholarship through exploring domestic service as it operated within Wales. Instead of focusing on the supply of servants to England, it will be argued that south Wales was itself a region that continued to experience a high level of employer demand, providing ample employment opportunities for local people and migrants alike. Furthermore, this study seeks to locate the daily experiences of servants within the wider context of the sector in which they were engaged, exploring the scale of the industry, the underlying supply and demand factors that influenced it and contemporary discourse surrounding the availability of servants during the period.

The first section of this chapter reveals the size of the workforce in Wales and the geographical variations that underlie the national figures. The second section contrasts the level of employer demand for servants with the number of workers entering the sector. It will be demonstrated that demand continuously outstripped supply but that this was not the result of a decline in the number of servants in south Wales. Instead it will be argued that increased internal competition from public institutions and businesses, which often siphoned the supply of workers away from private households, helped heighten the perception of a servant shortage. Public discourse on this 'servant problem' from the late nineteenth century onwards is examined, revealing how education and organised migration schemes were key concerns even though they had limited impact (particularly in the latter case) on servant numbers before the First World War. However, the debate, which centred both on the quality of servants and their availability, illuminates many of the concerns householders held and provides an insight into the complex social divisions that shaped the sector. Through examining the development of the domestic service industry in this way, this study contributes a new perspective on the economic history of Wales, challenging the perception of both the sector and the wider Welsh economy. Despite its perception as an intensely male arena, the significant role played by women in the Welsh economy is highlighted, and in doing so amends the traditional image of Welsh women as economically inactive. While some were, this was not exclusively the case, as exemplified by the experiences of Ada and Bessie at the start of this chapter. However, before examining the development of the sector, it is first necessary to clarify the parameters of the industry and the research methods adopted in trying to uncover its development during the study period.

DEFINING DOMESTIC SERVICE

A broad approach to domestic service has been adopted, defining it by the nature of the duties performed rather than the location in which they were undertaken.[7] Therefore, the title 'domestic servant' is applied to all those who legally performed personal, non-medical assistance, and/or engaged in tasks that promoted cleanliness, comfort and convenience, in return for financial remuneration. This definition encompasses servants engaged in businesses and public institutions as well as private households. Consequently, a more nuanced understanding of the evolution of service emerges that reflects the perception of the industry as understood by contemporary society, and as evidenced in multiple forms of primary source material, such as local newspapers, oral testimony and the official census tables. In addition, domestic service is also regarded as an industry owing to a discernible scale of pay, a recognisable occupation hierarchy and the existence of trade organisations. This approach accords with Mark Ebery and Brian Preston's study of service in England. They claimed that 'the most singular feature of the Victorian-Edwardian economy was that its greatest industry was not an industrial one'.[8] In doing so, the authors posit the notion that domestic service formed a distinguishable industry that was of great importance to the English economy.

This 'whole industry' approach contrasts greatly with much of the British literature on domestic service that has frequently confined itself to examining the experiences of 'maids of all work' or country-house staff. Many studies have been influenced by the women's history movement in drawing heavily on first-hand testimony and with the stated goal of unearthing the lives of those marginalised by history. A particularly good example of this is Rosemary Scadden's *No Job for A Little Girl*, which explores the experiences of Welsh maids during the interwar period. Similarly, the closure of many country homes in the mid-twentieth century provoked an upsurge of interest in those who had once worked and lived within them. While most of these studies examined English estates, Merlin Watson's study of Erddig House stems from this period and is reflective of broader interests in country-house servants. Given these dual strands of academic interest, it is of little surprise that the first wave of literature on domestic service in Britain occurred during the 1970s.[10] Despite the sector experiencing something of a renaissance in recent years, these two approaches continue to influence the related literature both at a British and Welsh level.

To reconcile these two strands with the 'whole industry' perspective, quantitative and qualitative material has been drawn upon to provide an insight into the significance of the sector to the Welsh economy. The most prominent statistical source used in this study is the *Census of England and Wales*, accessed via official census tabulations and the *Digest of Welsh Historical Statistics*. These have provided an insight into both the industry and its workforce. However, a note of caution should be issued when analysing such statistics. For example, servant birthplace data have facilitated an analysis of servant migration patterns. Yet, while many servants migrated in search of a position, others would have relocated when accompanying relatives, who moved to the area to take up posts in other industries. Likewise, job advertisements published daily in the *Western Mail* offer an indication of the level of demand and supply in the service sector as well as the type of service occupations most frequently sought. However, once again, attention must be given to the limitations of the source material. 'Situation vacant' advertisements were not the sole method of recruiting staff and the cost of placing an advert may have deterred servants seeking new positions from advertising. To alleviate the limitations of the numerical data, they have been scrutinised in conjunction with a range of published and archival sources to arrive at a more accurate understanding of the role of service in attracting and retaining workers in Wales. First-hand testimony has also been incorporated in the form of both published correspondence and oral history accounts gathered as part of the Swansea Valley Oral History project during the 1970s. These locate individual experiences within the wider industry and illuminate some of the underlying reasons behind the data.

Despite their limitations, the census reports provide one of the most accurate ways to examine the changing size and occupational composition of the service workforce at both national and county level. In addition, a case-study of the census enumerator records for Aberdare, Bridgend and Carmarthen during the years 1871, 1891 and 1911 has been undertaken. The towns were selected owing to their varied locations, population demographic and economic characters. Although the case study is in no way representative of domestic service in Wales as a whole, it provides a genuine insight into the diversity that existed in south Wales through bridging the gap between the coalfield, rural Wales and a location that conformed to neither representation.[11] Aberdare, located on the south Wales coalfield, had the largest population of the three case-study towns. *Kelly's Directory* of 1901 describes how its 'collieries afford employment to many thousands of persons, and give the town its chief support'.[12] In contrast, being situated just south of the coalfield, Bridgend had a more diverse economy, encompassing 'a brewery, a tannery, and iron and brass foundry' as well as manufacturing agricultural implements and lime quarrying.[13] In addition, Bridgend also had a significant role as a market town and an administrative centre for the local district.[14] Despite possessing the smallest population of the three towns, it greatly benefited from its proximity to Cardiff, Swansea and the coalfield, being a convenient location for new state institutions such as hospitals and white-collar commuters who took advantage of its good transport links.[15] In contrast, Carmarthen had a more westerly and isolated location. Its economy was largely characterised by its rural setting and agricultural hinterlands. By the commencement of the twentieth century, fishing and farming were claimed to be the most notable aspects of its economy.[16] Yet, similarly to Bridgend, Carmarthen was an administrative centre and a market town. In addition, it also had an important role as a college town, housing institutions such as teacher training and Presbyterian colleges.[17] A comparison of these three towns facilitates a deeper awareness of the adaptability of the domestic service industry and its ability to integrate into a range of local economies.

GEOGRAPHICAL VARIATION IN WORKFORCE SIZE

The most prominent statistical trend within the industry has been the changing size of the workforce. Despite remaining the biggest employer of women in Wales, accounting for almost 55 per cent of all occupied females in 1871, the proportion steadily declined during the late nineteenth century and by 1911 servants constituted 45 per cent of working females. In contrast, the largest employment category for men in the country, 'mines and quarries', accounted for only 19 per cent of occupied males in 1871 and approximately 32 per cent in 1911. However, to truly comprehend the dominance of domestic service as a source of income for women in Wales, we may compare it to the percentage of occupied females in England engaged in service, which never reached more than 39 per cent during the same period. This comparison highlights the significance of the domestic service industry for the Welsh female labour market during the era.

Another notable contrast with England becomes apparent when examining the actual number of servants rather than the proportion of the overall workforce they accounted for. While the number of domestics in England declined, in Wales numbers remained buoyant up to 1911, after which the First World War led to a fall in the servant figures as recorded in the census of 1921 (see Table 3.1). Overall, Wales experienced an increase of around 15,000 domestics between 1871 and 1921, while England's workforce declined by nearly 74,000. The losses were largely confined to urban manufacturing and commercial centres, such as Manchester, Newcastle, Bristol and London. This has been largely attributed to the growth of alternative forms of female employment.[18] Meanwhile, the buoyancy of the sector in Wales can be ascribed to the decline in the number of agricultural positions and the dominance of the coal trade, an industry largely prohibited from recruiting women since 1842. For instance, the large number of industrial centres present in Glamorgan greatly influenced the high servant figures in the county. In 1871 Glamorgan accounted for 23 per cent of all domestics in Wales. By 1911 the proportion had increased to 36 per cent, reflecting the actual increase in servant numbers from 20,494 to 37,350.[19] Towns within the county that were dominated by the coal industry, such as Aberdare, experienced the largest expansion in the number of servants. This was not only the result of the limited alternative employment opportunities for women, but also the dramatic growth in the town's overall population and the high level of employer demand for domestic help due to coalfield-generated prosperity.

Table 3.1: The size of the servant workforce in Wales, 1871–1921

	Number of servants			**Servants as proportion of overall workforce (%)**		
Year	Male	Female	Total	Male*	Female **	Total
1871	6,133	83,896	90,029	1.3	54.9	14.5
1881	10,240	88,221	98,461	2.1	57.0	15.3
1891	4,848	105,390	110,238	0.8	54.9	14.4
1901	11,459	88,878	100,337	1.7	49.3	12.0
1911	14,792	90,496	105,288	1.8	42.0	10.3
1921	8,024	78,481	86,505	0.9	36.8	7.9

Source: Williams, *Digest of Welsh Historical Statistics*, p. 96.
* Male servants as a proportion of the total male workforce in Wales.
** Female servants as a proportion of the total female workforce in Wales.

The decline in the number of agricultural positions also led many women in more rural Welsh counties to relocate in search of service positions in more industrial areas, further augmenting servant numbers. In nine out of the thirteen Welsh counties, workforce patterns reflected the decline or expansion of the overall population, revealing how developments such as rural depopulation influenced the distribution of servants throughout Wales. Westerly counties such as Cardiganshire, Merionethshire and Pembrokeshire experienced the most significant decline as many young girls moved further south or across the border into England.[20] This trend can be perceived in Carmarthen where the number of women engaged in agriculture fell to a low of 1,444 in 1891, while the overall population figures also fell from 12,926 to 10,221 during the study period as its staple trades such as fishing, farming and weaving declined.[21] The expansion of Llanelli and various towns in Glamorgan exacerbated this trend as many workers sought better paid positions in the new industrial areas.[22] For instance, in 1871, more than half (53.7 per cent) of domestics working in Aberdare had been born outside Glamorgan, with the largest proportion having originated from more rural counties in Wales. This reveals the importance of service as a vehicle for rural to urban migration within the country during the late nineteenth and early twentieth century. The high proportion of migrant servants in this area reflects the novelist Allen Raine's portrayal of Glamorgan as the 'El Dorado of the Welsh peasants' in her 1897 publication, *A Welsh Singer*.[23] The novel follows the story of Myfanwy, a Carmarthenshire shepherdess, who leaves home to take up a position as a maid in Glamorgan and eventually becomes a celebrated opera star. The novel suggests that the popular perception of Glamorgan was as an area of opportunity and that this extended beyond those seeking work in the heavy industries.

Consequently, of the three case-study towns, it was only Carmarthen that experienced a reduction in the size of its service workforce from 286 in 1871 to194 in 1911. The decline may have been even more pronounced had it not been for its role as a college town. Such areas frequently had many boarding and lodging houses owing to the high student population, each of which required domestic staff.[24] This reflected the high levels of female boarding-house servants in the English educational centres of Cambridge, Cheltenham and Rugby.[25] The census statistics have, therefore, proved instrumental not only in highlighting how the industry in Wales developed in a divergent manner to that of England, but also how local variations have greatly influenced the size of the sector within individual towns and counties.

SERVANT SUPPLY

The overall increase in servant figures in Wales has important implications for broader histories of domestic service seeking to establish the role of supply and demand factors in determining the development of the industry in Britain. Much of the existing literature has sought to explain the fall in servant numbers through examining the appeal of the industry to workers and the demands of householders for domestic assistance. Yet, a study of Wales, where servant numbers were increasing rather than declining, provides an opportunity to cast light upon the interplay of supply and demand factors in more depth. For example, although the influence of agricultural decline and heavy industry's dominance in Wales is undeniable, it is too simplistic to attribute the robustness of the country's domestic service sector solely to a ready supply of young girls with limited alternative employment opportunities.

Women entered service for a range of different reasons, as demonstrated by the earlier accounts of Ada Carter and Bessie Hopkins. For many it was a stopgap until marriage; for others, a lifeline during times of personal or financial difficulty; a few viewed it as a respectable long-term career option; while some were drawn to the opportunities for migration and even marriage. Social concerns over the respectability of women employed in various heavy industries was a recurring issue for those interviewed as part of the Swansea Valley Oral History project. Many of the interviewees revealed that their fathers favoured service as a more respectable alternative to working in the various forms of heavy industry. As one retired maid, Mrs Landon, explained: 'my father wouldn't let me work in a tin works or anything like that . . . you know they [the workers] were rough and ready'.[26] Meanwhile, another ex-servant, Mrs Kelly, decided to enter service to escape her job at the local tin works after gaining experience cleaning her manager's house, which the female workers were compelled to do on rotation.[27] Their testimony suggests that, for many girls in south Wales, service was the most respected occupation available to young women in the area.

However, rather than simply being a 'lesser evil', service was deemed an attractive option by some workers. The enduring appeal of domestic service is most evident in its continuing ability to attract male workers into the sector. Between 1871 and 1911 the industry experienced a continual increase in the number of male workers entering its ranks, despite the abundance of alternative positions available. Regardless of the multiple employment opportunities for male workers in the heavy industries, both the number and proportion of men in the service workforce increased. During the period, the number of male servants in Wales increased from 6,133 to 14,792. Even in an area of heavy industrialisation such as Glamorgan the percentage of men employed in the service sector increased from 4 per cent to 11 per cent by 1911.[28] In Carmarthen, men constituted just over 5 per cent at the start of the study period and nearly 11 per cent by its end. In the aftermath of the First World War they still accounted for more than 10 per cent of all servants in Glamorgan and almost 7 per cent of those in Carmarthenshire.[29] The high level of male workers in the domestic service industry in Wales is in stark contrast to England, where males generally accounted for around one in twenty-two servants.[30] A 'preponderance of male servants' in England has been perceived as an indicator of a 'military influence' in an area. For instance, in Windsor, where the number of 'officers living in private residences was particularly abnormal', their tendency to engage male household staff served to inflate the number of male domestics in the region.[31] Likewise, as male servants also commanded higher wages than their female counterparts, their presence, in towns such as Hastings, has been interpreted as an indicator of the region's prosperity.[32] Similarly, the presence of middle-class employers in Bridgend (the case-study town with the highest number of male servants) was facilitated by the presence of white-collar professionals such as doctors and solicitors, public house and hotel owners, as well as mine-related officials such as engineers and managers.

The motivations behind male workers seeking employment in the service industry were as multifaceted as the factors that compelled women to do so. While most men entered the sector through personal preference or family connections, it also proved a viable occupation for the disabled and elderly who were perhaps unsuited to heavy-industry positions. In the aftermath of the First World War, the government identified domestic service as a credible employment option for injured soldiers.[33] To encourage employers to engage ex-servicemen, insurance equality measures were introduced for disabled veterans in receipt of a Home Office pension.[34] This meant that employers paid lower insurance premiums for veterans than they would if engaging other disabled servants. Therefore, service was thought to provide a viable alternative employment option for those who could not or did not wish to enter the heavier industries.

EMPLOYER DEMAND

However, supply factors alone do not fully explain the continued expansion of the sector in south Wales. Without high employer demand the industry would not have been able to develop at such a pace. The historical evidence suggests that the demand for servants in south Wales was considerable throughout the period. The *Western Mail*'s 'situation vacant' advertisements for the years 1871–1921 show that the number of employers seeking staff was continually higher than the number of domestics seeking positions.[35] In 1871, on average fourteen advertisements per day were placed by prospective employers. In contrast, there were only three such advertisements placed by servants seeking positions. This pattern continued throughout the era, with newspaper advertisements remaining an important method through which workers could locate new positions. However, the peak decade in which this form of recruitment was utilised was the 1890s, when around 125 'situation vacant' and thirty-two 'situation wanted' advertisements for domestic positions were being published each day in the *Western Mail* alone.[36] Despite their limitations as an indicator of the number of people seeking domestic positions owing to the cost of placing an advert, they do conclusively show that vacancies for domestic helpers were plentiful. So extensive was this demand that one journalist described how

> one hears that servants cannot be procured, or, if procured, that they have developed the all too human tendency of doing what they ought not and leaving undone that which it is their duty to do. From Land's End to John o Groat's and from Caergybi to Caerdydd the melancholy cry goes up, and the 'wants' columns of the newspapers groan in vain with appeal of mistresses.[37]

The high level of demand for staff was both a cause and an effect of the high level of servant turnover, as many domestics frequently held individual positions for only a short duration of time. The high turnover suggests that a considerable number of vacancies were available as many workers could resign their positions without fear of being unable to locate another. The Swansea maid Bessie Hopkins had five employers in the years immediately following the First World War, with each post lasting between three and sixteen months. New posts were easily obtained, as she recollected when explaining why she remained with an overly demanding mistress for so long: 'three or four of their [her employers] friends asked me if I would go and work with them. I could have gone I think perhaps I would have had a better place but you don't like jumping from one job to another and I was near my sister and I was young. She was keeping an eye on me you see'.[38]

Such was the level of demand that a significant number of servants were attracted to south Wales to find work, suggesting that the region possessed a thriving domestic servant labour market. Many domestics initially travelled to south Wales while accompanying a family member in search of work in one of the heavy industries. This may explain why, of the three case-study towns featured in this chapter, it was the colliery town of Aberdare that had the highest proportion of servants born elsewhere in Wales. However, a significant proportion travelled to south Wales specifically to take up work in service. Indeed, many Welsh employers purposely sought staff from outside the region, with vacancies for positions in towns such as Newport and Cardiff being advertised in English regional publications such as *The Bristol Mercury* and *The Hampshire Advertisement*, as well as national papers such as *The Morning Post*.

Table 3.2: Birthplaces of servants in Aberdare, Bridgend and Carmarthen (selected years)

Where born (%)	1871			1891			1911		
	Aberdare	Bridgend	Carmarthen	Aberdare	Bridgend	Carmarthen	Aberdare	Bridgend	Carmarthen
In town of enumeration	22.7	21.6	39.9	46.5	17	44.6	42.9	17.3	44.3
Elsewhere in county	23.6	44.9	44.1	16.5	48.6	33.7	21.1	37.8	31.5
Elsewhere in Wales	47.3	14.4	11.1	26.4	11.5	16.7	17	15.4	13.9
Elsewhere in Britain	6.4	19.2	4.9	10.6	22.5	4.8	16.2	28.8	10.3
Other	0	0	0	0	0.5	0.2	2.8	0.6	0

Source: Census Enumerators' Books, 1871, 1891, 1911.

Figure 3.1: The butler's pantry, Tredegar House, *c.*1890]

Figure 3.2: The housekeeper's room, Tredegar House, *c.*1890

Source: Peoples Collection Wales, ©Newport City Council

Larger households such as Baglan House, Tredegar House and the Llanover Estate were also particularly keen to recruit long-distance migrants, often through utilising London-based employment agencies such as that of a Mrs Hunt that catered for higher class and aristocratic employers.[40] Census enumerator records have shown that many country-house staff, generally considered the *crème de la crème* of the industry, were frequently drawn from outside Wales.[41] For instance, in 1891, at Tredegar House, twenty-four servants were listed as being resident, fifteen of whom were born in England and one came from Elgin in Scotland. The appeal of stately houses to prospective servants centred, in part, on the social prestige attached to such positions. However, the superior working and living conditions (see Figures 3.1 and 3.2) also held great appeal and stood in stark contrast to the often harsh conditions of more modest households. Numerous accounts published in the editorial column of the *Western Mail* detail many of these hardships, such as the inadequacy of the accommodation, the absence of basic provisions and the general lack of privacy.[42] Establishments such as Tredegar House, therefore, presented an attractive option that could entice some of the most skilled and experienced servants to migrate considerable distances.

A high number of migrant workers is also visible in the town case-study data. The birthplace composition of the servants in Bridgend strongly suggests that south Wales was a region with high internal demand for servants as it had the smallest proportion of domestics who were native to the town itself. The rural counties in the south-west of England were a prime place of origin for the town's domestic staff, although some had travelled from even more distant counties such as Yorkshire and Norfolk. There were also a small number of foreign servants from countries such as Australia and Italy.[43] Despite being located to the south of the coalfield, by 1911 long-distance migrants accounted for 44 per cent of servants in Bridgend. To place this in perspective, 75 per cent of servants in London were migrants, while only 33 per cent of domestics in York had relocated to the city.[44] Even in Carmarthen, despite its westerly location and largely rural character, 16 per cent of domestics originated from outside Carmarthenshire in 1871 and 24 per cent in 1911. Although Carmarthen's service workforce was more insular than in the other two case-study towns, this level of migrant workers was not insignificant. Instead they were comparable with English towns such as Colchester, where 25 per cent of the workforce originated from outside the town. Therefore, while the dominance of domestic service in the female labour market has been attributed to the lack of alternative sources of employment in south Wales, the increasing number of migrant workers reveals a level of demand so considerable it frequently attracted workers from beyond its own borders.[45]

PUBLIC DISCOURSE ON SERVANT SHORTAGES

The failure of worker supply to meet the ever-increasing employer demand gave rise to widespread concerns over a servant shortage. Despite the generally increasing number of domestic staff in Wales, the proportion of the workforce engaged as servants gradually contracted as other industries began to expand more rapidly.[46] In 1871 almost 15 per cent of the Welsh workforce was engaged in domestic service occupations. By 1911 this had declined to just over 10 per cent.[47] The difficulty some employers faced in obtaining staff led to a widespread belief that young women were avoiding entry into the sector. The subsequent discourse surrounding the 'servant problem', as it was labelled by the press, centred heavily on two issues: the availability of maids and their quality (which appears to have been determined by both their competency and respectability). The expansion of state education and the organisation of migration schemes by various charitable and religious groups were two notable developments that served to heighten public fears over a shortage of reliable domestic assistants.

A study of the public discourse on the issue, as featured in the editorial columns of the local press, has revealed that the potential for social mobility afforded by the increased accessibility of education in the late nineteenth century influenced many of the opinions expressed by local householders. For instance, a newspaper report from March 1900 claimed that good maids were becoming as hard to source as 'blue roses'.[48] The anonymous writer lamented the provision of state education (compulsory school attendance was introduced in the 1870s) and asked: 'what is to be done? For with the spread of education there is a constant increase in the number of women who don't like doing dirty work and want it done for them'.[49] This is echoed in the account of a Cardiff-based employer, who told of the 'great mischief' that 'lies in school board teaching' as girls are

> trained to consider themselves far above the occupations of servants, and, in some instances, when engaging to fulfil the offices of servants coolly ask if they have time to practice their music on your piano. Talk of introducing pianos into board schools! Where will poor 'Mistresses' be able to find a servant capable or qualified to take upon her the usual and necessary offices of a servant?[50]

The expansion of alternative forms of female employment in the retail, clerical and nursing sectors led many employers to believe that decent girls were being educated above their station and would no longer contemplate entering service.[51] Although many of these new positions were inaccessible to servants, some were not. Brian Abel-Smith has noted that the newly professionalised nursing sector continued to recruit many of its members from among the 'servant class' throughout the nineteenth century as servants often possessed the necessary skills and experience to care for patients, having cared for babies, invalids and elderly employers.[52] Likewise, they also had the correct knowledge to maintain standards of cleanliness and were used to long hours and hard work. The First World War provided impetus and opportunity for many women to change occupation. Despite the often temporary nature of these developments, it broadened personal horizons and emphasised the flaws in the service industry.[53] Yet, while these developments may have slightly curtailed the expansion of the sector, it did not lead to a decline in the number of servants.

However, such fears chimed with a popular contemporary belief that the expansion of education was a 'sign of the collapse of domestic authority' as it sharpened 'class-consciousness and inculcated in the young a distaste for domestic service'.[54] These fears were not entirely unfounded, as by 1919 the National Union of Teachers had begun to raise objections to the inclusion of compulsory domestic science classes in both primary and secondary school curriculums. The Rhondda representative of the NUT, a Miss Griffiths, explained to fellow members that mothers in her district were reluctant to allow their daughters to attend domestic science lessons for fear that it would hamper their wider education. She claimed:

> If they [school girls] wasted their time at cookery schools, they were handicapped in their educational work. The mothers [of the young girls in the Rhondda] were afraid that if this kind of training was to be introduced into the continuation schools it was with the idea of making highly efficient domestic servants for the use of the employing class.[55]

This is in striking contrast to the first-hand accounts of pre-war servants who claimed that their parents would not sanction any other available form of occupation for their daughters. This was not purely the result of any stigma surrounding the undertaking of 'dirty work' but was also the consequence of changing social attitudes in the aftermath of the First World War, when mothers increasingly resented their daughters being channelled into service.[56] This account draws stark class lines that did not necessarily reflect the actual class divide between many servants and their employers. However, it shows how service was imbued with social conflict and that the recognised potential for social mobility placed great strain on householders struggling to recruit competent staff.

Aside from expanding education provision, fears of a servant shortage were further compounded by the existence of organised emigration schemes such as those established by the Salvation Army and the Girls Friendly Society (GFS). Wales and Ireland were thought particularly good recruitment areas for potential migrants during the agricultural recession of the late nineteenth century and the economic depression of the interwar years.[57] While their impact on depleting servant numbers in Britain was low, owing to limited take-up and their frequent exclusivity (targeting upper-working or middle-class women), the existence of these schemes was a cause for concern for many servant-employers. As one newspaper correspondent explained: '[if] things go on drifting from bad to worse, and if the Canadian boom sets in it is hard to see what the British mistress will do . . . the few desirable servants make their way steadily across the ocean, there to settle down happily and to become in time the mistresses of other servants drawn in their turn from our distressful islands!'[58] This was a very optimistic assessment of the opportunities that awaited the migrants in their new countries, but in a climate of fear over servant shortages, the impact of organised migration added to public concerns.

Organised migration schemes aimed to encourage the safe movement of women out of Britain to assume posts in service overseas. The demand for women in the British colonies was high and servants were rare, with it being estimated that there were sixty potential employers for every one maid.[60] While many were forced to rely on indigenous servants, the lack of British domestics was believed to be a deterrent to many middle-class women to emigrate.[61] So acute was the desire for middle- and upper-class women to relocate to the colonies that organisations such as the Women's Emigration Society had been established to encourage their migration. It was hoped that this would not only increase their numbers overseas but would also provide a solution to the problem of a surplus of unmarried women in Britain.[62] As one writer argued:

> To several, if not most of the colonies young women are carried free, and on their arrival in the colony employment is always awaiting them. There is plenty of reason why many young women who are now pining for husbands and comfort should find both by taking advantage of some of the means of emigration, under which they are protected as well as aided.[63]

If the estimates of their regional agents are to be believed, then this scheme enjoyed a notable level of success with 8,000 British females relocating to New South Wales alone between 1881 and 1884.[64] To further encourage the movement of 'respectable' women, other schemes were established to ensure that the women who did emigrate would be able to find British servants to labour in their colonial households. The Salvation Army played a key role in setting up programmes to find Welsh servants positions with British mistresses abroad. Advertisements featured in the local press read:

> superior girls wanted at once for domestic service in Canada; to sail October 4th or 18th; personally conducted to destination, and good situations guaranteed; best part of fares advanced to suitable applicants; lady Canadian representative here to advise – Call or write to Miss W. Leal, c/o Salvation Army Emigration Bureau, 5 Denmark Street, Bristol.[65]

The involvement of the Salvation Army reassured young women of their personal safety and made movement as easy as possible.[66]

The GFS also assisted many young servants to migrate to the colonies. The GFS was an organisation set up in association with the Anglican Church to safeguard rural working-class girls hoping to source employment in British towns and cities.[67] However, it also assisted those seeking employment overseas. The organisation's annual reports reveal their role in locating jobs, protecting girls *en route*, and providing accommodation on arrival.[68] However, the annual reports from the emigration department of the GFS for the Llandaff diocese suggest that take-up was not very high. In 1893 only three girls emigrated from the diocese.[69] Unusually, one wished to migrate to a warmer climate for the winter and so temporarily relocated to Egypt, while the other two servants emigrated permanently to America, one of whom was accompanied by her family. In 1902 numbers were still relatively low, with only two members recorded as having emigrated. One was conveyed to America where she was met by the organisation's American associate, and the other, a lady's maid, had, like many women of her occupation, travelled privately with her mistress to Burma.[70]

The relatively small number of women who emigrated, despite in some instances free passage and guaranteed work, may partly be attributed to the selectivity of the host countries. Australia was particularly discerning about the type of girls recruited into service posts, with the Australian Board of Immigration closely monitoring the nature of the girls being admitted to the country.[71] For instance, the GFS associate in Adelaide reported to her colleagues in Britain that the settlement had 'no openings for companion helps in the colony', nor did they wish to receive any sickly servants as the climate was especially not 'beneficial in cases of consumption'.[72] Meanwhile, the correspondent in South Africa reported that Cape Colony possessed many 'openings for Nursery Governesses, Companion Helps, Matrons, and Working Housekeepers', while 'it is a great happiness to add that the climate is so fine that there have been some cases of delicate health which, under the advice of an experienced physician, it has been possible to recommend for employment. These persons are all greatly improved in health, and everyone is self-supporting'.[73] This suggests that the programmes did not just facilitate the migration of servants but also helped to shape it according to the demands of the different reception countries.

Such schemes were the forerunners of larger government-run programmes introduced during the interwar era, such as that established by the Australian government to coax British girls into its service sector.[74] However, only a minority of girls actually emigrated in the interwar era and it seems unlikely that more low-key schemes would have had a larger impact on the service workforce in the nineteenth century, when domestic work was plentiful, voyages were longer and return tickets were seldom offered. Yet despite their limited impact on depleting servant numbers, the existence of such schemes continued to heighten concerns over a servant shortage in Wales. Despite these fears, the supply of servants did not dry up before the First World War, it simply failed to keep up with employer demand in the area. Meanwhile, the expansion of other forms of female employment such as nursing constricted the proportion of the overall workforce that service accounted for. Rather than a decline in the availability of staff owing to emigration or education, it was the internal diversification of the sector that greatly increased competition for staff.

DIVERSIFICATION IN THE DOMESTIC SERVICE SECTOR

It is important to note that the discourse surrounding servant shortages was largely confined to household staff as opposed to servants based in business premises and public institutions. As the period progressed, private household service was considered a less attractive form of employment in comparison to the increasing number of positions becoming available in businesses and institutions. Although the duties and even job titles often reflected those of private households, greater job security and improved working conditions rendered these occupations a more appealing prospect for many people.[75] Both Bridgend and Aberdare experienced an increase in the number of domestic staff located outside private homes.[76] This was in response to several social trends such as the development of the leisure industry, the expansion of municipal governance and even an increase in civic pride.[77] These trends led to significant changes in the urban environment, such as the creation of parks, hospitals and hotels, all of which required domestic workers to maintain them.[78] Therefore, would-be employers of household servants increasingly had to compete with these alternative workplaces. Their ability to compete with the newly emerging businesses and institutions was severely hampered by monetary restrictions. Girls in hospitals, for instance, had regular rates of pay, fixed duties, set hours and had the camaraderie of working alongside others.[79] In contrast, those employing household servants were restricted to offering lower wages and engaging only one domestic who was required to perform a far great number of tasks. Consequently, household positions emerged as a less secure and less appealing option.

The decline in the appeal of household service impacted most on lower-middle and working-class employers who appear to have found it particularly difficult to recruit and retain good staff. Far from being confined to the wealthier upper classes, by the mid-nineteenth century servant keeping had been adopted by an increasingly diverse range of householders. The emergence of the middle classes stimulated demand for domestics throughout Britain, and south Wales was no exception. While professionals generally accounted for between one third and a half of servant-keeping householders in towns such as Carmarthen and Bridgend, the more modest households of miners and general labourers also on occasion engaged domestic help.[80] Although the proportion of servant-employers emanating from the working classes varied from place to place, the census case study of Aberdare, Bridgend and Carmarthen suggests that areas with high male employment had a larger number of lower class employers. Of the three towns, Aberdare had the largest number of 'unskilled' or 'partly skilled' employers, with them accounting for 14 per cent of all sampled households in 1871. As men on the coalfield could secure incomes at an early age, so they were able to marry and establish households at an earlier age, thus increasing the number of working men requiring or desiring domestic assistance.[81] However, in all three towns, the most dominant employer occupation was that of shopkeeper, merchant and dealer, whose income and social class could vary greatly.[82]

Correspondence published in the *Western Mail* suggests that these lower status householders were particularly vilified by maids and were blamed for many of the problems that were thought to blight the industry. A common sentiment expressed by one Newport maid in 1892 was the belief that 'mistresses used to respect their servants and were looked up to in return, but such mistresses now are few and far between. There are so many "ladies" who have been domestics themselves that we cannot expect them to make good mistresses'.[83] A housemaid from the Rhondda valley claimed that 'so-called ladies who have just jumped up do not know how to treat a servant',[84] while other maids described their less affluent mistresses as 'half-trained ladies' with 'no idea of housekeeping, but a good idea how to dress'.[85] This chimes with the popular belief that social status was as important to servants as to their employers.[86] However, one correspondent to the *Western Mail* provided an alternative explanation for the fraught relationship between lower income employers and their servants. He claimed: 'I noticed that the complaints do not come so much from those who live in wealthy houses, where there is more than enough to spare, but from those who give assistance to mistresses with very limited incomes who must manage economically in order to pay their way honourably'.[87] Here household tensions were attributed to the hardships induced by limited resources rather than socially insecure mistresses or maids. Yet, regardless of the underlying reasons, lower income households were particularly fearful that the supply of good-quality staff would cease as demand continued to escalate in the late nineteenth century, and it is in this sphere that class antagonism and social tensions were most greatly felt. A consideration of the increasingly diverse range of employers who sought domestic assistants helps explain why many contemporary observers lamented the existence of a servant shortage. While the number of domestics in Wales continued to increase, they were being sought by an increasing number of potential employers and it was in those lower income householders, where social tensions were at their highest and work conditions often at their lowest, where the apparent shortage was most acute.

CONCLUSION

Regardless of the social tensions that plagued the industry throughout the period, domestic service remained an important and enduring part of the Welsh economy and society. While domestic service in south Wales has often followed a different trajectory to that experienced in England, an examination of the Welsh sector has significant implications for our perception of the wider British industry. The importance of considering the interplay between the factors of supply and demand, as well as locality and industry, has proved pivotal in generating a more nuanced understanding of domestic service. An exploration of domestic service in south Wales has also revealed the interconnectedness of the area with the rest of the United Kingdom and beyond. Consequently, south Wales has emerged as an area that continued to experience a high level of internal employer demand for domestic service workers. Meanwhile, the study of service also challenges perceptions of the Welsh economy as a male arena. Domestic service was an important industry that provided workers of both sexes with the opportunity to become active economic agents. While the sector has often been viewed as the 'lesser evil' of the employment opportunities available to women, the increasing proportion of men in the sector and the first-hand testimony of retired servants has suggested that service was an attractive option for many workers. The accounts of Bessie and Ada have especially revealed the multiple experiences of service and that servants were as diverse as the people who recruited them. It is only through placing the individual servants into the broader context of domestic service as a 'whole industry' that their true contribution to the Welsh economy can be fully appreciated.

NOTES

1 South Wales Miners' Library: South Wales Coalfield Collection [hereafter SWCC] AUD/482, Bessie Hopkins's account recorded as part of the Womens' Work Experiences in the Swansea Valley Audio Collection.

2 Bessie Hopkins, Swansea Valley Audio Collection.

3 National Library of Wales: NLW ex 1906, Reminiscence of Ada Carter.

4 L. J. Williams, *Digest of Welsh Historical Statistics*, vol. 1 (Cardiff: Welsh Office, 1985), p. 96.

5 R. Scadden, *No Job for a Little Girl: Voices from Domestic Service* (Llandysul: Gomer Press, 2013); M. A. Williams, 'The new London Welsh: domestic servants 1918–1939', *Transactions of the Honourable Society of Cymmrodorion*, 9 (2003), 135–51.

6 C. Howells, 'Wales's hidden industry: domestic service in south Wales, 1871–1921' (unpublished PhD thesis, Swansea University, 2014).

7 Although not as broad as the classification proposed by Ebery and Preston who list wig makers and rat-catchers among the servant ranks: M. Ebery and B. Preston, *Geographical Papers: Domestic Service in Late Victorian and Edwardian England, 1871–1914* (Reading: University of Reading, 1976).

8 Ebery and Preston, *Geographical Papers*, p. 2.

9 For example, J. Musson, *Up and Down Stairs: The History of the Country House Servant* (London: John Murray, 2009); and P. Sambrook, *Keeping their Place: Domestic Service in the Country House 1700–1920* (Stroud: Sutton Publishing, 2005).

10 P. Horn, *The Rise and Fall of the Victorian Servant* (Dublin: Gill and Macmillan Ltd, 1975); T. McBride, *The Domestic Revolution: The Modernisation of Household Service in England and France 1820–1920* (London: Croom Helm Ltd, 1976).

11 R. M. Jones, 'Beyond identity? The reconstruction of the Welsh', *Journal of British Studies*, 31 (1992), 349.

12 *Kelly's Directory of Monmouthshire and South Wales* (London: Kelly's Directories Ltd, 1901).

13 *The Post Office Directory* (1871).

14 H. J. Randall, *Bridgend: The Story of a Market Town* (Newport: R. H. Johns Ltd, 1955), p. 1.

15 J. Light, ' "Of inestimable value to the town and district?" A study of the urban middle classes in south Wales with particular reference to Pontypool, Bridgend and Penarth *c.*1850–1890' (unpublished PhD thesis, Swansea University, 2003), p. 33.
16 *The Post Office Directory* (1871); *Kelly's Directory* (1901).
17 W. Spurrell, *A Guide to Carmarthen and its Neighbourhood* (Carmarthen: W. Spurrell, 1882), pp. 28–31.
18 Williams, *Digest of Welsh Historical Statistics*, p. 96; Ebery and Preston, *Geographical Papers*, p. 25.
19 Williams, *Digest of Welsh Historical Statistics*, p. 113.
20 Williams, *Digest of Welsh Historical Statistics*, pp. 109, 114 and 117.
21 Williams, *Digest of Welsh Historical Statistics*, pp. 62 and 110; *The Post Office Directory* (1871); *Kelly's Directory* (1901).
22 J. Lodwick and V. Lodwick, *The Story of Carmarthen* (Carmarthen: St. Peter's Press, 1995), p. 194.
23 A. Raine, *A Welsh Singer* (London: Hutchinson and Co., 1897), p. 63.
24 Ebery and Preston, *Geographical Papers*, p. 26.
25 Ebery and Preston, *Geographical Papers*, p. 25.
26 South Wales Miners' Library: SWCC AUD/399, Mrs Landon's account recorded as part of the Womens' Work Experiences in the Swansea Valley Audio Collection.
27 South Wales Miners' Library: SWCC AUD/490, Mrs Kelly's account recorded as part of the Womens' Work Experiences in the Swansea Valley Audio Collection.
28 Williams, *Digest of Welsh Historical Statistics*, pp. 96, 110 and 113.
29 Williams, *Digest of Welsh Historical Statistics*, pp. 96, 110 and 113.
30 Horn, *The Rise and Fall of the Victorian Servant*, p. 84.
31 Ebery and Preston, *Geographical Papers*, p. 74
32 Ebery and Preston, *Geographical Papers*, p. 74.
33 P. Horn, *Life Below Stairs in the 20th Century* (London: Sutton Publishing Ltd, 2001), p. 29; J. Flanders, *The Victorian House* (London: Harper Perennial, 2004), p.xxi; L. Lethbridge, *Servants: A Downstairs View of Twentieth-Century Britain* (London: Bloomsbury, 2013), p. 154.
34 West Glamorgan Archive Service: D/D CV 4/655/1-2, Servant Insurance Policy, 16 October 1920.
35 'Situations Vacant', *Western Mail*, 1871, 1881, 1891, 1901, 1911 and 1921.
36 'Situations Vacant', *Western Mail*, 1871 and 1891.
37 'The Servant Problem', *Western Mail*, 9 June 1900.
38 Bessie Hopkins, Swansea Valley Audio Collection.
39 'Situations Vacant', *The Bristol Mercury*, 19 October 1872; 'Situations Vacant', *The Hampshire Advertiser*, 10 June 1874; 'Situations Vacant', *The Morning Post*, 28 April 1892.
40 Glamorgan Archive: D/D/LIF300, Baglan House Records, a pamphlet advertising Mrs Hunt's agency based in London.

41 For further discussion of country-house recruitment and migration patterns, see A. Williams, *A Detested Occupation? A History of Domestic Servants in North Wales 1800–1930* (Llanrwst: Gwasg Carreg Gwalch, 2016).

42 Editorial, *Western Mail*, October–November 1892.

43 *The Census of England and Wales*: Bridgend, 1871, 1891 and 1921.

44 McBride, *The Domestic Revolution*, p. 35; L. Davidoff and C. Hall, *Family Fortunes: Men and Women of the English Middle-Class 1780–1850* (London: Hutchinson Education, 1987), p. 309.

45 Davidoff and Hall, *Family Fortunes*, p. 389; Colchester was a largely rural market town. In the mid-nineteenth century, most inhabitants worked in small shops or agriculture. A third of the population were employed in craft work, one fifth were engaged in domestic service and only one in twenty worked in service. J. Cooper and C. R. Elrington, 'Modern Colchester: Economic Development', *A History of the County of Essex: Volume 9: The Borough of Colchester* (London: Victoria County History,1994), *www.british-history.ac.uk* (accessed 29 May 2017), pp. 179–98.

46 F. V. Dawes, *Not in Front of the Servants: A True Portrait of Upstairs, Downstairs Life* (London: Century in Association with the National Trust, 1973), p. 28.

47 L. J. Williams, *Was Wales Industrialised? Essays in Modern Welsh History* (Llandysul: Gomer Press, 1995), p. 65.

48 'The Ways of Women', *Western Mail*, 10 March 1900.

49 'The Ways of Women', *Western Mail*, 10 March 1900.

50 'Experience of Sixty Years, Cardiff', *Western Mail*, 19 December 1892.

51 E. S. Turner, *What the Butler Saw: Two Hundred and Fifty Years of the Servant Problem* (London: Penguin Publishers, 2001), p. 233.

52 B. Abel-Smith, *A History of the Nursing Profession* (London: Heinemann Educational Books Ltd, 1970), pp. 4–5.

53 Dawes, *Not in Front of the Servants*, pp. 152 and 164; G. Braybon, *Women Workers in the First World War* (London: Routledge, 1989), pp. 181–3.

54 M. Beetham, 'Domestic Servants as Poachers of Print: Reading, Authority and Resistance in Late Victorian Britain', in L. Delap et al., *The Politics of Domestic Authority in Britain since 1800* (London: Palgrave Macmillan, 2009), p. 187; Turner, *What the Butler Saw*, p. 233.

55 'Girls and Service: Rhondda Objection to Domestic Training', *Western Mail*, 25 April 1919.

56 L. Delap, 'Kitchen sink laughter: domestic service humour in twentieth-century Britain', *Journal of British Studies*, 49 (2010), 624; L. Delap, *Knowing their Place: Domestic Servants in Twentieth-Century Britain* (Oxford: University Press, 2011), p. 33; 'Girls and Service' *Western Mail*, 25 April 1919.

57 'General News', *Birmingham Daily Post*, 16 November 1875: Williams, 'The new London Welsh', 143.

58 'The Servant Problems', *The Western Mail*, 9 June1900.
59 P. Hamilton and B. W. Higman, 'Servants of empire: the British training of domestics for Australia, 1926–31', *Social History*, 28 (2003), 68.
60 Lethbridge, *Servants*, pp. 100–1.
61 Lethbridge, *Servants*, pp. 100–1.
62 'The Women's Emigration Society', *The Morning Post*, 26 December 1883.
63 *The North Eastern Daily Gazette*, 10 September 1883.
64 'The Emigration of Women', *The Morning Post*, 5 July 1884.
65 'Situations Vacant', *The Western Mail*, 15 September1911.
66 'Situations Vacant', *The Western Mail*, 15 November 1911.
67 Girls Friendly Society, *http://girlsfriendlysociety.org.uk/what-we-do/our-history/* (accessed 16 October 2017).
68 Cardiff Central Library [herafter CCL]: Girls Friendly Society Llandaff Annual Reports, 'Department for GFS Members Emigration', 1892, p. 69.
69 CCL: Girls Friendly Society Llandaff Annual Reports, 'Emigration Department-Llandaff', 1893, p. 19.
70 CCL: Girls Friendly Society Llandaff Annual Reports, 'Emigration', 1902, p. 23.
71 CCL: Girls Friendly Society Llandaff Annual Reports, 'Department for GFS Members Emigration', 1892, p. 69.
72 CCL: Girls Friendly Society Llandaff Annual Reports, 'Department for GFS Members Emigration', 1892, p. 67.
73 CCL: Girls Friendly Society Llandaff Annual Reports, 'Department for GFS Members Emigration', 1892, p. 69.
74 Hamilton and Higman, 'Servants of empire', 67–82.
75 M. Higgs, *Tracing your Servant Ancestors: A Guide for Family Historians* (Barnsley: Pen and Sword Books Ltd, 2012), p. 22.
76 *The Census of England and Wales*: Bridgend and Aberdare, 1871, 1891 and 1911.
77 C. Cook, *The Routledge Companion to Britain in the Nineteenth Century, 1815–1914* (Abingdon: Routledge, 2005), p. 116; P. Horn, Pleasures and Pastimes in Victorian Britain (Stroud: Amberley Publishing, 2011), pp. 20–2.
78 Horn, *Pleasures and Pastimes*, pp. 22 and 292; Cook, *The Routledge Companion to the Nineteenth Century*, p. 106.
79 Higgs, *Tracing your Servant Ancestors*, p. 22.
80 *The Census of England and Wales*: Bridgend and Carmarthen, 1871, 1891 and 1911.
81 D. Jones, 'Counting the Cost of Coal: Women's Lives in the Rhondda, 1881–1911', in A. V. John (ed.), *Our Mother's Land: Chapters in Welsh Women's History, 1830–1839* (Cardiff: University of Wales Press, 1991), p. 113.
82 M. J. Winstanley, *The Shopkeeper's World 1830–1914* (Manchester: Manchester University Press, 1983), p. 43.
83 'A Servant, Newport', *Western Mail*, 5 December 1892.

84 'Housemaid, Rhondda Valley', *Western Mail*, 9 December 1892.
85 'A Swansea Servant', *Western Mail*, 12 December 1892; 'A Poor Servant, Cardiff', Western Mail, 1 December 1892.
86 Dawes, *Not in Front of the Servants*, p. 62.
87 'A Non Unionist, Cardiff', *Western Mail*, 21 December 1892.

FROM PATERNALISM TO INDUSTRIAL PARTNERSHIP

THE EVOLUTION OF INDUSTRIAL WELFARE CAPITALISM IN SOUTH WALES, c.1840–1939

STEVEN THOMPSON

IN AN important essay published in 1980, L. J. Williams noted the great strides that had been made in Welsh 'labour history' to that point in time and the extent to which this area of historical inquiry had broadened to include a variety of different aspects of working-class life. At the same time, he argued, this broadening of the perspectives of Welsh labour historians had not extended so far as to include a consideration of the individuals who employed all these Welsh workers in the first place. In his particular focus on coalowners as a group, Williams noted that two generations had passed since they had been nationalised out of existence and yet, despite the importance of employers in the stories of strikes and struggle that had engaged the attentions of labour historians, still very little work had been done to advance understanding beyond stereotypes and myths.[1] Another two generations have passed since that essay was published and yet we still lack the histories of employers, whether coalowners or other industrialists, that could help to broaden and re-enliven interest in the Welsh industrial past and offer a more rounded portrait of industrial communities.[2]

Williams's essay offered a series of penetrating thoughts on different aspects of the history of the coalowners, including their economic functions and roles as employers, on the one hand, and their place in the community on the other. As part of the latter focus, he considered the character, extent and effects of efforts made by coalowners to enhance the social capital, institutions and facilities of coalfield communities, largely in the form of chapels, churches, schools, libraries, institutes and hospitals.[3] This industrial welfare forms the subject of this chapter and while a study of this aspect of the history of employers cannot possibly make good the lacuna of studies of employers in the Welsh industrial past, it nevertheless goes to the heart of a major aspect of the popular and scholarly perception of industrialists in modern Wales. Again and again, they have been portrayed as heartless, self-serving tyrants determined to extract the highest possible profit from their collieries no matter what the consequences for their workers and with no regard for the communities in which their enterprises were situated.[4] Popular myth in Cardiff, for example, states that the inscription on John Cory's statue unveiled in Cathays Park in 1906, 'John Cory, Coalowner and Philanthropist', is a contradiction in terms, while Sir W. T. Lewis, the coalowners' leader in the late nineteenth century, was memorably described by Sidney Webb as the 'best hated man in south Wales'.[5] The current study, therefore, is offered as a first step in a new history of Welsh industrial employers that subjects such views to some measure of scrutiny.

While Welsh historians have failed to focus their attentions on the history of employer paternalism, historians of other countries and regions have devoted a great deal more time and effort to this matter.[6] In particular, Joseph Melling has offered a number of studies of industrial welfare and has usefully noted three different approaches that might be utilised.[7] First, an empirical approach considers the range and content of services that were provided by employers to their workers. Secondly, purposive analyses attempt to explain the variety of motives that led the employer to make provision for worker welfare. Lastly, functional interpretations assess the functions that the provision seems to fulfil, whether they were intended by the employer or not. Crucially, he also notes that such approaches need to be sensitive to the particular historical contexts under consideration.[8] This essay utilises these different approaches to industrial welfare and attempts to situate them within the particular social, cultural, political and economic contexts of the south

Wales coalfield. It does so through a series of case studies in which a single company or employer is examined in three important periods of industrialisation in south Wales to illustrate some of the general themes and developments in industrial welfare provision. It is not suggested that the case studies somehow encapsulate the periods under consideration in their entirety, only that they constitute some of the most interesting and illuminating instances of provision in the region. Through such case studies, a sense of the significant shifts in industrial welfare over the course of a century is revealed and located in the broader industrial context of the region.

Different parts of south Wales came to experience a process of industrialisation from the latter decades of the eighteenth century and certain forms of employer paternalism were evident from the beginning. Industrialisation in the region was most evident in the rise of the iron industry in the northernmost parts of Glamorgan and Monmouthshire, especially in the area around Merthyr Tydfil, and in the development of copper smelting in the region around Swansea.[9] Such was the development in the former that by the 1830s, roughly fifty iron furnaces were in operation in an arc of towns from Ystradgynlais in the west to Pontypool in the east. Merthyr, at the centre of these developments, witnessed its population increase from 7,705 in 1801 to 46,378 in 1851.[10] Copper development did not bring about the same growth in population and the industry only employed about 2,000 workers by 1841, though due to its effect in stimulating other industrial concerns, whether coal mining to serve the copper smelting directly or other, related metallurgical processes and chemical works, far more people than this looked to the copper industry for their means of support.[11]

Certain paternalistic practices were evident in these two districts from an early phase. Common to both forms of industrialisation were the appointment of 'works surgeons' by the employers in the respective industries. A works surgeon was appointed to serve the needs of the workers of Cyfarthfa ironworks, for example, while the Sirhowy and Tredegar ironworks appointed a doctor in 1813, Nantyglo ironworks engaged a surgeon from 1817, and the Hirwaun ironworks did likewise from at least the mid-1820s.[12] Many employers also combined such medical provision with friendly benefits offered through works-based schemes. At the Llanelly Copperworks Co. in 1806, for example, 2d per week was stopped from each man, though the fund had to be supported initially by the company, and benefits of 7s. a week were paid to sick or injured workers unable to work. A further 1d a week was collected from the pay of workers to fund the employment of a surgeon-apothecary and the free provision of any medicines where the affliction was not due to the misconduct of the worker.[13]

The motivations of employers in making or supporting these forms of provision were varied. Ideas of Christian charity and the need to create a public profile were clearly evident, but, more interestingly, employers also looked to use such paternalism to attract and retain labour. This was a serious consideration in the late eighteenth and early nineteenth centuries as industrial concerns were established in sparsely populated areas. Moreover, a traditional form of defence against employer exploitation was for workers to simply leave their place of employment. The eligibility for friendly benefits, built up through service to the company involved, however, discouraged this mobility of labour and helped employers retain a stable and settled workforce.[14] Therefore, employer paternalism in the early years of industrialisation was largely intended to attract, retain and discipline a new industrial workforce that had to be adapted to life in a new setting.

EARLY VICTORIAN PATERNALISM

The supposed financial, moral and other benefits of paternalism were evident in employer motivations in the region from the early period of industrialisation, therefore, but they were to assume a new importance in the mid-century period. The growing pains of industrialisation, evident in the years up to 1830, were to give way to the turmoil and crises of adolescence in the 1830s and 1840s as south Wales was rocked by industrial strife, political instability and outbreaks of serious violence.[15] In this frenzied atmosphere, industrial paternalism took on an added significance and many individuals looked to industrial labour policies as part of the means of restoring balance and preserving peace. The crucial figure in framing and advocating employer paternalism as a means to promote social cohesion and political stability was Hugh Seymour Tremenheere.[16] Tremenheere was a barrister by training and, on 8 December 1839, just a few short weeks after the Newport rising, he was appointed to conduct an investigation into educational provision in south Wales.

In his role as an educational and, just a few years later, mines inspector through the 1840s and the 1850s, Tremenheere was determined to consider all the various factors that determined the quality of life of the working population.[17] Similar to other reform-minded politicians and individuals in the 1830s and 1840s, he believed firmly that the social conditions that prevailed in industrial communities led to dissatisfaction, intemperance and immorality, but also to trade unionism, political radicalism and violent revolt. As he later wrote about Welsh industrial workers in the 1830s and 1840s:

> Dirt, neglect and discomfort surrounded their dwellings almost universally; the means of education were scarcely more than the very humble and scanty ones which satisfy a people in the lowest state of intelligence; and sensuality, ignorance, and perverted views, with a reckless sacrifice of their children to their own cupidity, were preventable to a lamentable degree.[18]

While other observers might have attributed such failings to immorality and fecklessness on the part of the poor and working class, Tremenheere clearly attributed at least some responsibility to structural factors and the policies of employers. The answer, he believed, was for employers to recognise their responsibilities to their workers, their families and the communities in which they lived. 'Property has its rights as well as his duties', he claimed, arguing that 'where great fortunes are made from the labour of thousands of the working classes, a great debt is due to them', and likening the relationship between an employer and his workers to that of a parent and his child.[19] What was needed, he argued, were benefits clubs to guard against the risks of old age and sickness, sanitary improvements to improve living conditions, temperance efforts to eradicate drunkenness, weekly rather than monthly payment of wages to prevent debt, the abolition of 'truck' shops so as to remove a source of exploitation, and provision of places of worship to improve moral standards.

Interestingly, and tellingly, Tremenheere shared the widespread distrust of trade unions. In his view, they encouraged workers to take action against their employers that resulted in disruption to production, with its attendant costs, and a higher labour cost in the form of wage increases, both of which resulted in higher selling costs of iron and coal and a fall in competitiveness and profits.[20] Indeed, through organisation and agitation in trade unions, workers imperilled Britain's international standing,

> by . . . destroying the very foundation of our national advantages as a manufacturing people . . . crippling the capital that keeps in motion this vast system of manufacturing industry, encouraging foreign competition, rendering nugatory the superior intelligence of the manufacturer . . . paralysing the energy and enterprise of the merchant in seeking out . . . foreign and distant markets, and dragging down and extinguishing the very trade that is their mainstay for future employment.[21]

Tremenheere used his position during the mid-century decades to advocate more paternalistic labour policies on the part of employers in the region and worked to persuade industrialists that their financial and industrial relations interests were best served if they made provision for their workmen.

The most complete realisation of Tremenheere's ethos of industrial labour management came in the case of the Dowlais Iron Company. From a relatively basic system of provision in the early part of the century, its various forms of provision were developed further during the 1830s and 1840s to form an integrated system of relief, medical care and education. By the 1850s, 4d in each pound was stopped from the wages of all workers and was divided for the purposes of different areas of provision: 2d went towards the sick funds, 1½d was paid towards the cost of medical attendance and medicines, and the remaining ½d went to funding the schools. Weekly payments of 2s. to the colliers and 2s. 6d to iron miners and furnace workers were made after six months' membership in the schemes, though accident cases disabled from working were given immediate support.[22] To a large degree, therefore, these forms of paternalistic provision involved workers providing for their own welfare by the payment of compulsory deductions while in work to gain eligibility for sickness benefits when they were unable to work. At the same time, while the medical funds returned a profit for the company, the cost of the educational provision exceeded the sum raised to a greater degree and the company found itself subsidising the programme of welfare schemes each year to ensure their survival.[23]

These various efforts were intensified with the appointment of G. T. Clark as manager of the company in 1856. By the late 1860s, the medical schemes and sick funds covered all of the 8,000 to 9,000 workmen employed by the company and, as such, covered roughly 30,000 people when their families are also counted. In addition, the company built cottages or else granted leases on their land for workmen to erect their own houses, supported the parish church, established a savings fund for workmen, provided a reading room and library, promoted musical and other cultural endeavours in the community and, from 1869, provided a hospital of eight beds through the agency of Clark's wife and supervised by the company's head surgeon.[24] In his thoughts on provision for his workers, Clark adopted a literal interpretation of paternalism and viewed himself as the father of his workmen:

> My own men are like my own children, and I should as soon think of refusing to listen to my own child as of refusing to listen to any man who comes to me on any matter, because I think it of equal importance that my men and I should be on good terms as that I should be on good terms with my own family.[25]

Contrasting his own superintendence of his firm favourably with joint stock companies in the Pontypool region in which the same closeness between master and men was not possible, Clark believed, in terms very similar to Tremenheere, that it was to the mutual benefit of employer and worker that the moral and physical conditions of the labouring population be raised to such an extent that they become sober, industrious and independent workers.[26] Schools would provide the 'moral training' that would stand children in good stead in their later lives as workers, while savings schemes would foster that spirit of independence that was even more important than the actual funds that would keep a man off the Poor Law.[27] Sick funds obviated the need for recourse to the parish authorities, while the fact that the medical schemes secured the same medical services to the men and their families as were enjoyed by Clark and his family demonstrated his interest in their wellbeing and the common bonds between them.[28] In such a relationship, trade unions were a particular problem since, in Clark's view, they came between a master and his men, interfered with the principles of free trade and personal freedom of action, and tended to increase the costs of industrial products and thereby decrease industrial competitiveness, both of which acted against the interests of both the employer and his workers.[29]

Such paternalism was accepted by the workers to a large degree but could be the cause of dissatisfaction at moments of crisis. Such a moment came with the visitation of cholera in 1866. In his capacity as a major industrialist and as chairman of both the Local Board of Health and the Poor Law Guardians, Clark was energetic in his response to the crisis and quickly set about co-ordinating the response to the epidemic in Merthyr. His actions did not prove popular with his workers, however. A public meeting was held at which were passed resolutions that objected to the conveyance of victims to the 'hospital' where circumstances permitted their care in their own homes, the burial of victims in graves not chosen by the families, the destruction of bedclothes without compensation, and the continuation of Cresswell as the medical attendant at the works.[30] Clark's reply to the men indicated the extent of his wound at this rejection of his paternalism. In a long letter, he pointed out the instances over the preceding years in which he had personally interceded, often at their request, to improve the welfare schemes provided through the company or to assist them in some particular difficulty.[31] This appeal seemed to work and a meeting of the workmen a number of months later decided that the schemes continue as before. Nevertheless, here was a clear revolt against the company's influence and control, albeit in the particular circumstances of a cholera epidemic, that perhaps defined the boundaries of employer paternalism.[32]

By the late 1850s Tremenheere was convinced that the efforts made by employers in the region during the 1840s and 1850s had brought about a transformation in industrial and social relations, and had consequently ended the possibility of revolt and rebellion that had been so evident in the 1830s. Following the Newport rising of 1839, he opined that most employers had undertaken at least some measure of ameliorative reform and had attempted to improve the lives of their workers in at least some way.[33] A test of the transformative potential of employer paternalism came in 1858, Tremenheere believed, when depression in the iron trade caused a fall in wages and the introduction of short-time working. Workers, he was able to report with much satisfaction, accepted the changes without murmur, such was the 'better understanding' and 'mutual confidence' that existed between masters and men. In this instance, Tremenheere argued, could be seen evidence 'that the great body of the masters do, in fact, care for their people' and that 'the workpeople are naturally disposed, when the time of pressure comes, to listen fairly to their masters' representations'.[34] The precise impact of employer paternalism is difficult to measure accurately and certainly Tremenheere was keen to attribute better industrial relations to the types of employer benevolence that he advocated. The better performance of the Victorian economy in the third quarter of the century undoubtedly eased industrial tensions, but, nevertheless, Tremenheere was convinced that more enlightened labour policies on the part of Welsh employers were an important factor in this improvement in relations between capital and labour.

LATE NINETEENTH-CENTURY COAL CAPITALISM

It is perhaps no surprise that the most notable instances of employer paternalism in the mid-nineteenth century came within the iron and other metallurgical industries rather than in coal. The greater premium on skill and the cash- rather than labour-intensive nature of metal production meant that companies in these different industries took a different view of the advisability of expenditure on paternalistic provision.[35] This means that it is difficult to point to any coal company in south Wales during the nineteenth or twentieth centuries that undertook the same breadth of paternalistic provision as the Dowlais Iron Company during the middle decades of the nineteenth century. Nevertheless, some coal companies did make provision for their workers in the latter part of the century and were moved to do so for their own particular reasons.

In particular, the latter decades of the nineteenth century witnessed the advent of new forms of industrial welfare provision and these new developments were intended to mitigate the impact of certain statutory interventions that affected the profits that employers might expect from the coal industry. Significant political and public discussion of the relationship between workers and their employers in this period focused on the fate of men injured during the course of their work, and the first generation of 'miners' MPs' were instrumental in placing employers' liability and workmen's compensation on the political agenda.[36] Legislation passed in 1880 and 1897 meant that the work-related injuries of industrial workers became a significant cost that employers sought to manage and, given the greater incidence of injury and disease in the coal industry, and the correspondingly higher financial burden, it was coalowners who gave these matters the greatest proportion of their time and efforts.

Crucial in these new developments was William Thomas Lewis. Born in Merthyr Tydfil, Lewis became apprenticed as an engineer to his father at the Plymouth ironworks and later became the third Marquess of Bute's mining engineer in 1864. This important position, in addition to his own industrial acquisitions and ventures, made Lewis one of the foremost industrialists in south Wales by the 1870s and 1880s, and this is evident in his crucial role in establishing a coalowners' association for the Cynon valley in 1864, which became the Monmouthshire and South Wales Coal Owners' Association in 1871. As the dominant figure in that association, Lewis was integral to the creation of the sliding scale that pegged miners' wages to the price of coal for the rest of the century and was instrumental in the direction of the association's industrial policies in the period.[37] Significantly, Lewis was an Anglican in an overwhelmingly nonconformist region, a Conservative in a Liberal heartland, and militantly anti-trade union in a working-class district in which unionism was gaining ground.

Lewis was integral to the development of three new areas of paternalistic provision in the last two decades of the nineteenth century and all were intended to address problems that coalowners perceived were due to employers' liability and workmen's compensation legislation. These were the South Wales and Monmouthshire Miners' Permanent Provident Society, the ambulance brigade movement and the establishment of cottage hospitals. The permanent provident society movement was initiated in the north-east of England coalfield in the wake of the Hartley disaster in 1862. A provident society was established to provide financial aid to the widows and 'orphans' of men killed in the disaster but also, more generally, to the families of men killed in smaller accidents that claimed a life or two at a time; the society also paid 'disablement benefits' to men prevented from working as a result of injury.[38] In the years that followed, further permanent provident societies were established in other coalfields, but efforts in south Wales to imitate the movement were abortive in the 1870s, largely as a result of worker opposition. Among the reasons for the opposition was a fear that such a measure could disrupt the passage of the Employers' Liability Bill, the lack of any old-age or sickness benefits, the failure to include payments to widows whose husbands died of ill health, and a fear that the proposed subscription would endanger workers' support for existing friendly societies.[39]

The context changed with the passage of Employers' Liability Act of 1880. The legislation made employers responsible for the financial losses experienced by workers injured at work and gave such workers, in theory at least, the right to take legal action against their employers to secure financial recompense. In response to the passage of the Act, Lewis and his fellow coalowners forced the creation of a South Wales and Monmouthshire Miners' Permanent Provident Society, despite opposition from workers' leaders, and used a variety of methods, some more legitimate than others, to encourage as many miners as possible into membership. The advantage to the employers was that membership of the society involved workers 'contracting out' of their rights under the legislation (that is, waiving the rights granted to them by the legislation) since the 'joint provision' for injured and deceased miners was allowed to stand in place of the provision made by the Act.[40] The fund from which such payments were made was accumulated from weekly contributions from member workers, donations from the great and the good, and a contribution from the employers which, in south Wales at least, amounted to 25 per cent of the total contributed by each coalowners' workers.

The motivations for the establishment of the permanent provident society were, therefore, many and varied. First, it was an anti-statist measure intended to frustrate the workings of the statutory framework of employers' liability, through the 'joint provision' that required workers to 'contract out'. However, it was also anti-statist in the sense that employers used the permanent provident fund movement as part of an effort to oppose suggested extensions or amendments to employers' liability during the 1880s and suggested workmen's compensation legislation in the 1890s.[41] 'Joint provision' by workers and employers, it was argued, was far more beneficial than a statutory legal framework to govern the relationship between the two parties since it brought them into close co-operation in support of the wellbeing of workers.[42] Secondly, rather than bear the cost of injured miners' incapacity themselves, as they would have done under the legislation, employers were able to lessen their financial liabilities through their voluntary, paternalistic contributions: injured workers, in effect, paid for their own death and disability benefits and the scheme was more dependent on self-help than employer support. Last, the permanent provident society movement worked to undermine the appeal of trade unions since the provision of 'friendly' benefits such as sick pay and disability payments was one of the main inducements used by British trade unions during the nineteenth and early twentieth centuries to persuade workers into membership.[43]

Lewis was central in the efforts to establish and administer the permanent provident society and it stood at the heart of his philosophy of labour management. He looked to buttress its role through two other developments that are evident from the 1880s. The first was the creation of ambulance brigades at workplaces where workers would be trained in first-aid techniques that could be utilised immediately a worker was injured. A more general move towards first-aid training was evident across British society in these years, with the formation of the St John Ambulance Brigade in 1877 the most obvious manifestation. Lewis looked to extend this movement into the region and used his position on the board of the permanent provident society to get it to give formal encouragement to the formation of classes at collieries connected to the society.[44] Large numbers of such ambulance brigades were indeed founded across south Wales in the years that followed, trained by the local doctors, many of whom had close links with the colliery companies, and supported by employers through the provision of ambulance halls and ambulance brigade competitions.[45]

The second initiative was to give support to the foundation of hospitals in industrial districts. The most notable example came with Lewis's considerable financial support for the Merthyr General Hospital opened in 1888 and, again, Lewis drew an explicit link with the permanent provident society. In a banquet at Aberdare to celebrate his knighthood in 1886, Lewis extolled the virtues of the society, mentioned that he had assisted with the administrative work of the small cottage hospital provided by the Marchioness of Bute at Aberdare, and opined that such hospitals could work closely with the society to aid injured workers.[46] Less than a month later, it was announced that the Marquess of Bute, for whom Lewis still acted as agent, was to donate £1,000 towards the erection of a general hospital at Merthyr if an additional £2,000 could be raised by other means.[47] Lewis himself donated the 35,000 pennies (£145 16s. 8d) he received from the (35,000) members of the permanent provident society on the occasion of his knighthood and stated his hope that the society would be able to subscribe to voluntary hospitals at some point in the future.[48] In later years, Lewis was also instrumental in the erection of hospitals at Porth in the Rhondda Fawr valley and at Aberdare in the Cynon valley.[49]

Lewis saw his support for the permanent provident society, ambulance brigades and cottage hospitals as being part of a broader, connected strategy that was intended to accomplish several different aims. Apart from the desire to undermine any calls for statutory intervention into the relationship between employers and workers, and apart from the efforts to undermine the appeal of trade unions, these initiatives were also intended to lessen the financial liabilities placed on employers by employers' liability and, later, workmen's compensation legislation. This was because both primary and secondary care, in the form of first aid and hospital services, worked to minimise the degree of temporary or permanent impairment and, consequently, the levels of compensation payments for which employers were liable. The period once again demonstrates the extent to which industrial welfare was utilised by employers to pursue a variety of aims and the degree to which the wellbeing of workers and their families was not necessarily the main priority.

For their part, miners and their leaders seem to have been willing to accept the worth of ambulance brigades and cottage hospitals, and threw their support behind them with few exceptions. Workers volunteered for ambulance brigades and took pride in their work as 'dusty doctors' because they saw, and indeed experienced, the suffering that accompanied accidents in the workplace and could see the benefits that appropriate first-aid care could bring to injured colleagues. For their part, trade union lodges pressed employers to provide the necessary first-aid materials at collieries required by the Coal Mines Regulation Act of 1887.[50] As far as cottage hospitals were concerned, employers were keen to see them established but were largely content to see workers take on the running costs and assume administrative responsibility for the institutions; there were few struggles for control between employers and workers in the context of hospital provision.[51]

The permanent provident society was a different matter, however, and quite significant disagreement came to characterise relations between workers and employers in relation to the fund through the second half of the 1890s and into the new century. The crucial factor here was the passage of the Workmen's Compensation Act in 1897 that provided for more generous payments that were enforceable more easily through law than was the case under the Act of 1880, thereby making the permanent provident fund far less attractive to workers. The new South Wales Miners' Federation attempted to extricate its members from the society in the years after 1898 and despite various inducements and some attempts at coercion on the part of the employers, miners in the region deserted the society in their droves in the early years of the century as this form of industrial welfare was rejected overwhelmingly.[52]

INTERWAR INDUSTRIAL WELFARE

The breakneck development of the coal industry up to 1914 came up hard against the economic downturn of the immediate postwar years and the longer term decline of the interwar period. Economic depression, rationalisation and consolidation, mass unemployment and fractious industrial relations scarred industry in south Wales during the 1920s and 1930s, and gave rise to new attitudes towards industrial welfare. In addition, an industrial welfare movement, originating in various developments during the First World War, and given institutional form in an Industrial Welfare Society established in 1918, served to once again alter the philosophy behind such policies, the types of provision made and the aims behind such activities. The Industrial Welfare Society was supported by many employers from across Britain throughout the interwar period. Indeed, it came to be captured by the employers who regarded it as preferable to any organisation or initiative that was controlled or sponsored by the state. It emphasised the utility of industrial co-operation and harmonious relations between workers and employers, guided by scientific methods of labour management, as the means by which to increase efficiency, productivity and profitability.[53]

While some coal companies in south Wales did take notice of the industrial welfare movement and did indeed undertake some provision for their workers, it was away from the coal industry that the most significant developments in the region took place. In particular, Sir Alfred Mond, owner of the nickel refinery at Clydach in the Swansea valley was an important figure in twentieth-century industrial welfare and industrial relations, and his company pioneered significant innovations in industrial welfare provision. The company, Brunner, Mond and Co., was founded by his father, Ludwig, and John Brunner in 1873, and soon developed into a major chemicals company, before amalgamating with a number of other concerns in 1926 to form Imperial Chemical Industries, one of the largest companies in Britain and one responsible for 40 per cent of chemicals production in that period.[54]

The refinery at Clydach started production in 1902 and the company immediately implemented the welfare provision that characterised the company's industrial concerns elsewhere. Both Ludwig Mond and John Brunner were keenly interested in industrial welfare provision. As a Unitarian, Brunner held a strong belief in the responsibility of employers for the moral and material wellbeing of their workers, and a determination that the state should not interfere with that responsibility.[55] Alfred Mond took over from his father and shared such views, and was also clearly aware of the industrial welfare and industrial relations policies of employers across Britain, Europe and America.[56] He argued that an equal partnership existed in modern industry between shareholders, management and labour, and that 'the recognition of each of these three factors as equal and essential parts of the industrial organism' was essential. He stated that the slogan to guide industrial relations should be 'Partnership in work, pay, play and profits'.[57]

As such, workers at Clydach worked an eight-hour day; a model village that contained modern, relatively spacious houses was built for key workers; a recreation hall was erected; works clubs were formed including a band, a choir, a photographic society and various sporting teams; canteens were provided to feed workers; and a shareholding scheme was implemented to enable workers to purchase shares at reduced prices.[58] Such developments continued during the interwar period: a medical centre staffed by a full-time medical officer was provided from 1924 onwards; the company introduced paid holidays for workers – one of the first in Britain to do so; and a generous pension scheme was introduced for employees. These various initiatives were part of a broader package of labour management policies that included: a central labour department to consider labour management policies at its numerous concerns; a system of works councils to facilitate communication between workers and Mond himself as head of the company; the creation of a workers' staff grade to which workers with more than five years' service were eligible for promotion (and which carried privileges such as entitlement to a month's notice of termination of employment and a weekly wage rather than an hourly rate); a shareholding scheme in which workers could purchase shares at less than market price; and the creation of a works magazine to keep employees informed of company matters, including various social and cultural activities. The keynotes to this approach to 'industrial co-operation', argued Mond, were 'personal contact, improved status, increased security, co-partnership, and information'. With such developments, he opined, 'I am confident that we will be entering upon a new era of prosperity and entering also upon a new ascent in the long climb towards a higher and better civilization'.[59]

Mond's nickel refinery at Clydach did not suffer the industrial turmoil that afflicted the coal industry in south Wales during the interwar period. An article on Mond's policies published in *Industrial Welfare*, the journal of the Industrial Welfare Society, in 1927 was keen to emphasise the 'half-century of industrial peace' that had characterised the company's industrial relations to that point, including all those years in which the refinery at Clydach had been in operation.[60] Through the rest of the 1920s and into the 1930s, still the refinery was free of the industrial disputes and difficulties that affected the coal industry in the region. It is also interesting to note that Mond hoped to extend his philosophy of labour management beyond his own enterprises and apply it more widely to British industry in order to soothe industrial relations during the troubled interwar period. In the spring of 1927, and immediately following the tumultuous events of 1926, Mond arranged a meeting between a group of large industrialists and the Trades Union Congress in the hope of working towards more harmonious industrial relations. This meeting was dismissed by the miners' leader A. J. Cook as 'Mond moonshine'[61] but it does signify an attempt on the part of some employers, especially in the 'new' industries of the interwar period, to place industrial relations on a more harmonious basis that recognised workers' needs and that hoped to increase the productivity and efficiency of their enterprises through the application of more modern theories of labour management.[62] This approach stands in contrast to that adopted by most other employers in south Wales during the period and especially those in the older, heavy industries such as coal. Nevertheless, and despite the acceptance of his policies by his workers at Clydach, the British labour movement viewed Mond's efforts towards industrial harmony with intense suspicion and considerable opposition, indeed as an attempt to emasculate it, and he was not able to solve the numerous problems that afflicted British industrial relations in that period.[63]

CONCLUSION

The evolution of industrial welfare in south Wales can perhaps be encapsulated through a consideration of three individuals. G. T. Clark, William Thomas Lewis and Alfred Mond, through their respective industrial concerns, can be said to illustrate many of the main currents and developments during the century or so up to the Second World War. From paternalistic provision in the early to mid-Victorian period, to a more institutional and bureaucratic approach in the late nineteenth century, and to an emphasis on industrial partnership in the interwar period, the approaches of these three men to the welfare of their workers offers a broad chronology of developments in provision in the region. Furthermore, the focus on the iron, coal and metallurgical/chemical industries in turn, in these three periods, with their particular forms of company organisation, from family owned firms to limited liability companies and to large multidivision corporations, also tells us something about the course of the Welsh economy during this period and the context in which innovations in welfare capitalism took place. The attitudes of the three men, and the conduct of their respective businesses, cannot be described as representative of employers as a whole – each of the three men owned or managed some of the largest concerns in their respective periods, and certainly smaller companies were not able to mobilise the same resources in provision for their workers. But each of these three examples gives an insight into the dominant aims, forms and outcomes of industrial welfare provision in each of the three periods and give a broad sense of the dominant ideals behind such provision.

At the same time, despite change over time, it is possible to discern certain common themes across the period as a whole. One of the most obvious is the desire to attract, retain and control a stable and efficient workforce. This was crucially important in the early phase of industrialisation as efforts were needed to attract workers to previously isolated and sparsely populated areas, but it was just as significant by the interwar period in more technical and skilled occupations such as those found in nickel production. A second common theme, connected to this first motivation, was the hope of advocates and practitioners of industrial welfare that beneficent labour management policies would create a better relationship between the worker and the company, and develop a form of loyalty to the employer that would undermine any support for trade unionism. Clark, Lewis and Mond were quite clear in their opinions on the harmful influence of trade unions and the extent to which they militated against the interests of both employers and workers in industry. That this aim was less successful in relation to Lewis than it was for Clark or Mond is as much to do with the particular form of industrial relations in each industry as it is to the effectiveness of their particular forms of industrial welfare. As a labour- rather than capital-intensive industry in which a lesser premium was placed on skilled labour, the coal industry was subject to greater disagreement and industrial strife over the matter of wages than other industries. Lastly, regardless of the industry or the period considered, employers shared a distrust of state intervention and looked to retain control over their relations with their workers; in this regard, it felt at times that employers were as opposed to state interference as they were to the interventions of trade unions.

It seems, therefore, that industrial welfare was a broad and flexible entity that could be adjusted to the particular circumstances facing employers in any period and then used to pursue a variety of industrial, social, financial and political aims. The variety of different policies available to any employer, and the ease with which they could be tailored to meet the particular needs of that employer at any point in time, meant that industrial welfare was a useful tool across various industries and in different periods. If we are to understand the policies and actions of the labour movement, as labour history sets out to do, and if we are to move beyond an understanding of employers that is based on myth and stereotype, then we need a new industrial history of Wales that considers the actions and policies of employers as much as workers, and see industrial relations in a more holistic way that emphasises the actions and motivations of all actors. It is perhaps time that Welsh employers found their historian.

NOTES

1 L. J. Williams, 'The Coalowners', in David Smith (ed.), *A People and a Proletariat: Essays in the History of Wales 1780–1980* (London: Pluto Press, 1980), pp. 94–5.

2 One exception is R. Griffiths, *The Entrepreneurial Society of the Rhondda Valleys, 1840–1920: Power and Influence in the Porth-Pontypridd Region* (Cardiff: University of Wales Press, 2010).

3 Williams, 'The Coalowners', pp. 106–11.

4 This essay defines 'industrial welfare' as 'the provision of a service by an employer on a non-wage basis for his employees'; J. Melling, 'Employers, Industrial Welfare, and the Struggle for Work-place Control in British Industry, 1880–1920', in H. F. Gospel and C. R. Littler (eds), *Managerial Strategies and Industrial Relations: An Historical and Comparative Study* (London: Heinemann Educational, 1983), p. 56.

5 J. R. Wilson, *Memorializing History: Public Sculpture in Industrial South Wales* (Aberystwyth: Centre for Advanced Welsh and Celtic Studies, 1996), p. 10 (I am grateful to Neil Evans for this reference); N. Evans, 'Cardiff's labour tradition', *Llafur*, 4/2 (1985), 78.

6 One exception in the Welsh context is A. Burge, 'Exorcising demonologies: coal companies and colliery communities in south Wales', *Llafur*, 9/4 (2007), 101–9. Among studies of other regions, see, for example: E. C. McCreary, 'Social welfare and business: the Krupp welfare program, 1860–1914', *Business History Review*, 42/1 (1968), 24–49; S. D. Brandes, *American Welfare Capitalism, 1880–1940* (Chicago: University of Chicago Press, 1976); A. Tone, *The Business of Benevolence: Industrial Paternalism in Progressive America* (London: Cornell University Press, 1997); W. D. Kinzley, 'Japan in the world of welfare capitalism: imperial railroad experiments with welfare work', *Labor History*, 47/2 (2006), 189–212.

7 See his 'Employers, Workplace Culture and Workers' Politics: British Industry and Workers' Welfare Programmes, 1870–1920', in J. Melling and J. Barry (eds), *Culture in History: Production, Consumption and Values in Historical Perspective* (Exeter: University of Exeter Press, 1992), pp. 109–36; 'Industrial strife and business welfare philosophy: the case of the South Metropolitan Gas Company from the 1880s to the war', *Business History*, 11/2 (1979), 163–79.

8 Melling, 'Employers, Industrial Welfare, and the Struggle for Work-place Control', pp. 56–7.

9 R. O. Roberts, 'The Smelting of Non-ferrous Metals since 1750', in G. Williams and A. H. John (eds), *Glamorgan County History. Volume V: Industrial Glamorgan from 1700 to 1970* (Cardiff: Glamorgan County History Trust, 1980), pp. 47–95; S. Hughes, *Copperopolis: Landscapes of the Early Industrial Period in Swansea* (Aberystwyth: Royal Commission on the Ancient and Historical Monuments of Wales, 2000).

10 T. Boyns and C. Baber, 'The Supply of Labour', in G. Williams and A. H. John (eds), *Glamorgan County History. Volume V: Industrial Glamorgan from 1700 to 1970* (Cardiff: Glamorgan County History Trust, 1980), p. 315.

11 D. G. Evans, *A History of Wales 1815–1906* (Cardiff: University of Wales Press, 1989), pp. 17–19.

12 O. Jones, *The Early Days of Sirhowy and Tredegar* (Newport: Starling Press, 1972), p. 70; K. M. Bryant, *The Health of a Nation: The History and Background of the National Health Service with Thoughts on its Future* (Farncombe: Kenneth M. Bryant, 1998), pp. 30–1; Report of the Lords Committee on the

Poor Laws (400), 1818, v, minutes of evidence, p. 143; Royal Commission on Children's Employment in Mines and Manufactories, *First Report (Mines and Collieries)* (380), (381), (382), 1842, xv–xvii, pp. 553, 621.

13 *Report of the Lords Committee on the Poor Laws*, pp. 131–2.

14 S. Webb and B. Webb, *Industrial Democracy* (London: Longmans & Co., 1920 edn), pp. 550–1.

15 See, for example, G. A. Williams, *The Merthyr Rising* (London: Croom Helm, 1978); D. J. V. Jones, *The Last Rising: The Newport Insurrection of 1839* (Oxford: Clarendon, 1985); D. J. V. Jones, 'The Scotch Cattle and their black domain', *Welsh History Review*, 5/3 (1971), 220–49; I. G. Jones, *Communities: Essays in the Social History of Victorian Wales* (Llandysul: Gomer Press, 1987), pp. 322–62.

16 D. G. Paz, 'Tremenheere, Hugh Seymour (1804–1893)', *Oxford Dictionary of National Biography* (Oxford: Oxford University Press, 2004; online edn, January 2008), *http://www.oxforddnb.com/view/article/27695* (accessed 5 November 2012).

17 *Minutes of the Committee of Council on Education, Part II, 1839–40* (254), 1840, xl, appendix II, pp. 207–8.

18 *Report of the commissioner appointed, under the provisions of the act 5 & 6 Vict. c. 99, to inquire into the operation of that act, and into the state of the population in the mining districts* [hereafter, *Report of the commissioner . . . into the state of the population in the mining districts*], *1850* [1248], 1850, xxiii, p. 64.

19 *Minutes of the Committee of Council on Education, 1840–41* [317], 1841, xx, p. 17; *Report of the commissioner . . . into the state of the population in the mining districts, 1856* [2125], 1856, xviii, p. 26.

20 *Report of the commissioner . . . into the state of the population in the mining districts, 1847* [844], 1847, xvi, pp. 9–14.

21 *Report of the commissioner . . . into the state of the population in the mining districts, 1847*, p. 14.

22 Glamorgan Archives, Dowlais Iron Company Collection, 'Arrangements at these Works for providing the men employed with Medical assistance & Drugs, Relief during Sickness, and Education for their Children, May 1853'.

23 Dowlais Iron Company Collection, 'Doctors Fund, Receipts and Expenditure, 3 years ending 31 March 1859'; 'Dowlais Iron Company Collection, Summary of income, expenditure, profit and loss of various funds, *c.*1862'.

24 For this range of provision and a more detailed consideration of Clark's activities, see G. P. Smith, 'Social control and industrial relations at the Dowlais Iron Company c.1850–1890' (unpublished MSc Econ. thesis, University of Wales, Aberystwyth, 1981). See also Clark's testimony in the *Fifth Report of the Royal Commission to inquire into the Organization and Rules of Trades Unions and other Associations, Minutes of Evidence* [3980-I], 1867–68, xxxix, pp. 82–93; *Merthyr Telegraph*, 30 October 1869, 2.

25 *Fifth Report of the Royal Commission to inquire into the Organization and Rules of Trades Unions*, p. 84.
26 *Fifth Report of the Royal Commission to inquire into the Organization and Rules of Trades Unions*, p. 88.
27 Smith, 'Social control and industrial relations at the Dowlais Iron Company', pp. 15, 30–1, 56–114.
28 Smith, 'Social control and industrial relations at the Dowlais Iron Company', pp. 28, 29.
29 *Fifth Report of the Royal Commission to inquire into the Organization and Rules of Trades Unions*, pp. 82, 83, 88.
30 Dowlais Iron Company Collection, 'Resolutions passed by a public meeting of the Dowlais workmen, 1866'; with draft of reply by G. T. Clark on behalf of the Dowlais Iron Company relating to the sick fund, schools and stoppages from wages.
31 'Resolutions passed by a public meeting of the Dowlais workmen', 1866.
32 Smith, 'Social control and industrial relations at the Dowlais Iron Company', pp. 140–6; *Fifth Report of the Royal Commission to inquire into the Organization and Rules of Trades*, p. 86.
33 *Report of the commissioner . . . into the state of the population in the mining districts, 1856*, pp. 24–7.
34 *Report of the commissioner . . . into the state of the population in the mining districts, 1858* [2424], 1857–8, xxxii, p. 30.
35 See D. Geary, 'The Myth of the Radical Miner', in S. Berger, A. Croll and N. Laporte (eds), *Towards a Comparative History of Coalfield Societies* (Aldershot: Ashgate, 2005), p. 57.
36 'Miners' MPs' were Members of Parliament, often former or current miners' leaders, elected from mining constituencies and active in their representation of the miners' interests in parliament. On these, see H. A. Clegg, A. Fox and A. F. Thomson, *A History of British Trade Unions since 1889, Volume 1: 1889–1910* (Oxford: Clarendon Press, 1964), pp. 239–49, 269–304, 364–422; K. Gildart, 'Labour Politics', in K. Gildart (ed.), *Coal in Victorian Britain, Part II: Coal in Victorian Society, Volume 6, Industrial Relations and Trade Unionism* (London: Pickering & Chatto, 2012), pp. 385–94.
37 For a hagiographical portrait of Lewis, see E. Phillips, *A History of the Pioneers of the Welsh Coalfield* (Cardiff: Western Mail, 1925), pp. 193–204.
38 J. Benson, 'Coalminers, coalowners and collaboration: the miners' permanent relief fund movement in England, 1860–1895', *Labour History Review*, 68/2 (2003), 181–94; G. L. Campbell, *Miners' Insurance Funds: Their Origin and Extent* (London: Waterlow & Sons, 1880).
39 *Western Mail*, 15 November 1878, 3; 19 November 1878, 3; 26 November 1878, 3; 23 December 1878, 2.
40 The societies in different coalfields varied in this regard, with some, such as Durham and Northumberland, not requiring that members contract out of

their statutory rights; P. W. J. Bartrip and S. Burman, *The Wounded Soldiers of Industry: Industrial Compensation Policy, 1833–1897* (Oxford: Oxford University Press, 1983), pp. 171–2.

41 An excellent example can be found in *The Employers' Liability Act (1880) Amendment Bill; A Few Words Thereon to Miners, by J. Pringle, Lately a Working Miner at Barrington Colliery, Northumberland* (London: Liberty and Property Defence League, 1883).

42 See, for example, Cymdeithas Ddarbodawl Barhaol Mwnwyr Swydd Fynwy a Deheudir Cymru, *Anerchiad gan Mr. W. Thomas Lewis* (Aberdare, 1881), p. 6. See also, for example, *Western Mail*, 9 February 1881.

43 J. E. Vincent, *John Nixon: Pioneer of the Steam Coal Trade in South Wales – A Memoir* (London: John Murray, 1900), p. 242. More generally, see S. Thompson, 'The friendly and welfare provision of British trade unions: a case study of the South Wales Miners' Federation', *Labour History Review*, 77/2 (2012), 189–210.

44 *Western Mail*, 7 November 1882, 23 November 1882.

45 For an example, see the ambulance hall erected at Fochriw with support from Guest, Keen, and Co.; *Evening Express*, 15 Mehefin 1908, 3.

46 *Merthyr Express*, 30 January 1886, 8.

47 *Merthyr Express*, 20 February 1886, 4, 5, 7; 27 February 1886, 5; 13 March 1886, 4, 6. Bute eventually donated £3,000 to the foundation of the hospital; *Merthyr Express*, 6 October 1888, 5.

48 *Merthyr Express*, 16 October 1886, 7.

49 A. Lewis, 'The story of Merthyr General Hospital', *Merthyr Historian*, 4 (1989), 105; Phillips, *A History of the Pioneers of the Welsh Coalfield*, p. 200.

50 The term 'dusty doctors' was used by B. L. Coombes in his *I am a Miner*, 23 (London: Fact, 1939), p. 74.

51 See S. Thompson, 'To relieve the sufferings of humanity, irrespective of party, politics or creed: conflict, consensus and voluntary hospital provision in Edwardian south Wales', *Social History of Medicine*, 16/2 (2003), 247–62.

52 For examples of union opposition to the society, see South Wales Miners' Library, Monthly Reports of the Rhondda No.1 District of the Miners' Federation, 4 January 1904, 4 February 1904, 6 February 1905, 21 August 1905. Membership of the society fell from more than 76,000 members in 1897 to 22,000 in 1902, and further to 1,000 in 1907 after a further amending Act in 1906; Monmouthshire and South Wales Miners' Permanent Provident Society, Annual Report, 1920, p. 15.

53 R. Fitzgerald, *British Labour Management and Industrial Welfare 1846–1939* (London: Croom Helm, 1988), pp. 203–7.

54 Fitzgerald, *British Labour Management and Industrial Welfare*, pp. 115–16, 118–25.

55 Fitzgerald, *British Labour Management and Industrial Welfare*, pp. 118–19.

56 For examples of Mond's awareness of the policies of other employers, see A. Mond, *Industry and Politics* (London: MacMillan & Co., 1927).

57 *The Spectator*, 5 November 1927, 6. See also Mond's *Industry and Politics*, esp. pp. 1–12.

58 A. C. Sturney, *The Story of Mond Nickel* (Plaistow: Curwen Press, 1951), p. 28; J. Goodman, *The Mond Legacy: A Family Saga* (London: Weidenfeld and Nicolson, 1982), p. 135; H. Bolitho, *Alfred Mond, First Lord Melchett* (London: Martin Secker, 1933), p. 162.

59 *The Spectator*, 5 November 1927, 7. Interestingly, Mond appointed his own son as labour director to implement these various ideas; Bolitho, *Alfred Mond*, p. 305.

60 *Industrial Welfare* (October, 1927), 317.

61 South Wales Coalfield Collection, Glyn Evans pamphlets; A. J. Cook, *The Mond Moonshine: My Case against the 'Peace' Surrender* (London: Workers' Publications Ltd, c.1927).

62 H. F. Gospel, 'Employers' labour policy: a study of the Mond-Turner talks 1927–33', *Business History*, 21/2 (1979), 180–97.

63 One pamphlet described 'co-partnership and welfare schemes' as the 'machinery to undermine the resistance of the workers' and linked industrial welfare to non-political (or 'scab') unions; Labour Research Department, *The Non-Politicals* (London: The Labour Research Department, 1928), p. 14.

THE AFFLUENT STRIKER

INDUSTRIAL DISPUTES IN THE PORT TALBOT STEELWORKS, 1945–1979

BLEDDYN PENNY

As GREAT BRITAIN made the transition from war to peace following the Second World War, the town of Port Talbot embarked on its own transformation. The decision, made during the war, by the Steel Company of Wales (SCOW) to locate Europe's largest steelworks, the Abbey works, in the town had a profound effect on the locality, bringing employment, vast new housing estates and a plethora of opportunities for recreation and leisure. To contemporary observers and residents, it appeared that the arrival of the Abbey works had precipitated a rapid rise in the town's fortunes as Port Talbot entered a halcyon era of prosperity and expansion. Writing in 1951, the year of the Abbey works's official unveiling, a reporter encapsulated the general mood when he wrote that Port Talbot 'became a real boom town. To shop keepers, cafe proprietors, barbers, to all business men in the town, the erection of the huge steel city on the stretch of sand dunes between the town and sea spelt prosperity.'[1] In the new steelworks itself, however, the mood was not so harmonious. Despite rising wages and a renewed emphasis on employee welfare, the years between 1945 and 1979 were marked by a persistent series of strikes and industrial disputes. The Port Talbot steelworks even attained a degree of national notoriety with the press dubbing it the 'the strike works' and 'a new Dagenham'[2] (a reference to the woeful state of industrial relations at Ford's Dagenham car plant). Where the plant once embodied visions of a brighter postwar future and the promise of modern industrial production, in the 1960s and 1970s it became emblematic of the widening malaise in British industrial relations. Against a backdrop of widespread material and economic improvement, how did the state of industrial relations at the plant degenerate so rapidly?

In this regard, the state of industrial relations at the Port Talbot works was not entirely unique. Localised stoppages and unofficial strikes were emerging as a pervasive characteristic of industrial relations in postwar Britain. David Gilbert has argued that, by the 1960s, 'a consensus seemed to be developing that Britain's industrial relations were distinctive in a number of ways, particularly in the frequency of small stoppages and in the unofficial and unconstitutional status of most strikes.'[3] The scale of the issue provoked a national inquiry, the 1968 Royal Commission on Trade Unions and Employers' Associations, popularly known as the Donovan report after its chairman Lord Donovan.[4] Among those firms called to submit evidence to the inquiry was the SCOW, the only Welsh steel firm to do so. For the report's compilers, the SCOW made for an interesting case study; not only was the firm the largest, and therefore the most economically important, steel manufacturer in the region, but it also had a poorer record of industrial relations than any of its rivals. The causes underlying the disputes at the Port Talbot works were multifarious, with issues such as wages, workplace control and jobs emerging as common themes among the strikers' grievances. However, the reasons why steelworkers struck also reveal how they understood their workplace and the complex relations within it. The factious and localised stoppages that occurred at the plant during this period were as likely to bring workers into conflict with each other or their trade union leaders as with their managers. Workplace loyalties and alliances thus proved to be fluid, and local affiliations and sectional interests could assume greater significance than class-based solidarities. Aside from the economic damage they caused, the wave of strikes that hit the Port Talbot works were important indicators of how steelworkers interpreted the social relations of the workplace, their own occupational identities and sense of class.

Class has loomed large in the written history of industrial conflict. In both academic and popular conceptions, the negotiation of power in industry is often seen as a bilateral class struggle: between workers and their collective organisations on the one hand, and managers or owners on the other. In Richard Hoggart's analysis, '[t]he world of "Them" is the world of bosses', against which the 'Us' of the working-class defined itself.[5] With social history in the ascendancy during the 1960s, the history of trade unionism and strikes were posited as emblems of class consciousness and class struggle. The social history movement's leading exponent, Eric Hobsbawm, articulated this narrative when arguing that 'working-class experience gave the labouring poor the major institutions of everyday self-defence, the trade union and mutual aid society, and the major weapons of such collective struggle, solidarity and the strike'.[6] Industrial disputes were never apolitical but the types of conflict that emerged at the Port Talbot steel industry defy a purely bilateral analysis. As the influence of Marxist theory waned, some historians began to question the extent of class consciousness and solidarity among workers. Ross McKibbin, for example, presents class as a fluid concept that existed alongside other categories of identity and was, thus, subject to numerous interpretations (and reinterpretations) and meanings. In this understanding, workers' 'political communication and group loyalties became multilinear: men could unite against masters, equally they could unite with them.'[7] Such an approach not only pays greater consideration to the internal divisions within the working class but also recognises the importance of individualistic, as well as collectivist, orientations among workers. Port Talbot's steelworkers rarely struck for political reasons, but their motives for taking industrial action, nonetheless, reveal broader truths about working-class culture and values.

The Marxist-inspired analysis of historians, such as Hobsbawm, provided a pertinent framework for the new generation of Welsh historians who, in the 1970s and 1980s, passionately presented the case for a new, albeit highly politicised, historical understanding of modern industrial Wales. Industrial conflict figured prominently in their analyses of the creation of an industrial Welsh society and a politically aware Welsh proletariat. Strikes and workplace disputes were the subject of a number of influential works on modern Welsh history, such as Gwyn A. Williams's *The Merthyr Rising*, R. Merfyn Jones's *The North*

Wales Quarrymen, and Hywel Francis's *History on our Side*, and figured prominently in numerous studies of the south Wales miners, such as E. W. Evans's *The Miners of South Wales*, Hywel Francis and Dai Smiths's *The Fed*, and, most recently, Ben Curtis's *The South Wales Miners*.[8] The unity of the working class is a recurring theme in these works and industrial disputes are often posited as emblematic outbursts of hostility to capitalism and bourgeois control. Julie Light, commenting on Dai Smith's interpretation of the 1910 Tonypandy riots, for example, noted 'that this is an example of a historian wishing to portray the community as a source of resistance to capitalism.'[9] Writing against the backdrop of the miners' strikes of the early 1970s and the epochal 1984/5 strike gave these works a contemporary relevance and message. Within the context of these contemporary political struggles, historians were more eager to celebrate the Welsh working class's history of struggle and solidarity than question its internal differences and complexities. *The Fed*, for example, has been described as 'a guide to standing up for ourselves and fighting back against the state even when things are desperate.'[10]

This singularly heroic image of the Welsh working class, however resonant and stirring it may be, has fixed our understanding of working-class culture within certain limited parameters. Welsh industrial workers undoubtedly exhibited traits of class-consciousness and political radicalism, albeit at certain times and places, but caution must be exercised when evaluating how reflective these views were of the Welsh working class as a whole. Both Mike Lieven and Julie Light have argued that the working-class communities of the south Wales coalfield were more internally divided and less homogenous than they appeared through the lens of labour history.[11] Stepping outside the coalfield, there were also those industrial workers whose lives were not primarily conditioned by coal: the tinplate workers of Llanelli, the copper workers of Swansea and the steelworkers of Port Talbot, to name but a few. The diversity of the Welsh industrial economy was mirrored in the diversity of its working class, but this, thus far, has not been adequately represented in the historiography. In this context, then, the historical study of other groups of Welsh workers, such as steelworkers, can add to our wider understandings of working-class culture and society. Chris Williams has specifically addressed this issue and argued that 'without a history of steelworkers, our understanding of the nature of industrial society in, for example, Ebbw Vale and Dowlais, remains incomplete;'[12]

Martin Johnes, meanwhile, has related this concern to broader debates on class, noting that 'more studies are needed of other industries, notably steel, if the extent of class consciousness is to be understood.'[13] If the history of the Welsh miners presents an understanding of working-class culture predicated on solidarity and homogeneity, the history of Wales's steelworkers reveals a more fluid concept that defies any rigid political simplification. Class, while being conceptually important, was also malleable, producing its own internal tensions and hierarchies as well as formidable displays of loyalty and resistance.

Understanding how workers interpreted their workplace, with its associated grievances and struggles, requires a focus on the individual as well as the collective. Oral history is of the utmost significance in this regard, offering personal perspectives on wider issues. As Joanna Bornat has argued: 'by means of the interview, oral historians are able to access personal experiences, eye witness accounts and the memories of people whose perspectives might otherwise be ignored or neglected.'[14] As part of the research project on which this chapter is based, over thirty former Port Talbot steelworks employees were interviewed.[15] Drawn from a variety of occupations and positions within the plant, these workers' testimonies and memories of industrial action, both as participants and observers, reveal the personal and sometimes conflicting motives that led individuals to strike. Memory is, of course, fallible and workers' recollections of past events are subject to continual reinterpretation within a present context.[16] At the time the events in this chapter took place, few steelworkers could have anticipated the dramatic contraction their industry would go on to experience, yet this undoubtedly influenced the way they understood their own pasts and coloured the evidence provided in their oral testimonies. Nonetheless, any understanding of past societies must be predicated on the individuals that inhabited them. Without an understanding of the thoughts, feelings and beliefs of the individual in history, the past is easily reduced to a series of neatly defined collectives reacting to wider economic and political forces. Individual agency, however, has also been a powerful instrument of historical change and is integral to understanding the changing dynamics of the industrial workplace.

This chapter begins by assessing the impact the arrival of the Abbey works had on the material and economic lives of those who worked there and their families. It will argue that while the benefits of affluence were not shared equally, through rising wages and sustained investment in local housing and welfare, the majority of the plant's workers came to enjoy a standard of living that would have been unthinkable to the preceding generation. Why, then, did this improvement in the economic and material conditions of Port Talbot steelworkers coincide with an unprecedented period of industrial unrest at the plant? The remainder of the chapter will focus on the causes underlying the steelworkers' discontents: the plant's unwieldy system of multitrade union bargaining and the arbitrary pay differentials that consequently emerged between different groups of workers. Although the disputes that arose from these issues often defied traditional class loyalties, workers were nonetheless motivated to act over basic issues of parity and fairness, which remained fundamental to their understanding of working-class values.

TREASURE ISLAND: PORT TALBOT THE 'BOOM TOWN'

The opening of the Abbey works in 1951 was heralded as an industrial marvel and a symbol of Britain's postwar reconstruction. Reporting on the occasion of the plant's official unveiling, a reporter for *The Daily Telegraph* described it as a 'landmark in steel history.'[17] Meanwhile, *The Times* wrote that '[i]t is claimed that there has been no single project of this size in the British isles since the great days of the railway age.'[18] As far away as Australia, New South Wales's *Cootamundra Herald* celebrated the plant's opening as a 'showpiece of Britain's post-war recovery'.[19] It was the people of Port Talbot itself, however, and those who went on to find work in the plant who would be the Abbey's biggest beneficiaries. It was not without exaggeration that the local newspaper, the *Port Talbot Guardian*, described the event as the 'most important day in Port Talbot's history'.[20] In 1948 the plant's proprietors, the SCOW, employed 4,337 employees at its Port Talbot works. By 1960, after building and extending the new Abbey works, that figure had risen to 18,102.[21] Even accounting for the contraction of other local industries, such as coalmining and tinplate, the demand for labour from the Abbey works guaranteed the availability of work for those who wanted it.

Such was the voracious demand of the SCOW for labour that the firm set about actively encouraging workers from throughout Great

Britain to relocate to Port Talbot to fill the new posts available at the plant. Even during the plant's construction phase, the firm expressed doubts that they would be able to recruit sufficient labour locally. SCOW director, Julian Pode, informed the Welsh Board of Health in 1947 that '[a]t least 3,000 [workers] would have to be recruited from the areas outside daily travelling distance.'[22] By 1961 there were 10,000 more people living in Port Talbot than there had been in 1939. According to one estimate, between 1946 and 1958 the population of the wider township grew by 25 per cent.[23] New houses were needed to accommodate this burgeoning influx of migrant workers, which, through protracted negotiations between the SCOW and the local council, led to the creation of Sandfields housing estate. Once complete, the new estate dwarfed all other residential developments in the region and grew to be the second-largest housing estate in Wales.[24] In the space of twenty years, from 1945 to 1965, more than 4,500 houses had been erected on the site, providing homes for 16,000 people, 4,000 of whom were steelworkers.[25] Although the reputation of postwar housing estates declined in later years, contemporaries were often delighted by the vision of modernity these new homes offered. Electricity throughout the home, indoor toilets and fitted baths were revelations to those who had been used to living in the town's ageing Victorian terraces.[26] The image of Port Talbot as a boom town was, thus, fast gaining credence. As Chancellor of the Exchequer, Hugh Gaitskell told the assembled audience at the opening of the Abbey works: 'You are a boom town now. People are coming in from all directions and you are building up a great new community stimulated and reinforced by new blood from all over these islands.'[27] When compared to the fortunes of other Welsh industrial towns, such as Merthyr Tydfil and Llanelli, whose declining populations were symptomatic of their diminishing industrial importance, Port Talbot's resurgence appeared remarkable to contemporaries and was duly celebrated.

In contrast to their parents' generation, Port Talbot's steelworkers not only enjoyed the prospect of improved housing but could also hope to receive better pay. During the 1950s and 1960s, the economic position of Port Talbot's steelworkers improved significantly with the condition of full employment facilitating a substantial increase in wages across the period. Wage differentials within the workforce remained considerable but the overall trend was undoubtedly up. According to E. O. Smith, 'the 1950s . . . gave rise to buoyant market conditions in which SCW and other companies conceded large wage claims', making Port Talbot's steelworkers among the best paid in the industry and among Britain's working class more generally.[28] In 1954 average weekly earnings in the SCOW's 'Steel Division' (Port Talbot) were £13 6s. 11d compared to £11 4s. 1d at its Newport works.[29] In the context of a period of national wage inflation, the average wage differential between Port Talbot's steelworkers and those of British manual workers in general was greater still, with the average manual weekly wage in 1954 standing at only £9 17s. 8d.[30] During the period 1948–59, one sociologist alleged that 'the differential between average earnings in steel production and those in all other industries increased so that even during the 1960s . . . there was parity between unskilled process workers in steel and skilled workers in other industries.'[31] Up until 1970, then, it could be confidently claimed that most of Port Talbot's steelworkers had, financially at least, 'never had it so good'.

The SCOW also resorted to other methods to attract and retain the large numbers of workers they required for their new plant. This was most apparent in the substantial efforts the firm made to improve employee welfare and work-based opportunities for recreation and leisure. In 1949 the company established its own Sports and Social Club and soon followed this by erecting a new Works clubhouse in 1952. In its glowing appraisal of the clubhouse, the *Western Mail* described it as 'the best-equipped, most up-to-date sports club built in Britain since the war' and noted its extensive sport facilities, including playing fields, 'first-class tennis courts', bowling greens, recreational areas and 'a large ultra-modern bar, with a kitchen behind.'[32] The *South Wales Evening Post* concurred, describing it as 'a magnificent new pavilion comparable with anything of the kind' and one 'which might well turn Port Talbot into one of the principle cricket and sports centres in Wales'.[33] The initial cost of the clubhouse development borne by the company was considerable, totalling £71,781,[34] and continued investment in extensions and renovations over the following decade brought the overall amount sanctioned on the clubhouse's development to over £100,000 by 1962.[35] In a competitive labour market, it was clear that the firm was compelled to make every inducement to maintain the goodwill of their employees, creating what was generally regarded as the largest corporate welfare infrastructure in the region.

DIVISIONS OF LABOUR: NEGOTIATIONS IN A MULTI-UNION WORKPLACE

This cosy image of affluent steelworkers and benign employers, however, fails to account for the growing unrest that was emerging within the plant. The increased prevalence of unofficial strikes and stoppages from the 1950s onwards marked a break with the steel industry's pre-existing industrial relations culture. After the 1926 general strike, the industry enjoyed a prolonged period of quiescence in industrial relations, characterised by a nationally low strike rate and amicable working relations within individual steel plants. Served by a moderate trade union, mostly benign employers and well-established negotiation machinery, workplace disputes were rare and most were amicably resolved through official channels. After 1926, Carr and Taplin argued that 'it was usually found possible to settle issues of wages and conditions without recourse to extreme measures.'[36] The industry's largest trade union, the Iron and Steel Trades Confederation (ISTC), had a long-standing culture of moderation and antimilitancy in the way it directed its membership. Unlike the strident political rhetoric of the National Union of Mineworkers, the ISTC prided itself on its tempered approach and its close working relations with the industry's managers. Kenneth O. Morgan positioned the union's leadership within the 'right-wing' and 'Gaitskellite' faction of the trade union movement,[37] and until the national steel strike of 1980, the union remained largely averse to condoning strike action. In an open letter sent to Port Talbot's staff workers in 1968, the union's general secretary, Dai Davies, outlined the union's industrial relations philosophy:

> BISAKTA [ISTC] believes in conducting its affairs in a responsible and intelligent way and has never regarded itself as one of two sides ranged against each other in a state of permanent hostility but rather as part of a joint enterprise where divergent interests can be reconciled by discussion and negotiation against a background of common interest in an efficient, thriving and prosperous industry.[38]

The wave of unofficial strikes that took place at the Port Talbot works were, thus, highly antithetical to the moderate and conciliatory tone struck by the steelworkers' union leaders.

The ISTC, however, was not the only union representing employees at the Port Talbot works. In 1967 there were nine trade unions representing manual workers alone in the plant, with memberships ranging from nine to 6,915.[39] The number of trade unions operating in the Port Talbot works represented the diverse range of occupations and professions the plant contained. In the popular imagination, the steelworker is most readily associated with the image of the rollerman or the blastfurnaceman, typically bespectacled, clad in an apron and cloth cap and standing in the glare of the furnace. The iron and steel industries, however, have always been characterised by a high degree of occupational diversity and steelworkers were among the most occupationally heterogeneous groups of Britain's industrial workforce. Among this diverse and specialised workforce, however, three broad occupational groups can be discerned: process workers, who undertook most of the activities directly relating to making steel and included occupations such as blastfurnacemen and crane drivers; craftworkers, who were primarily engaged in maintenance and repair work and included the plant's electricians and bricklayers among other trades; and staff workers – a diverse group encompassing senior managers through to junior laboratory assistants and typists, who were all characterised by their removal from manual work. While process workers were mostly organised by the steel unions, the ISTC and the National Union of Blastfurnacemen, the trade union membership of the plant's craftworkers corresponded to their particular trade: the Electric Trades Union for electricians, for example. Complicating this picture further, during the 1950s and 1960s, the emergence of the so-called white-collar unions succeeded in unionising much of the Abbey works's previously unorganised staff workers. By 1968 it was estimated that half of the industry's white-collar workers were unionised.[40]

In their dealings with the plant's management, each trade union acted in a largely autonomous manner, with separate negotiating bodies and boards conducting deals in isolation from the other unions. Until the creation of the Slimline Committee, latterly known as the Joint Trade Union Committee, in 1980, there was no mechanism for collective multi-union bargaining within the Port Talbot works. While the SCOW conducted its negotiations collectively, through the employers' association, the Iron and Steel Trades Employers' Federations, the trade unions acted separately, creating a complex and unwieldy system with profound implications for the climate of industrial relations in the plant. For the ISTC, collective bargaining was facilitated by several negotiating bodies, where workers' and employers' representatives finalised national agreements on a variety of issues, such as pay, working hours and holiday entitlements. Deals struck by the Heavy Steel Trades Board, for example, covered Port Talbot steelworkers employed in the 'heavy' steel producing end of the industry, while the Sheet Trades Board negotiated on behalf of workers in the plant's rolling and finishing departments. None of these agreements, however, applied to the plant's craft and staff workers who had their own negotiation machinery, such as the National Joint Trade Union Craftsmen's Iron and Steel Committee. The nationalisation of Britain's steel industry, with the creation of the state-owned British Steel Corporation (BSC) in 1967, brought about some rationalisation of the industry's complicated negotiating structure, but multi-union bargaining remained the defining characteristic of industrial relations at the Port Talbot works. Inequality was an inevitable product of this, with pay and benefits being distributed unevenly among different groups of workers based on the differing collective strength of their respect bargaining mechanisms.

These unions not only negotiated separately but often had fundamentally different outlooks on politics and industrial relations. When in 1970 a local ISTC organiser at Port Talbot wrote in alarm to his general secretary of his concerns at the possibility of a '"Red Cell" being set up' within the plant, he was expressing a long-standing ideological rift between the dogged moderation of the process workers' unions and the, allegedly, radical tendencies of the craftworkers' unions.[41] An Abbey works electrician who represented his union on the plant's multi-union health and safety committee also remembered the diverging political outlooks of the different unions. 'Craft people, craft safety reps who were there, and any shop stewards, were very militant', he remembered. 'The people who were on production tended to lean towards management'.[42] Suspicion, rather than solidarity, characterised the relationships between the plant's trade unions and this often manifested itself in the internecine power struggles between them in the workplace. The most common source of these inter-union tensions was the issue of demarcation, where certain working practices and job roles within the plant were reserved for members of a particular union. Although designed to bring clarity to each union's role within a complex multi-union workplace, demarcation contrived to pit unions against each other in a constant battle for members and influence. The ISTC, for example, complained bitterly throughout the 1950s and 1960s that the Transport and General Workers' Union were trying to poach their members in the Abbey works strip mill. 'Another case of the Transport Union trying their infiltration methods' was how a local ISTC branch officer described one such infringement to his area organiser.[43] This was not an isolated incident. In its evidence submitted to the Royal Commission on Trades Unions and Employers' Associations in 1966, the SCOW conceded that they were presently dealing with no fewer than 116 separate demarcation disputes and cases of restrictive practice at their Port Talbot works.[44] Demarcation disputes could also erupt into outright industrial action. In 1957, for example, the plant's general manager, Fred Cartwright, incredulously recorded that,

> The beginning of the introduction of automatic drinking machines caused a sit-down strike on the 20th August. The men and women employed in the canteens demanded that the machines should be filled by Confederation [ISTC] members and that all food made for these machines should be packed by Confederation members.[45]

Rather than explicitly targeting the plant's management, industrial action of this kind was designed to check the advance of other trade unions and ensure that each union's individual organising rights were not compromised. The result was to amplify and internalise industrial conflict, whereby trade unions were more likely to enter into disputes with each other than with the plant's managers.

STRIKES: PAY, STATUS AND FAIRNESS

Demarcation disputes could prove to be a costly and disruptive nuisance for the plant's managers, but when asked about the main reasons for strikes in the plant, most steelworkers had few reservations in proffering a single issue: pay. A former chairman of the plant's multi-union committee maintained that working conditions 'and the pay packets were the two main issues. I mean, they'd go on strike for a penny. Those were the two issues I think that drove people's morale'.[46] For much of the postwar period, the high correlation between wage claims and industrial stoppages was a well-recognised national phenomenon. A contemporary sociological study, conducted during the 1970s, of a steelworks in the north of England revealed that, during industrial disputes, 'issues relating to wages and to other pay issues (bonus, conditions, overtime and lost-time) were clearly predominant.'[47] Hobsbawm, meanwhile,

Table 5.1: Chronology of industrial disputes at Port Talbot steelworks, 1952–77

Year	Dispute
1952	Bricklayers' strike. Strike arose over a company decision to suspend sixteen bricklayers over a dispute about manning.
1954	Coke-oven workers' strike: 300 Iron and Steel Trades Confederation members at the Margam coke ovens went out on an unofficial strike over pay.
1958	Three industrial disputes within the space of a month. In February, 450 Cold Mill workers went on strike and 560 members of the BISAKTA Abbey no. 11 branch also went on strike.
1959	10,000 BISAKTA members walked out after it was claimed that a works' clerk had been unfairly dismissed.
1960	Ninety-two draughtsmen and female tracers employed at the plant came out on strike over a wage claim.
1961	Bricklayers' strike: 350 bricklayers and 700 bricklayers' mates struck resulting in the closure of the plant.
1962	Bricklayers' strike. The dispute was over the 'job and finish'.
1963	Amalgamated Engineering Union strike. The AEU's members struck for a wage increase of £5 to £8 a week.
1967	Bricklayers' strike. The dispute arose over management's intention to withdraw certain 'privileges' that had been afforded to bricklayers, such as the right to switch shifts.
1969	Blastfurnacemen's strike over pay.
1971	National blastfurnacemen's strike. The National Union of Blast-furnacemen were demanding a national pay rise of 35 per cent.
1971	Two thousand clerical workers at the Port Talbot, all members of the ISTC, went out on strike over a wage claim.
1974	The plant's craftsmen struck in June when negotiations with management over the manning of the new no. 5 blastfurnace collapsed.
1974	Eighty design and surveying staff struck over wage differentials.
1975	Five thousand and six hundred process workers walked out in June over proposed changes to working practices, such as weekend working and manning levels.
1977	Electricians' strike. The strike's catalyst was the refusal of five electricians to man the newly commissioned sinter plant, but the crux of the dispute centred on pay for 'specialised' work.

describing the national picture, elaborated that 'the periods of maximum strike activity since 1960 – 1970–2 and 1974 – have been the ones when the percentage of pure wage strikes have been much the highest – over 90 per cent in 1971–2.'[48] Strikes at the Port Talbot works were capable of containing a range of different issues and grievances, but wage claims were the most commonly recurring feature of unofficial stoppages at the plant throughout the 1950s, 1960s and 1970s. Indeed, across these three decades there were no fewer than sixteen significant strikes at the works in which wages were a significant contributory factor (see Table 5.1).

As a result of the fractured nature of bargaining at the plant, however, these wage claims were always advanced by the representatives of a particular section of the workforce, either by an individual department within the plant or a local trade union, and, therefore, never mobilised the entirety of the works' employees. Moreover, these strikes were often unofficial and locally instigated. They usually lacked the official approval of the national trade union leadership or were only sanctioned retrospectively, typically as a means to swiftly expedite a return to work by union leaders. As in other industries, such as the automotive industry, the unofficial strike emerged as a relatively new phenomenon in the industrial relations culture of Britain's steelworks. Writing in the *Western Mail* in 1969, a south Wales steelworkers' trade union official despairingly commented that '[t]here have been more unofficial stoppages in the past few years than in my previous 30 years as a full-time trade union official'.[49] Their unofficial status, however, did not mean that these strikes were not significant. Both in terms of the disruption they caused and the national media attention they generated, these strikes were highly damaging to the profits and reputations of the SCOW and its successor, the BSC. The highly integrated nature of modern steelmaking, reliant as it was on a number of interdependent processes, allowed a proportionately small group of workers to halt the plant's production entirely. This was the case in 1969, when a strike by the works' 1,300 blastfurnacemen halted production for seven weeks, slashing steel production by 750,000 tons and prompting a formal inquiry by the Secretary of State for Employment, Barbara Castle.

With wages at the heart of these industrial disputes, the media were quick to denounce the strikers at the Port Talbot works as selfish and avaricious. As Port Talbot's steelworkers were already among the highest paid manual workers in the country, the press reduced the strikers' motivations to pure greed and self-interest. Reports on the strikes invariably contained exaggerated estimations of the wages the strikers were earning alongside the usual tropes associated with the lavish lifestyles of Port Talbot's steelworkers. Describing a strike by bricklayers at the plant in 1961, the *Western Mail*, for example, outlined the greedy motives of the strikers: 'The desire for a bigger and bigger share in the profits of the works led the bricklayers into successive demands for bonuses and special payments that put them among the elite of the steelworks with pay packets around £35 a week.'[50] Reporting on the same strike, the *Daily Mail* elevated the bricklayers' alleged wages to '£50 a week' in an article tendentiously headlined, 'Me, my shares, and my Jag, by the striker.' The article went on to paint the strike's leader as an overpaid, Jaguar-driving opportunist, who cynically manufactured industrial disputes to boost his own wages and those of his fellow bricklayers.[51] That this particular bricklayers' strike was actually instigated over proposed changes to working practice rather than wages seemed to matter little in the media's coverage.

The understanding of industrial conflict as being increasingly driven by material objectives and devoid of solidaristic instincts was also frequently observed by academics and came to dominate much of the national debate on the widening prevalence of strikes during this period. For some on the political left, the increased frequency of unofficial disputes, centred on sectional wage claims, was endemic of 'the disintegration of the working-class' and the dissipation of class solidarities among industrial workers.[52] In 1978 Hobsbawm encapsulated the general despondency that had beset Britain's left-wing intelligentsia. He argued that 'it would be a mistake' to believe that affluence 'has made the working-class more homogeneous. On the contrary', he went on, 'it seems to me that we now see a growing division of workers into sections and groups, each pursuing its own economic interests irrespective of the rest.'[53] For Hobsbawm these trends constituted a fundamental shift in the attitude of industrial workers and industrial conflict. He argued:

> It now often happens not only (as sometimes occurred even 100 years ago) that groups of workers strike, not minding the effect on the rest – e.g. skilled men on labourers – but that the strength of a group lies not in the amount of loss they can cause to the employer, but in the inconvenience they can cause to the public, i.e. to other workers (e.g. by power blackouts or whatever).[54]

Ironically, commentators on both the political left and right seemed united in maligning industrial workers for their avarice and abandonment of traditional class loyalties.

In their attempts to diagnose the industrial relations problems of the Port Talbot steelworks, contemporary commentators typically projected their own political agendas, rather than attempting to fully grasp the strikers' motivations and grievances. While some may have acted opportunistically, the majority struck in frustration at the institutionalised unfairness of their workplace, characterised by inequalities of pay and status that permeated the different sections of the plant's workforce. This was most apparent for the plant's craftworkers and the often fractious relationship between them and their process worker counterparts. Throughout the period, there was lingering resentment among the craftworkers that they were denied the financial rewards made available to the esteemed process workers. In contrast to Selina Todd's assertion that 'the British working-class was becoming more homogenous at the beginning of the 1970s . . . the divisions between skilled and unskilled workers were narrowing',[55] such distinctions remained an important and divisive feature of working life at the Port Talbot steelworks. Unlike the steelworkers, the plant's craftworkers had undertaken apprenticeships in their respective trades, often lasting as long as four years, conferring upon them a skilled status. Tensions arose, however, as it became felt that their skills were not being fairly rewarded, particularly in relation to the 'unskilled' process workers. A fitter and tuner at the Port Talbot works, for example, remembered: 'the production workers, who were the people in the mill or operating the mill, they had good money.'[56] A works electrician went further. When asked about the causes of the tensions between process and craftworkers, he elaborated:

> Well mainly I think because craft people thought they were better than production [laughs]. You know like a social standing sort of thing, but then again the production people were the ones who had the money, so when I was earning maybe £15 a week, somebody in the harbour who was driving a crane over there was on £20 a week, so that was a thing that got between us. We thought we were worth more than what we were. Well we thought we were worth more than what we were getting . . . we were skilled. They were

> labourers, what you call labourers, who were doing mill jobs, they were driving a mill just sitting there on a desk pulling levers, but we were skilled.[57]

Status and fairness, rather than greed, underpinned the craftworkers' discontents.

The craftworkers' frustrations were a product of the vagaries of the plant's pay structure. Among the working class, pay was important, not only as a means of material reward but as an indicator of a group's worth and significance. Ferdynand Zweig noted that, for the British worker, '[t]he wage-packet also gives social significance to his job . . . The workers never compare themselves with those far above them, but they watch closely those who are treading on their heels or are higher up but not far from their own position.'[58] Alongside the national negotiations, undertaken by the plant's respective trade unions, the expanding influence of bargaining on the shop floor became an increasingly important determinant of the individual steelworkers' wage. Most shop-floor bargaining was conducted via local branch officers and shop stewards.[59] The conduct of these negotiations was often informal and officialised by oral agreements, but, through this kind of bartering, lay union officials exercised considerable power to negotiate on a host of local pay arrangements. Of particular significance was the power branch officials and shop stewards exerted to negotiate bonus wage payments, which came to constitute an increasingly sizeable proportion of steelworkers' overall salaries. Indeed, the industry's complex wage structure, with as many as nine different components in determining a standard craftsman's pay, allowed considerable scope for haggling on the factory floor, particularly in relation to tonnage bonuses, fringe payments and 'special awards'.[60]

Although strong trade union branches in the plant were able to negotiate a host of favourable bonus and top-up payments for their own members, other workers looked on with increasing envy and resentment. The Cold Mill, for example earned the epithet 'the Gold Mill' due to the high wages the mill's sizeable ISTC branch was able to secure for its workers.[61] No section of the plant's workforce was more aggrieved than the craftworkers who, being solely involved in the maintenance of the plant, were not entitled to the production bonuses, based on tonnage output, which inflated the process workers' wages. Once the perceived link between skill and material reward (an important precondition of workers' acceptance of a capitalist logic) was thought to have been severed, the ensuing sense of injustice was readily channelled into organised protest. In Taylor's analysis, 'the result was a resort to inter-union disputes, damaging conflicts between work groups and a serious collapse in any sense of cohesion or solidarity at the point of production.'[62] Unofficial disputes, then, were often manifestations of a pervasive sense of unfairness among workers, but they also acted as expressions of frustration at the unwillingness of managers and national trade union leaders to address their grievances. Rather than expressing unrestrained greed, unofficial strikers were often united in intense displays of local solidarity, showing immense resilience in the face of overwhelming condemnation from managers, trade unionists and fellow workers.

The greatly enhanced importance that shop-floor negotiations assumed at the Port Talbot works was entirely congruent with broader postwar trends in British industrial relations. One of the primary motivations behind the government appointment of the Royal Commission on Trade Unions and Employers' Associations in 1966 was the widespread recognition of the disparity and dysfunctional relationship between the formal processes of national bargaining and the unrestrained bartering of the factory floor. The inherent problems of this dual system were adumbrated in the commission's findings, published in its report, which noted that 'workplace bargaining is fragmented because it is conducted in such a way that different groups in the works get different concessions at different times. The consequence is competitive sectional wage adjustment and disorderly pay structures'.[63] This consequent process of 'wage drift', whereby nationally negotiated wages bore diminishing relevance to workers' actual pay, posed a central dilemma to the works managers and senior trade unionists alike, both of whom had a vested interest in restoring their authority over local trade unionists and rationalising workers' pay structures. In its final verdict, the Royal Commission on Trade Unions and Employers' Associations was highly critical of existing wage systems and the machinery used to negotiate them. They concluded that 'it is apparent that considerable difficulties are encountered both in maintaining fair relatives between different groups of workers and keeping a reasonable amount of control over wage levels'. Moreover, they went on to note that '[i]f groups of workers see that other groups with whom they have hitherto enjoyed equality are able to improve their position because of the vagaries of the pay system it is not surprising if they feel indignation and seek to recover a position of parity.'[64] In Lord Donovan's analysis, unofficial strikes were not products of greedy strikers but inevitable symptoms of illogical and unfair methods of negotiating wages.

As the group of workers most disadvantaged by the dual system of wage negotiation at Port Talbot, the plant's craftworkers were the primary instigators of strikes throughout this period. Unofficial strikes were not the sole preserve of the craftworkers, with process and staff workers also walking out on several occasions, but of the four significant wage disputes that took place during this period, all were instigated by craftworkers.[65] A recurring characteristic of the craftworkers' strikes was the conspicuous lack of sympathy and support they received from their fellow steelworkers and other trade unions. In this regard, the 1963/4 engineers' strike is an illustrative example. Like other disputes, the decision to strike taken by members of the Amalgamated Engineering Union (AEU) at the Port Talbot works was primarily motivated by pay and the long-standing resentment between the worsening financial position of the plant's craftworkers in relation to process workers. Their action halted production at the plant for six weeks, suspending work for the entirety of the plant's workforce. The response of their fellow workers was one of resentment, rather than solidarity. In its reportage of the strike, the *Western Mail* commented that '[t]he men who have been laid off because of the fitters' strike are scathing about the AEU leadership.'[66] Recalling the several craftworkers' strikes of the period, a process worker described an almost absolute lack of sympathy for the strikers among other employees: 'because they put us all out of work', he explained, '[t]hey put us all out on the road didn't they? And what they put us out on the road for was to fatten their own pockets, not us. It didn't benefit us at all. In fact, we lost money because of it.'[67] Despite being designed to represent the occupational diversity that existed within the plant's workforce, the system of multi-unionism that emerged often served to accentuate these differences; rather than uniting behind a common cause, workers were increasingly being brought into conflict with each other as they pursued their own individual interests.

Such attitudes appear antithetical to the themes of working-class solidarity and unity that dominate labour history accounts of industrial conflict. Disputes of this kind, however, defy a purely bilateral and class-based interpretation of industrial relations and require an understanding of the tensions and incremental divisions of status within the working-class itself. For workers in the Port Talbot steel industry, the distinction between process workers and craftworkers was not purely occupational. Hierarchies that differentiated skilled and unskilled workers still conditioned the way steelworkers understood their own self-worth and their relationship with each other. One process worker remembered: 'I felt some of the craft workers did look down on us, the normal workers then – the steelworkers – they did look down on us, quite a few of them.'[68] Another process worker and trade union official commented on what he remembered as the perceived arrogance of the craftworkers; 'the craftsmen believed that because they did an apprenticeship that they were untouchable', he noted.[69] Even craftsmen themselves conceded that the two groups of workers inhabited separate spheres or, as one Port Talbot works fitter put it: 'they had their world and we had ours.'[70] Industrial disputes, such as the 1963/4 AEU strike, then, were militant manifestations of these intra-class tensions, with workers challenging each other as well as their managers. Moreover, they were recognitions that although the working class often shared similar goals – better pay, working conditions and greater autonomy – there were many ways of advancing them, some of which did not necessitate pan-worker solidarity.

In this understanding of industrial conflict, alliances were fluid and perpetually remade to suit particular needs and challenges. Workers and trade union leaders could unite against their managers but they could also ally with them to undermine the efforts of the strikers. Union-sanctioned blacklegging was not uncommon during the unofficial strikes of the period, as unions instructed their members to carry on working while others were on strike. Indeed, in his own account of his firm handling of the 1961 bricklayers' strike, the works' general manager confidently informed his fellow directors: 'the Company's action is supported by the overwhelming majority of our work force as indicated by the fact that, as yet, no Union has supported the bricklayer Union by refusing to work with staff who are laying bricks. This is a most unusual circumstance in modern unionized works.'[71] In doing so, the blacklegging workers were directly following the instructions of their trade union leaders who consistently formulated strategies to protect the interests of their own members, rather than 'the steelworkers' as a collective. A similar situation occurred in 1977 when the plant's electricians announced their intention to strike and the ISTC's national leadership responded by instructing their Port Talbot members not to lend any assistance to the strikers. In a directive that could have been issued by the plant's managers, the union's divisional organiser informed the national press: 'I have sent out circulars to my members at the Port Talbot steelworks telling them they are not to co-operate in any way with the strikers.'[72] Privately the union's divisional representatives went further still, assuring their national executive that they 'had applied pressure on the EETPU [Electrical, Electronic, Telecommunications and Plumbing Union] for a return to work' and 'would continue to do all in their power to restore the plant to normal working'.[73] Repeatedly, workers organised themselves in ways that protected their own interests, even when this brought them into direct conflict with other occupations within the plant. While the distinction between workers and management remained, their relationship was not axiomatically defined by hostility. In contrast to the antithetical understanding of class relations that underpin much of labour history, industrial relations at the Abbey works were not fixed by any single political paradigm. Rather, alliances and hostilities were continually remade to suit particular needs and situations.

As well as bringing workers into conflict with each other, unofficial strikes could also reveal tensions between workers and their trade union leaders. National trade union leaders had little reason to condone unofficial strike action that they regarded as an affront to the official agreements and the established national negotiating machinery from which they derived their power. When, in 1971, the majority of the ISTC's staff workers at Port Talbot staged an unofficial walkout in a protest over pay, the union's general secretary was emphatic in calling them back to work and beseeched them to adhere to the official negotiation machinery. In an open letter to the plant's staff workers, Dai Davies reiterated the union's orthodox response to unconstitutional action: 'The strike is an unofficial one', he wrote,

> And if it continues will remain such because there can be no question of the Executive Council supporting actions which are in breach of the Organisation's rules. On the contrary the Executive Council instructed me to inform your members that they should

> immediately call off their unofficial stoppage and resume normal operations so that their claim can be processed through the established negotiating machinery.[74]

The strident line taken by trade union leaders often promoted a similarly intransigent response from the strikers so that management-worker disputes over wages soon conflagrated into intra-union conflicts concerning issues of representation and power. The decision by the Electrical, Electronic, Telecommunications and Plumbing Union executive in 1977, for example, to not officially sanction the wage claim advanced by Port Talbot's electricians quickly escalated into a bitter feud between the union's Port Talbot members and their national leaders. At the height of the strike, the leader of the Port Talbot electricians even announced at a mass meeting that 'I am fighting the union more than the BSC, without a shadow of a doubt'.[75] Unofficial strikes over pay, then, could soon raise awkward questions about the nature of power within the trade union movement itself; specifically, where should the majority of power lie, who should wield power and for what aims? Working-class loyalty to their trade union leaders may have been loosely predicated on a sense of historical affinity and common politics, but it was much more dependent on their leaders' ability to advance their goals within the workplace. Once these leaders appeared unable or, indeed, unwilling to do this, loyalty quickly turned to hostility.

CONCLUSION

The period 1945–79 unquestionably marked the most tumultuous period in the history of industrial relations at the Port Talbot steelworks. Never before or since have strikes been such a pervasive feature in the lives of Port Talbot's steelworkers. Although the national steel strike of 1980 was the defining conflict in the history of Britain's steel industry, the prolonged period of harmony that followed revealed how uncharacteristically discordant the previous three decades had been. Unusually, these strikes were not set against a backdrop of depression and hardship, like the industrial disputes of the late nineteenth century and interwar period. Rising wages and, initially, full employment, allowed steelworkers to realise a standard of living that would have been unobtainable to their parents. Steelworkers' opportunities for leisure and recreation multiplied, as disposable income brought better shops and clubs to the town, and their employers developed new sports and welfare facilities. Clearly, the archetypal image of the oppressed industrial worker and the tyrannical boss, as painted by R. Merfyn Jones,[76] is of little relevance to the new kinds of industrial conflict that characterised postwar Port Talbot.

The lack of solidarity during these disputes, alongside the use of blacklegging and the fluid nature of the alliances they contained, represent further departures from the traditional narrative of workplace conflict. For some contemporary commentators, these kinds of behaviours were emblematic of 'the decline of the working class' and the erosion of traditional working-class values. During this period, the notion of working-class embourgeoisement gained considerable currency, suggesting that rising wages, new technologies and new ways of living, were creating a new middle class out of an atrophied and redundant proletariat. Investigating this thesis was the subject of Goldthorpe and Lockwood's highly influential affluent worker studies: three volumes examining the lives of car workers in Luton in the 1960s. While the authors cautioned against the existence of widespread working-class embourgeoisement, they nonetheless agreed that a 'process of convergence' was taking place between the working class and white-collar workers. One symptom of this, they argued, was 'an absence of solidaristic orientations . . . among our Luton workers not only in their pattern of out-of-work sociability but in their working lives as well, and in fact in the general way in which they interpreted the social order.'[77] Other academics went further, despairing at what they regarded to be the dissolution of traditional working-class culture. At the beginning of the 1980s, Gwyn A. Williams despondently wrote of 'the puny response from Wales to the repeated calls for protest and action from British trade union and Labour organizations' and appeared resigned that 'there seemed to be little response from a population readily accepting the values and arguments of the new dispensation.' They were, he concluded, 'a naked people under an acid rain.'[78]

Strikers at the Port Talbot steelworks, however, were not greedily aspiring to middle-class lifestyles nor were they ignorant of traditional working-class values. Rather, they were a working class emboldened by the relative security and certainty of the postwar world to challenge the perceived injustice and unfairness of their workplace. They were also emboldened to disregard the rigidities of the pre-existing social order and fight battles along lines of their own choosing. In the traditional Marxist narrative, collectivity is a strength but so too is independence and autonomy. For perhaps the first time in their history, postwar affluence gave Port Talbot's steelworkers the strength to proactively challenge the decisions and policies of their managers and trade unions, regardless of the opinions of their fellow workers. In doing so, they challenged the dominant interpretation ascribed to the ideology of the working class, rooted, as it is, in its sense of solidarity and hostility to capitalism. Whereas historians have often tried to rigidly frame industrial conflict within a particular political paradigm, workers' motivations to take industrial actions reflected a variety of grievances, ranging from the personal, the materialistic to the ideological. Old solidarities may have lost some of their significance, but the determination to improve conditions and pay remained at the heart of workplace struggles, showing a degree of continuity with the traditional aspirations of the organised working class. In its attitudes towards the workplace and society, the working class was changing but it was not disappearing.

NOTES

1 *Y Cymro*, 20 July 1951.

2 *Western Mail*, 17 February 1958; *The Financial Times*, 3 January 1964.

3 D. Gilbert, 'Strikes in Postwar Britain', in C. Wrigley (ed.), *A History of British Industrial Relations, 1939–1979* (Cheltenham: Edward Elgar, 1996), p. 137.

4 *Report of the Royal Commission on Trade Unions and Employers' Associations* (London: Her Majesty's Stationery Office, 1968).

5 R. Hoggart, *The Uses of Literacy: Aspects of Working-Class Life with Special Reference to Publications and Entertainments* (Harmondsworth: Penguin Books Ltd, 1958), p. 73.

6 E. J. Hobsbawm, *The Age of Revolution: Europe, 1789–1848* (London: Abacus, 1977), p. 210.

7 R. McKibbin, *The Ideologies of Class: Social Relations in Britain 1880–1950* (Oxford: Oxford University Press, 1994), pp. 7–8.

8 G. A. Williams, *The Merthyr Rising* (London: Croom Helm, 1978); R. M. Jones, *The North Wales Slate Quarrymen, 1874–1922* (Cardiff: University of Wales Press, 1981); H. Francis, *History on our Side: Wales and the 1984–85 Miners' Strike* (London: Lawrence and Wishart, 2015); E. W. Evans, *The Miners of South Wales* (Cardiff: University of Wales Press,

1961); H. Francis and D. Smith, *The Fed: A History of the South Wales Miners in the Twentieth Century* (London: Lawrence and Wishart, 1980); B. Curtis, *The South Wales Miners, 1964–1985* (Cardiff: University of Wales Press, 2013).

9 J. Light, 'Manufacturing the past – the representation of mining communities in history, literature and heritage: '. . . Fantasies of a world that never was'?, *Llafur*, 8/1 (2000), 22.

10 D. Leeworthy, 'The Fed', *https://historyonthedole.wordpress.com/inspirations/the-fed/* (accessed 2 July 2017).

11 Light, 'Manufacturing the past'; M. Lieven, *Senghennydd: Universal Pit Village, 1890–1930* (Llandysul: Gomer Press, 1994).

12 C. Williams, 'Going underground? The future of coalfield history revisited', *Morgannwg*, 42 (1998), 49.

13 M. Johnes, ' "For Class and Nation": dominant trends in the historiography of twentieth-century Wales', *History Compass*, 8/11 (2010), 1258.

14 J. Bornat, 'Reminiscence and Oral History: Parallel Universes or Shared Endeavour?', in R. Perks and A. Thomson (eds), *The Oral History Reader*, 2nd edn (Abingdon: Routledge, 2006), p. 457.

15 These interviews were conducted by the author while researching his PhD thesis, 'Class, work and community: Port Talbot's steelworkers, 1951–1988' (unpublished PhD thesis, Swansea University, 2016).

16 For a more detailed consideration of the theoretical issues surrounding oral history, see L. Abrams, *Oral History Theory* (Abingdon: Routledge, 2010).

17 *The Daily Telegraph*, 18 July 1951.

18 *The Times*, 18 July 1951.

19 *Cootamundra Herald*, 9 August 1951.

20 *Port Talbot Guardian*, 20 July 1951.

21 E. O. Smith, *Productivity Bargaining: A Case Study in the Steel Industry* (London: Pan Books Ltd, 1971), pp. 86–7.

22 The National Archives [hereafter TNA], Housing for Steelworkers, BD 11/1449, Housing for proposed Strip Mill at Port Talbot: Notes of meeting held in Conference Room, 21 February 1947.

23 G. F. Thomason, 'An analysis of the effects of industrial change upon selected communities in south Wales' (unpublished PhD thesis, University College of Wales, Cardiff, 1963), p. 220.

24 A. V. John, *The Actors' Crucible: Port Talbot and the Making of Burton, Hopkins, Sheen and all the Others* (Cardigan: Parthian, 2015), p. 5

25 *Western Mail*, 2 September 1951; *Western Mail*, 20 July 1964; Thomason, 'An analysis of the effects of industrial change upon selected communities in south Wales', p. 335.

26 Interview with D.T., 15 October 2013.

27 *Port Talbot Guardian*, 21 September 1951.

28 Smith, *Productivity Bargaining*, p. 24.

29 Shotton Record Centre [hereafter SRC], Steel Company of Wales Board Reports, 378/1 Box 12, Personnel Employed and Average Earnings for Week Ended 17 July, 1954.
30 Department of Employment and Productivity, *British Labour Statistics: Historical Abstract, 1886–1968* (London: HMSO, 1971).
31 P. Cooke, 'Inter-regional Class Relations and the Redevelopment Process', *Papers in Planning Research* (Cardiff: University of Wales Institute of Science and Technology, 1981), p. 34.
32 *Western Mail*, 2 December 1952.
33 *South Wales Evening Post*, 28 November 1952.
34 Richard Burton Archives, Fred Cartwright Papers [hereafter RBA, CART], 1/39/1, The Steel Company of Wales (Port Talbot) Sports and Social Club: Report on the financial assistance received from The Steel Company of Wales, 1957.
35 RBA, CART/1/39/2–3, The Steel Company of Wales Limited Sanction/ Expenditure to Date on Sports Clubs, 1962.
36 J. C. Carr and W. Taplin, *History of the British Steel Industry* (Oxford: Blackwell, 1962), p. 461.
37 K. O. Morgan, *Michael Foot: A Life* (London: Harper Press, 2007), p. 183.
38 RBA, Iron and Steel Trades Confederation General Secretary Correspondences [hereafter ISTC/F] 3, Open letter from Dai Davies, 29 January 1968.
39 Smith, *Productivity Bargaining*, p. 94.
40 Smith, *Productivity Bargaining*, p. 42.
41 RBA, ISTC/F/4, Letter from S. Biddiscombe to D. Davies, 23 December 1970.
42 Interview with P.A., 3 September 2013.
43 RBA, ISTC/F/21, Letter from G. Pugh to A. E. Vincent, 27 September 1960.
44 TNA, Royal Commission on Trade Unions and Employers' Associations – Productivity Bargaining: Evidence of the Steel Company of Wales, Lab 28/9, Supplement 1, Letter from D. John to J. Cassels, 6 June 1966.
45 SRC, Steel Company of Wales Board Reports, 378/1, Box 14, Steel Division: Report on Operations, August 1957.
46 Interview with D.F., 27 November 2013.
47 P. Bowen, *Social Control in Industrial Organisations, Industrial Relations and Industrial Sociology: A Strategic and Occupational Study of British Steelmaking* (London: Routledge & Kegan Paul, 1976), p. 182.
48 E. J. Hobsbawm, 'The forward march of Labour halted', *Marxism Today*, 22 (September 1978), 286.
49 *Western Mail*, 21 June 1969.
50 *Western Mail*, 16 October 1961.
51 *Daily Mail*, 27 September 1961.
52 See R. Taylor, 'The Rise and Disintegration of the Working-classes', in P. Addison and H. Jones (eds), *A Companion to Contemporary Britain, 1939–2000* (London: Blackwell, 2007).

53 Hobsbawm, 'The forward march of Labour halted', 284.
54 Hobsbawm, 'The forward march of Labour halted', 284.
55 S. Todd, *The People: The Rise and Fall of the Working Class, 1910–2010* (John Murray: London, 2014), p. 293.
56 Interview with T.J., 17 November 2014.
57 Interview with P.A., 3 September 2013.
58 F. Zweig, *The British Worker* (Harmondsworth: Penguin, 1952), p. 102.
59 Interview with K.W., 25 November 2013.
60 Smith, *Productivity Bargaining*, p. 45.
61 Interview with J.P., 9 October 2013.
62 Taylor, 'The Rise and Disintegration of the Working-classes', p. 381.
63 *Report of the Royal Commission on Trade Unions and Employers' Associations*, p. 18.
64 *Report of the Royal Commission on Trade Unions and Employers' Associations*, pp. 104–5.
65 See Table 5.1: 1963, 1969, 1971 and 1977.
66 *Western Mail*, 9 January 1964.
67 Interview with K.T., 26 September 2013.
68 Interview with K.T., 26 September 2013.
69 Interview with R.W., 13 November 2013.
70 Interview with T.J., 17 November 2013.
71 SRC, Steel Company of Wales Board Reports, 378/1, Box 15, Steel Division: Report on Operations, September 1961.
72 *Western Mail*, 1 April 1977.
73 Gwent Archives, Journals and Records of the Iron and Steel Trades Confederation, D3417/1/60, Minutes of Executive Council, 18, 19 and 20 May 1977.
74 RBA, ISTC/F/4(b), Letter from D. Davies 'To the Abbey Works Staff Members', 23 August 1971.
75 *Western Mail*, 30 April 1977.
76 See Jones, *The North Wales Slate Quarrymen*.
77 J. H. Goldthorpe, D. Lockwood, F. Bechhofer and J. Platt, *The Affluent Worker in the Class Structure* (Cambridge: Cambridge University Press, 1969), pp. 26 and 164.
78 G.A. Williams, *When Was Wales? A History of the Welsh* (Harmondsworth: Penguin, 1985), pp. 298, 299 and 305.

FROM MARGAM TO MAURITANIA

THE STEEL COMPANY OF WALES AND THE GLOBALISATION OF IRON ORE SUPPLIES, 1952–1960

LOUISE MISKELL

BY THE twentieth century Wales already had a long-established reputation as a metal smelting centre, though it was not a position it had achieved thanks to an abundance of metal ore reserves of its own. As Chris Evans's chapter elsewhere in this volume has shown, in the case of copper it was the availability of excellent local coal for use in smelting furnaces that gave Swansea an unassailable locational advantage as a smelting centre from the early eighteenth century onwards. Little of the copper ore smelted there was mined in Wales, with most coming from Cornwall and, from the 1830s onwards, from as far afield as Chile, Cuba and South Australia. In the Welsh ferrous sector the story was a little different. Local ore was utilised in the early years of the iron industry. Ironstone outcrops in the upper reaches of the south Wales coalfield led, in the late eighteenth century, to the establishment of ironworks in situ, in a formidable industrial arc stretching from Blaenavon in the east to Hirwaun in the west.[1] But Welsh iron ore did not sustain these works for very long. As early as the 1820s the leading Welsh firms began buying in supplies as local reserves became depleted and richer ores were obtainable from further afield.[2] Initially these came from the north-west of England; later from northern Spain.[3] The need to import ores for smelting meant that the location of iron and steel works on the coast made better economic sense. The story of this geographical shift is well known,[4] and underpinned a growing economic divergence between the valleys and the south Wales coastal strip as the former grew ever more dependent on the mining of coal, while the latter attracted new investment, especially at the processing and finishing end of the metal industries. Less well known is the story of how Welsh firms responded to the problem of sourcing sufficient iron ore during the period of rapid growth in the steel sector after 1945. Much like the copper firms before them, postwar Welsh steel producers were faced with a rapidly globalising picture of ore supply. Continued profitability in the industry demanded not just a willingness to purchase iron ore from new places, but also an active participation in exploiting new reserves and bringing them into the marketplace. From the early 1950s, Wales's largest steel firm, the Steel Company of Wales, did just that.

This chapter examines the involvement of the Steel Company of Wales (SCOW) in an iron ore mining venture in the West African country of Mauritania, a French colony until it gained independence in 1960. In doing so, it offers a new perspective on the impact of globalising trends on Wales's largest steel firm in the postwar period. The SCOW was formed in 1947 from the merger of four older Welsh steel companies, as part of a five-year plan to modernise the industry in the UK, drawn up in 1945 by the British Iron and Steel Federation (BISF).[5] By the 1950s SCOW had established an international reputation for steel modernisation, based principally on its success in building the new Abbey steelworks at Margam on the south Wales coast. Yet, as the evidence in this chapter will show, its ability to exert leadership and influence over international iron ore exploitation projects was limited. Such projects were, by necessity, the work of multinational corporations in which the views of particular participants, let alone of individual companies, were diluted. Moreover, participation in the French-led Mauritanian scheme required SCOW to reorient its gaze towards Europe, having for the previous decade looked more to America as the exemplar nation for steel modernisation. SCOW's involvement in the Mauritanian scheme revealed some of the uncomfortable realities of this realignment from a British perspective. It was the era of decolonisation, growing economic co-operation between the nations of continental Europe and the rise of new industrial powers like Japan and Brazil. Nevertheless, the insights SCOW gained from being able to scrutinise and discuss plans for West African iron ore mining and shipment helped the firm to keep abreast of change in the rapidly shifting world of steel production in the 1960s. In particular, involvement in the transportation planning for the Mauritanian ore scheme helped alert SCOW to the crucial role that harbour accommodation would have on the cost efficiencies of European steelmaking sites. As a result, it prioritised harbour modernisation as a key part of its development planning in the 1960s and was able to retain significant locational advantages over rivals.

POSTWAR STEEL AND THE PROBLEM OF ORE SUPPLY

The first two decades after the Second World War were boom years for steel. Growing demand for steel in the production of motor cars, the construction industry and a range of consumer goods created an expansionist climate. The industry become a totem of Britain's economic reconstruction and ambitious new capital expenditure projects were funded with the aim of modernising plant and processes. South Wales was a major beneficiary. In fact, it was an era of dizzying modernisation in the Welsh ferrous smelting sector, with the disappearance of many local and family firms, operating on a small scale using mainly cold-metal steelmaking practice, where scrap steel and pig iron would be purchased, melted down and made into ingots before being sent on to finishing plants for processing.[6] In their place came amalgamated companies with greater resources at their disposal, operating on a much larger scale and with the latest automated equipment.[7] The SCOW built the new Abbey works at Margam, which opened in 1951, and the Trostre tinplate works near Llanelli, where production began in 1956. Another south Wales firm, Richard Thomas and Baldwins, built the Spencer works (later known as Llanwern) near Newport. Both the Abbey and Spencer works were equipped with hot strip mill technology, designed to increase the output and quality of sheet steel and tinplate. Demand for sheet steel in particular was on the rise, especially for the manufacture of cars and consumer goods. The effect was to propel the region to the forefront of the UK industry. By the mid-1950s, the BISF acknowledged that, in terms of tonnage, south Wales and Monmouthshire was, 'the most important of Britain's ten steel-making districts', producing 4,607,000 tons of crude steel, or 23.3 per cent of Britain's total output in 1955.[8]

The investment in hot strip mill technology for bulk sheet steel production at the new Abbey works changed the scale of production. As Table 6.1 shows, it established the Steel Company of Wales as Britain's largest consumer of iron ore, eclipsing the Teesside firm of Dorman Long, famous for its structural steel, used in bridge construction, and the Scottish firm of Colvilles that produced heavy steel products such as bars and rails. With this new-found status came a greater share of the responsibility for securing the availability of iron ore and, as a result, SCOW found itself at the forefront of debates over the sourcing of future supplies.

Table 6.1: Share of total iron ore usage by principal UK consumers, 1958 (%)

Steel Company of Wales	15.73
Dorman Long	14.68
Colvilles	10.15
Summers	9.66
Guest Keen	8.66
Richard Thomas and Baldwins	7.77
Consett	6.12
South Durham	5.76
United Steel Company	4.75
Ford Motor Company	2.77
Skinningrove	2.42
Barrow ironworks	2.29

Source: Warwick Modern Records, MSS 365/BISF/357 Reports, Minutes and Correspondence of ad hoc committee on Mauritania, 1958–9, appendix 1

In the early years of SCOW's operations at Port Talbot, the bulk of iron ore consumed in Britain's steel plants was sourced domestically. In 1949, for example, almost 12.5 million tons of iron ore, mined in Derbyshire, Leicestershire, Nottinghamshire and Lincolnshire and elsewhere, supplied the blast furnaces of Britain's steelworks, compared to almost 8 million tons of imported ores, from countries including Sweden,

France, northern Spain and Sierra Leone.[9] The drive to increase output in the steel industry placed increasing pressure on the consumption of iron ore during and after the Second World War. The United Nations Economic Commission for Europe's report in 1949 raised doubts that current ore sources could continue to meet demand,[10] and by the early 1950s steel firms were beginning to look beyond their traditional supplies for longer term solutions to the problem of supplying an industry whose ethos was to maximise output. The BISF estimated that some 22 million tons of imported ore would be needed by British steel producers by the mid-1960s and noted that, in Europe too, increasing reliance on imported ores was likely given the number of new steelworks opening up on coastal sites such as Bremen, Rotterdam and Dunkirk.[11] Nor was the problem confined to Europe. America's domestic iron ore reserves were seriously depleted as demand for steel escalated during the war. Mining companies and leading steel producers undertook extensive survey work to locate new deposits and discovered some significant new sources. Exploitation of vast ore fields in the Canadian provinces of New Quebec and Labrador began in earnest in 1942, and the discovery of extensive iron ore reserves in the Cerro Bolívar mountains in Venezuela followed in 1947. Five American steel firms invested in the Canadian venture and, in Venezuela, the Orinoco Mining Company, a subsidiary of the United States Steel Corporation, was mining 10 million tons of iron ore per year by 1956.[12]

FROM AMERICA TO EUROPE

With American steel companies already involved in large mining ventures overseas, western European nations had a model to emulate, but also an incentive to act quickly to secure their own access to essential raw materials. The American steel industry had made huge advances in output levels during the Second World War and was the model to which the SCOW looked for guidance on many aspects of its plant and production. During the planning and building of the Abbey works in Margam, Port Talbot, in the immediate postwar years, the SCOW had drawn heavily on its contacts in American steel firms for guidance on design, layout and equipment, with a number of its staff making extended visits to American steelworks in the late 1940s and early 1950s to study their practices.[13] But by the 1950s the landscape was changing. The steel industries of France, Germany, Italy, Belgium and the Netherlands were undertaking their own ambitious modernisation programmes, with the adoption of wide strip mill technology, urged on in some instances by the demands of car manufacturers like Fiat and Renault, and partly funded by Marshall Aid.[14] The outbreak of the Korean War in the 1950s shifted the focus of America's attentions away from economic reconstruction, while in 1952 the creation of the European Coal and Steel Community paved the way for greater economic co-operation between former allies and enemy nations in Europe.[15] When it came to finding ways to secure future supplies of iron ore, then, it was towards Europe that SCOW's gaze turned. It was not the first time that UK iron and steel companies had joined forces with a European firm to this end. In 1873 the Dowlais Company, in partnership with Consett ironworks and the German firm of Krupp, purchased the Orconera Mining Company in Bilbao, one of around twenty British-owned mineral companies established in Spain in the 1870s.[16] By the second half of the nineteenth century, however, it was the mineral-rich colonial territories of European powers in North and West Africa that provided the potential solutions to the iron ore supply problem.

The scale of the iron ore deposits available and the practical challenges involved in mining and shipping large quantities of ore from remote regions of Africa exceeded what individual firms, or even nations, could shoulder in terms of the capital investment needed and the level of risk involved. Instead, it was the rise of the European multinational firm after the Second World War that provided the business framework for the exploitation of foreign ore fields. The pioneer historian of European multinational business noted the importance of the years from the mid-1950s to the early 1960s as a period of activity by European iron and steel companies in overseas iron ore mining ventures.[17] Typically featuring a head office in the 'parent' nation but with its business activities focused overseas, multinational mining corporations relied on capital from partner organisations in the main raw material consuming nations to fund expensive mining and transportation costs. In many ways, these corporations were built on inequalities of wealth and influence between the investor nations and the mining regions in which they operated, and their activities have attracted criticism from historians of neo-colonialism and decolonisation.[18] Perhaps because of this whiff of exploitation, the involvement of British steel firms in these initiatives is largely absent from steel industry histories, which, in any case, have focused more on mapping out the organisational structures of the industry as a whole than examining the activities of individual firms.[19] Yet, in the case of one such venture, the *Societie Anonyme des Mines de Fer de Mauritanie* (MIFERMA), archival records in the collections of the BISF and of the SCOW provide a detailed picture of British participation in this ambitious mining project and, in particular, the contribution of the Welsh firm to the evolution of the Mauritanian iron ore project.[20]

MIFERMA was established in 1952 as the successor to an earlier company, *Societies Francaise d'Explorations Minieres*, formed in 1948 to survey the iron ore deposits around Fort Gouraud in the interior of the French territory of Mauritania. Headquartered in Paris, MIFERMA's original shareholders were 40 per cent French, 40 per cent Canadian and 20 per cent British,[21] although the Canadian share was later sold to Italian and German steel interests. The British shares were held by BISC Ore Ltd, the ore-buying subsidiary company of the BISF, which purchased and shipped all imported ores and sold them at a standard price to British steel firms.[22] MIFERMA's remit was to facilitate the mining and transportation of an estimated 6 million tons of high-grade iron ore annually, for a period of about sixteen years.[23] The Mauritanian iron ore deposit had already attracted American interest. The Bethlehem Steel Corporation, based in Pennsylvania, had sent two geologists to survey and report on the deposit in 1949, and although they decided not to pursue extractive operations in the area, knowledge of American interests in locating new ore supplies gave the MIFERMA project a sense of urgency in the early 1950s. This was compounded by the knowledge that the successful exploitation of the reserves would take time; there were major obstacles to be overcome before iron ore from the Mauritanian mines reached any European consumers.

The political, technical and logistical challenges of the project were daunting. The iron ore deposits were located in the Kédia D'Idjil mountains, rising to 3,000 ft above sea level in the Mauritanian interior (see Figure 6.1). Previous investigations carried out had not comprehensively surveyed the whole ore field, so further drilling, sampling and mapping work was required to gain an accurate assessment of the exploitable iron ore. In a sparsely populated area, with negligible annual rainfall and prohibitively high temperatures for part of the year, even the organisation of this work was difficult.

Figure 6.1: Location of iron ore deposit and proposed railway in Mauritania

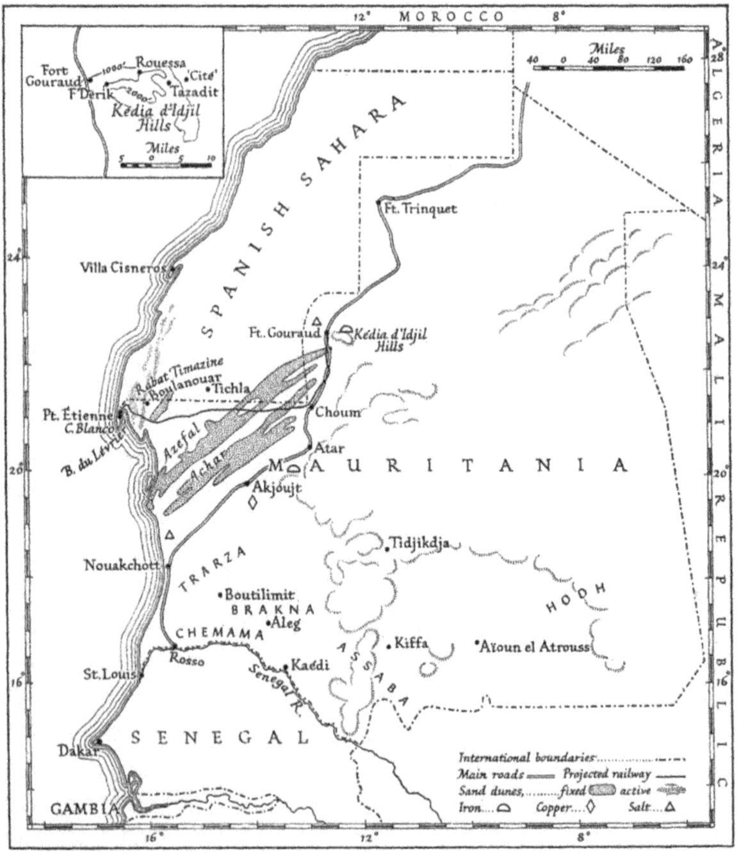

Source: R. J. Harrison Church, 'Problems and development of the dry zone of West Africa', *The Geographical Journal*, 127/2 (1961), 188. Reproduced with permission of the Royal Geographical Society.

A greater challenge still lay in the problem of conveying the ore to port for shipment to Europe. The shortest route to the coast involved crossing into Spanish territory in the northern Sahara, necessitating MIFERMA to enter into difficult negotiations with the Spanish government. The alternative route to the coast, entirely within French territory, was longer, requiring some 400 miles of road or rail construction, and involved negotiating areas of unstable sand dunes.[24] Aware that the costs of transporting the ore would be the likely factor determining the profitability of the project, the BISF wanted close scrutiny of these matters. The importance of the railway route and port, wrote one BISF member, 'cannot be too much stressed' and was 'of equal importance to the operation of the mine as is the study of the deposits themselves.'[25] An initial visit by MIFERMA representatives to examine the iron ore deposit came to similar conclusions. Their 1951 report stated, '[We] cannot too strongly emphasise the importance of a detailed study by experts in view of the importance to the enterprise of this railway, and of the dominating effect on its economy of the cost of construction and of operation of this essential part.'[26] It was over this key issue of transportation that the BISF sought to draw on expertise from the SCOW.

THE ROLE OF THE STEEL COMPANY OF WALES

SCOW has been identified as one of the 'most dynamic companies' in the postwar British steel industry.[27] As well as building Europe's largest new steelworks after 1945, the firm also built up a reputation for managerial talent. The construction and operation of the Abbey works was overseen by a formidable, and relatively youthful, trio comprising managing director, Julian Pode, finance director, David Young, and assistant general manager, Fred Cartwright. Together they presided over the company during a buoyant decade of expansion characterised by high wages, ongoing investment and increasing output levels. Their management ethos was based on new human relations ideologies, with attention to the quality of the workplace environment and the encouragement of employee participation in consultative forums.[28] Yet it was technical rather than managerial expertise that the BISF had in mind when they approached SCOW for advice on the MIFERMA project. In particular, they sought the help of Fred Cartwright (Figure 6.2) whose background was in engineering. Previously employed by Guest, Keen and Baldwins, Cartwright had played a key role in the building of the new Dowlais works at East Moors in Cardiff in the 1930s. By the mid-1950s he had visited most of the major steelworks sites in Europe and North America and consequently had an extensive international network of industry contacts. He was also an active disseminator of steel industry knowledge, giving occasional lectures and publishing on aspects of the modern steel industry.[29] Contemporaries viewed him as a moderniser and a formidable engineering talent.[30] Of significance, as far as the MIFERMA project was concerned, was also the fact that he had begun his engineering career with the Great Western Railway and was therefore well qualified to advise on the difficult issue of ore transportation route and costs.

In 1953 Cartwright was approached for advice on the MIFERMA project by C. R. Wheeler of the BISF, who had been overseeing British involvement in the project since 1951. Initially, attention had focused on the surveying of the mineral deposit and gaining an accurate idea of its size and accessibility. During this phase of the work the advisors on behalf of the British group were the geologist F. G. Percival and the mining engineer André Choubersky. By 1953, when the logistics of moving the ore to the coast were being considered, the need arose for additional

Figure 6.2: W. F. Cartwright, assistant general manager, Steel Company of Wales, *c*.1947

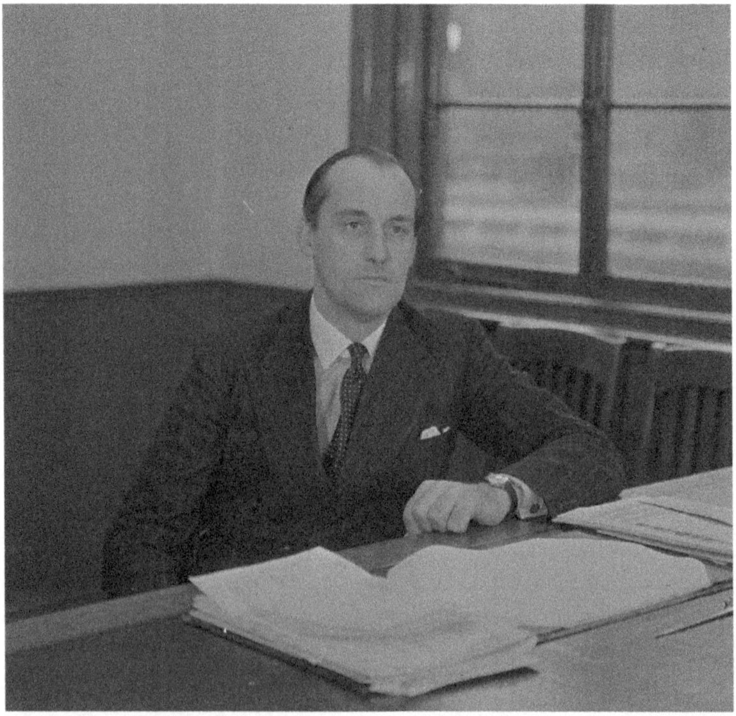

Source: Tata Steel. Peoples' Collection Wales.

expertise. Wheeler had close links with the Welsh steel industry through the firm of Guest, Keen and Baldwins, where he had been commercial manager in 1930, and a director in 1940,[31] and would have had first-hand knowledge of Cartwright's background. The role he envisaged for him was an advisory one, scrutinising the planning and costing of arrangements for the transportation of the ore on behalf of the British shareholders in the project. Alongside Cartwright, he also engaged the help of Dr W. MacGregor, director of the construction firm of George Wimpey and Co. Ltd, and these two became the nominated representatives of the BISF and its subsidiary, BISC Ore, for the next phase of the project planning.

It seemed that having built up a reputation for his work on two major steelworks construction projects, as well as having a background in railway engineering, had placed Fred Cartwright, and thereby SCOW, in a unique position as the only British steel firm to have direct involvement in the planning of the Mauritanian iron ore scheme. It was the beginning of an extensive commitment lasting for the rest of the decade, during which Cartwright made three trips to Paris for company meetings, hosted a visit by MIFERMA representatives to the Abbey works in Port Talbot, exchanged regular correspondence with other technical advisors to the company, and also joined a three-week fact-finding visit to Mauritania to survey the mines and the proposed railway route. His participation in this trip was as one of two representatives of BISC Ore in an eleven-man international party of engineering, mining, construction and railway experts. Cartwright's involvement in the expedition was relatively well known at the time. He wrote about his time in Mauritania for industry publications including *Ingot News*, the company newspaper of Richard Thomas and Baldwins, in which he described the experience of camping in the desert and eating a diet of gazelle meat.[32] His more formal reports and a diary account of the trip have not previously been utilised by steel industry historians. These provide a Welsh steel company perspective on the project as well as evidence of the extent to which an individual firm like SCOW could hope to make its voice heard and exert an influence in an increasingly transnational and globalised industry.

When first approached about the Mauritanian iron ore project in 1953, Cartwright was asked to look into the relative merits and costs of transporting ore over desert terrain by road and rail.[33] Cartwright's initial advice was that a railway should be built from the Mauritanian ore field to the coast via the shortest possible route, across the border and through Spanish territory to Villa Cisneros.[34] But these pragmatic observations took little account of political considerations. MIFERMA's negotiations with Spain over the railway route through its Saharan territory took place against a backdrop of international realignment with Franco's government. Ostracised from official relations with the west after the war, Spain had made small, incremental steps towards rehabilitation in the 1950s, with admission to UNESCO, the United Nations and the International Monetary Fund, but it remained ideologically distant.[35] A reluctance to have to rely on Spanish co-operation turned attention to alternative port options in French territory. André Choubersky explained to Cartwright that 'the French are pressing heavily to go to Port Etienne. This will involve 160 miles more track, a 3 kilometer tunnel through cliff to go round the Spanish border, and the crossing of the dunes. The sundry government survey parties all say it will be feasible, and port conditions are so much better at Port-Etienne, that the scheme will cost only £7,000,000 more'.[36] MIFERMA contracted Danish construction company Kampsax, who had previously had engineering oversight of the Trans-Iranian railway project in the 1930s,[37] to survey the possible routes and, although Cartwright commended the standard of the Danish company's report, he lamented that '[i]t is a sad commentary on the political state that we have to go to Port Etienne'.[38]

Cartwright also found that his views on other aspects of the scheme, though well received, were lost from view as the project progressed to the more detailed decision-making phase. The choice of materials and size dimensions for the rails and sleepers for such an extensive railway, for example, he considered 'a very fundamental one [which] . . . will affect any future development.' After a meeting with MIFERMA in Paris in March 1959, Cartwright wrote of his concerns over the preferences of the French for a relatively lightweight rail. 'American railroads are now using 132 lb rails almost everywhere and, as they [MIFERMA] are proposing to use the largest type of American diesel locomotive, I am afraid I remain unconvinced that their proposal to use 109 lb rails is wise.'[39] Cartwright's knowledge of the US steel industry dated back to the late 1940s and influenced much of his thinking on operational matters and productivity. More recently, a visit to the American iron ore mining operations in Venezuela in 1956 convinced him that MIFERMA needed to be more ambitious in their planning:

> My argument is, briefly, that if Fort Gouraud is to be developed on the scale now suggested, it is a proposition more on the scale of Venezuela than the other smaller mines with which Europeans have had experience. The Americans have steadily developed the heavier rail and in no case do I know of their deciding that a small rail could be used in place of a big one.[40]

Cartwright's recommendations about the railway demonstrated the extent to which he continued to regard American practice as the gold standard in the steel industry, despite the rapid advances made in European steel production in the 1950s. In some respects, this was not surprising. American strip mill technology had been fundamental to the reshaping of European steel production in the middle decades of the twentieth century.[41] The United States continued to occupy a commanding position in the world steel industry throughout the 1950s and 1960s, producing more crude steel annually than the whole of western Europe and the UK combined until the end of the 1960s.[42] More broadly, advances in productivity and management practices in US manufacturing industries instilled in many of Cartwright's generation a sense of lagging behind the Americans and a desire to learn from, if not always to adopt, their business methods.[43] Although there were no US partners in the MIFERMA project, the involvement of the Toronto-based mining company Frobisher Ltd, which originally held some 34 per cent of MIFERMA shares, brought a welcome North American perspective to the project as far as the BISF was concerned. Frobisher's withdrawal from the venture in 1957 after the completion of the exploration phase of the project, when its shares were bought by German and Italian steel companies,[44] was a disappointing development from the British point of view. In particular, Cartwright feared that the withdrawal of its Commonwealth partner would weaken the UK's ability to secure tenders for British companies.

His concerns about the ability of British firms to tender illustrates the extent to which the national interests of individual shareholders and their representatives loomed large. Even in an international mining venture in which all partners stood to benefit from the increase in ore supplies, the prospect of securing lucrative contracts for the supply of plant and equipment introduced an element of rivalry between collaborators. As a representative of a 20 per cent shareholder, Cartwright ultimately had little opportunity to influence decisions over the choice of contractors or the purchase of machinery, but this did not deter him from criticising some of the choices of equipment and suppliers made by the MIFERMA directorate. Although he laced his comments with concerns over equity of opportunity, ultimately his views on the tendering process were about advancing British interests. He urged, for example, that

> should the scheme go forward, the locomotive tenders issued would be very wide. Many makers are not mentioned in the report who are perfectly competent to build such locomotives and already have much experience in desert work. English Electric, who they brushed on one side, have I am pretty sure a great deal more desert experience than Alco, General Electric or Nydquist and Holm, mentioned as the preferred makers in the report.[45]

His Anglo-American preferences aside, Cartwright had put his finger on a problem that needed to be addressed by MIFERMA in order to secure wider financial backing for the Mauritanian iron ore project. In 1960 the company applied for a loan from the World Bank. Its support came with the requirement that all calls for tenders would be international in character. Consequently, early in 1959, MIFERMA wrote to nineteen firms in France, ten in Britain, ten in Germany, ten in Italy and six in Spain to outline the nature of the earth-moving and construction work needed.[46]

ECONOMIC DEVELOPMENT OR EXPLOITATION?

Equity of opportunity in the process of tendering for contracts was not the only issue MIFERMA had to consider in preparing its loan application to the World Bank. More broadly, the question of who would benefit economically from the iron ore mining scheme was one that had to be addressed explicitly in the project plans. The World Bank was established in 1947 with a remit to promote development in poor regions. In the context of decolonisation since the mid-1950s, the needs of new African nations loomed large,[47] making it an essential requirement of any loan application for economic activity in the region to generate wealth and bring economic benefits to the local population. For MIFERMA, this meant thinking not only about what the availability of Mauritanian iron ore would do for the European steel industry, but also about what the mining project would deliver for Mauritania. Such considerations had not traditionally featured in the planning and prosecution of other African mining ventures. Since the 1930s, the British-based capital investment firm DELCO's iron ore mining operations in Sierra Leone had epitomised colonial exploitation. By remunerating its mine workers just 9d per day, paying minimal taxes in Sierra Leone, and ensuring that all plant and equipment for the mine was imported from the UK, one study estimated that 'no less than 82.75 per cent of the total economic benefits generated by the Sierra Leone ore mines found its way back into the coffers of British capitalism'.[48] In the years immediately before and after the Second World War there were signs of change, with growing criticism of the exploitative business arrangements of some British firms in West African colonies.[49] In this climate, investors in new projects had to tread carefully. Reports on MIFERMA in the British press tried to reassure the public that UK steel industry involvement was justified. *The Times*, for example, presented the iron ore venture as a step towards greater self-determination for the French colony:

> Miferma plans to export between five and six million tons of iron ore a year, with a value of nearly £30 million. Since a substantial proportion of this will accrue, either directly or indirectly to Mauretania . . . the benefits of the Fort Gouraud mines should be felt by the whole population . . . talk of both a Mauretanian nation and ultimate independence will be more realistic than it is at present.[50]

Given these shifts in public opinion, it is surprising that there is no evidence that either the ethics of British involvement, or the issue of Mauritanian economic development, featured in the discussions of the MIFERMA scheme in SCOW or the BISF. Despite Cartwright's reputation as a moderniser in his approach to engineering and production, and his commitment to human relations in management arrangements at the Abbey works, he appeared conservative and unenlightened in his views on the indigenous population in Mauritania. His report on his Mauritanian visit in 1954, for example, belied a view of the local population as potential obstacles to, rather than possible partners in, the scheme. He concluded: 'All the Arabs we met were extremely friendly and I do not think one should encounter any trouble, should a railway be built, from Arab opposition, but that is by no means certain.'[51] The content of the plans put forward to the World Bank by MIFERMA suggest that he was not alone in holding these views. The labour requirements mapped out for the iron ore scheme incorporated a clear delineation between how African workers and European workers were viewed, with African labour envisaged as being deployed predominantly at the open-cast mine, rather than the port. MIFERMA's costings for the project also assumed the provision of a lower standard of housing for local workers than the type of accommodation needed to attract skilled staff from Europe. Presumably in anticipation of the scrutiny of the World Bank, the project did incorporate a proposed training centre for local workers to reduce reliance on manpower from overseas, but this appeared to be little more than a token gesture. Despite agreeing the loan to MIFERMA on the grounds that the creation of jobs at the proposed new port and mine would 'open up completely new opportunities for development' and 'put the country on its own feet financially', the World Bank nevertheless accepted that around one third of the estimated total workforce of 2,000, would be skilled personnel brought in from Europe, while labour for unskilled jobs would be recruited locally.[52]

With labour metrics like this built into the project from the outset, it is perhaps not surprising that historians of postcolonial Africa have been highly sceptical of the MIFERMA endeavour from the point of view of its impact on Mauritanian wealth and prosperity. The country gained independence from France in 1960 but, in practice, decades of under-investment in the region meant that it still needed outside support and the influence of the former colonial power continued. It was part of a pattern of economic activity in the region characterised by continuity, as '[i]mperial businesses did not collapse alongside colonialism, but instead successfully adapted their operations by highlighting their role in the economic development of the continent.'[53] A number of studies of the impact of MIFERMA's activities on economy and society in Mauritania have suggested that, for large sections of the native population, the Mauritanian iron ore project delivered no meaningful economic or political rewards. According to one study, even for those who gained work at the mine, low wages, poor housing and dangerous working conditions combined to produce 'a dramatic deterioration in their material situation.'[54] The damning verdict of one Algerian scholar was that European investment in Mauritania underpinned a neocolonial society in which a few prospered, but the majority were exploited as the mineral wealth of the region was 'pillaged'.[55]

MIFERMA was by no means unique in its activities. The first decade and a half after the Second World War saw a flurry of activity by international mining companies throughout Africa, mainly developing large-scale, opencast sites where production was predominantly for export.[56] Other multinational corporations like LAMCO, the Liberian American-Swedish Mineral Company, were formed to lead these initiatives, with capital provided from the key mineral-consuming nations.[57] While such ventures often failed to generate wealth and deliver employment opportunities in Africa, there is clearer evidence that they yielded the desired results for their European shareholders and iron ore consumers. Table 6.2 illustrates a significant increase in the volume of ore production from West Africa by the mid-1960s. Longer established ore-supplying nations were not supplanted by these developments, especially as it took time to put in place infrastructure and facilities for mining and transportation of new African supplies. In the early 1960s, SCOW continued to purchase the bulk of its iron ore from Sweden, with figures for 1963 showing that Swedish supplies accounted for 65 per cent; North African sources 19 per cent; with a further 9 per cent coming from West African mines and 5 per cent from France.[58] It was not until the second half of the 1960s that the Mauritanian iron ore deposit began to reach more significant levels of production, with more than 9 million metric tons mined in 1970.[59] Nevertheless, the direction of travel was clear.

Table 6.2: West African iron ore production, 1960–5 (in thousands of metric tons)

	1960	1965
Liberia	2,800	15,000
Sierra Leone	1,464	2,097
Mauritania	—	6,200
Guinea	776	800 (estimated)

Source: Adapted from Swindell, 'Iron ore mining in West Africa', 333.

THE CONSEQUENCES FOR PORT TALBOT

For SCOW, the greater diversification in iron ore supply to the UK steel industry and, in particular, the increase of non-European ores had knock-on effects for other aspects of investment and development planning throughout the 1960s. To take full advantage of the brave new world of long-distance iron ore importation, the SCOW had to address not only the challenge of developing mining and transport infrastructure in West Africa, it also had to rethink its own facilities at home. In particular, the prospect of receiving large shipments of iron ore from the new African mines prompted scrutiny of dock facilities. Port Talbot dock dated from 1898 and had been built to serve the needs of local coalowners.[60] It was designed to handle ships of 10,000 tons capacity, a size no longer suitable for the bulk ore-carriers that left Port-Étienne and other West African ports with cargoes of iron ore bound for Europe. When MIFERMA submitted its loan application to the World Bank in 1960, it envisaged developing Port Etienne to handle vessels of 60,000 tons and such was the pace of change in the scale of ore freight, this size of carrier was soon overtaken. The Liberian port of Monrovia was improved to handle 90,000-ton vessels in 1970.[61] Not only was Port Talbot dock dwarfed by this scale of development, there was no other port in Britain capable of receiving ore carriers of more than 35,000 tons. It was a problem that Fred Cartwright had raised in an address to the congress of the Institute of Transport, in 1962 in which he highlighted the 'utter inadequacy' of ore-receiving facilities at British ports and warned that the country's steel industry was 'operating under a severe disadvantage compared with the industries of western Europe based on big ports and adequate handling facilities.'[62]

The upgrading of facilities at Port Talbot was not necessarily viewed as the default solution to this problem. With the Spencer steelworks in operation, the expansion of Newport docks was one option put forward by the government in a White Paper published in 1965. Steel company executives at SCOW also briefly considered the possibility of financing developments at Milford Haven, some eighty miles away from Port Talbot, as an ore shipping port, but the prohibitive costs of onward transportation of the ore to the blast furnaces made the scheme unviable.[63] Instead, SCOW began investigating plans for a new tidal harbour at Port Talbot as part of an ambitious new phase of capital investment that also involved converting the plant to basic oxygen steelmaking (BOS).[64] This process, pioneered in Austria in the 1950s, had a transformative effect on rates of output, as the blowing of oxygen into the steelmaking vessels significantly speeded up production, enabling some 2,400 tons of steel to be produced from one 100-ton vessel in a twenty-four hour period.[65] The process was already in use at Llanwern, Ravenscraig and elsewhere by the time the SCOW development scheme was drawn up, and had proven itself to be more cost-effective than open-hearth steelmaking. By yoking it to the harbour development plan that would deliver savings in transportation costs, SCOW was able to forecast even greater efficiencies.

The new Port Talbot harbour was a joint project of the SCOW and the British Transport Docks Board, and was constructed over four years at a cost of £20 million. Even during the planning phase, SCOW continually revised upwards its estimate of the size of ore vessels that the harbour should be designed to handle, from 80,000-ton carriers to ships of 100,000 tons and over. At the time of its opening, Port Talbot was the only port in the UK capable of handling 100,000-ton ore carriers. The new facility was formally opened by the Queen and the Duke of Edinburgh on 12 May 1970. By this time, the steel industry in Britain had been nationalised and the SCOW no longer existed in name, but it left an ongoing legacy. Port Talbot's primacy as Britain's premier location for sheet steel production had been secured. Other steelmaking sites were unable to match the cost efficiencies now possible at the Port Talbot works, thanks to its access to a deep-water harbour as well as its use of the most technically advanced steelmaking processes.[66] On a national level it had prompted the steel industry to face up to the new challenges presented by the globalisation of the iron ore trade and helped it to remain competitive in the increasingly challenging environment of the 1960s. On an international level it ensured that the Port Talbot plant was well positioned to be able to reap at least a share of the benefits in the huge growth in world demand for sheet steel in the two decades after the Second World War

CONCLUSION

Fred Cartwright's participation in the MIFERMA project helped arm SCOW with detailed knowledge of the trajectory and scale of overseas iron ore mining developments. Even before Mauritanian ore had begun arriving on the market in large quantities, his access to the plans and forecasts of the firm, along with the opening up of mines elsewhere on the African continent, brought a sharp sense of urgency to SCOW's planning from the early 1960s, which paid dividends in the long term. It was just reward for Cartwright's lengthy and sometimes frustrating engagement with MIFERMA. Over the seven years of his involvement, his advice on details of the project had rarely prevailed and his preferences for American solutions to problems like bulk ore transportation meant that he sometimes lacked confidence in European approaches. He was also disappointed that British involvement in the Mauritanian scheme had failed to deliver wider economic benefits, most notably in the form of contracts for British firms. For a company that had become an acknowledged leader in the industry in Britain and a trusted source of expertise, having a relatively minor role in the MIFERMA project must have proved difficult. On the one hand, it was important that Wales's leading steelmaker had a seat at the international table during a transformative period, when the world's major steel producers were having to cast their nets ever more widely to source iron ore from remote regions, distant from the main centres of steel production. But just having a seat at the table did not necessarily guarantee influence for SCOW. For MIFERMA, the point of inviting shareholders like BISC Ore Ltd to send experts to represent them was as much about giving key investors a sense of involvement as it was about actually utilising this expertise. Ultimately, in a French-led project, the voices of individual experts representing minority shareholders were always likely to remain peripheral, even where these were based on clear financial and technical considerations.

The involvement of the SCOW, perhaps the flagship firm of the early postwar Welsh economy, in an exploitative iron ore mining scheme in one of the poorest regions of north-west Africa, raises some uncomfortable issues for historians of modern Welsh industry. It serves as a reminder that, as their raw material supply chains globalised, south Wales firms became the recipients of ore from regions where employment practices and standards of safety fell well below the levels acceptable in their own workplace. Moreover, as a major ore consumer they became direct beneficiaries of mining operations that were designed more to keep market prices low for purchasers than to boost the economic fortunes of the inhabitants of the ore-field regions. SCOW's silence on the question of what the MIFERMA investment might do for Mauritanian political and economic advancement suggests a rather hard-nosed attitude to the acquisition of new iron ore supplies. For them, and for the other partners in the scheme, financial considerations, rather than humanitarian ones, took precedence in planning for the mining and transportation of the ore. To some extent, the fact that they had only a bit-part in a French-led project meant that the Welsh firm could avoid having to confront some of the more tangled issues arising from the decline of colonialism and the realigning of relations between European states in the postwar period. What they could not avoid were the implications of the new global expansion of ore mining and shipping for the future competitiveness of the Welsh steel industry. When it came to responding to these challenges, SCOW's planning and investments in harbour facilities and its new BOS plant reaped lasting rewards.

NOTES

1 J. Elliott, 'The Iron and Steel Industry', in C. Williams and S. R. Williams (eds), *The Gwent County History, Volume IV: Industrial Monmouthshire, 1780–1914* (Cardiff: University of Wales Press, 2011), p. 76.

2 M. Atkinson and C. Baber, *The Growth and Decline of the South Wales Iron Industry, 1720–1880: An Industrial History* (Cardiff: University of Wales Press, 1987), pp. 25–34.

3 E. Jones, *A History of GKN Volume 1: Innovation and Enterprise, 1759–1918* (Basingstoke: Macmillan, 1987), pp. 257–9, 310–14.

4 See, for example, D. G. Watts, 'Changes of location of the south Wales iron and steel industry', *Geography*, 53/3 (1968), 294–367.

5 The four firms involved in the merger were Richard Thomas and Baldwins; Guest, Keen and Baldwins; Lysaghts; and Llanelly Associated Tinplate Companies. The British Iron and Steel Federation was an association of the major firms, formed in 1934 to increase centralisation of the industry during the Depression. See S. H. Friedelbaum, 'The British iron and steel industry: 1929–9', *The Journal of Business of the University of Chicago*, 23/1 (1950), 117–32.

6 C. Baber and J. Dessant, 'Modern Glamorgan: Economic Development after 1945', in G. Williams and A. H. John (eds), *Glamorgan County History. Volume V: Industrial Glamorgan* (Cardiff: Glamorgan County History Trust, 1980), p. 600.

7 S. Tolliday, 'Steel and Rationalization Policies, 1918–1950', in B. Elbaum and W. Lazonick (eds), *The Decline of the British Economy* (Oxford: Oxford University Press, 1986), p. 91.

8 British Iron and Steel Federation, *The South Wales Steel Industry* (November 1956).

9 R. Shone, 'The sources and nature of statistical information in special fields of statistics: statistics relating to the UK iron and steel industry', *Journal of the Royal Statistical Society. Series A*, 113/4 (1950), 467.

10 D. L. Burn, *The Steel Industry, 1939–1959: A Study in Competition and Planning* (Cambridge: Cambridge University Press, 1961), p. 325.

11 Warwick Modern Records [hereafter WMR], MSS 365/BISF/357, Draft Report on Mauritania, 12 August 1959.

12 For details of the Canadian mining ventures, see G. Humphrys, 'Mining activity in Labrador Ungava', *Transactions of the Institute of British Geographers*, 29 (1961), 187–99. For the Venezuelan project see Richard Burton Archives, Fred Cartwright Papers [hereafter RBA, CART], 1/49/1/10, W. F. Cartwright, Visit to Brazil, Venezuela and United States, October 1956: report.

13 For details see L. Miskell, 'Doing it for themselves: the Steel Company of Wales and the study of American industrial productivity, *c*.1945–1955', *Enterprise and Society*, 18/1 (2017), 184–213.

14 R. Ranieri and J. Aylen, 'Technological Trajectories. The Wide Strip Mill for Steel in Europe (1920 to the Present)', in C. Barthel, I. Kharaba and P. Mioche (eds), *The Transformation of the World Steel industry from the XXth Century to the Present* (Brussels: Peter Lang, 2014), pp. 363–80.

15 J. Gillingham, *Coal, Steel, and the Rebirth of Europe, 1945–1955. The Germans and French from Ruhr Conflict to Economic Community* (Cambridge: Cambridge University Press, 1991), pp. 228–9.

16 C. Harvey and P. Taylor, 'Mineral wealth and economic development: foreign direct investment in Spain, 1851–1913', *Economic History Review*, 40/2 (1987), 190.

17 L. G. Franko, *The European Multinationals. A Renewed Challenge to American and British Big Business* (London: Harper and Row, 1976), p. 66.

18 For example, M. Bennoune, 'Mauritania: formation of a neo-colonial society', *Middle East Research and Information Project Report*, 54 (February 1977), 3–13.

19 See, for example, Burn, *The Steel Industry*; H. Abromeit, *British Steel: An Industry between the State and the Private Sector* (Berg: Leamington Spa, 1986). Studies that have adopted a company-level perspective include, P. W. S. Andrews and E. Brunner, *Capital Development in Steel: A Study of the United Steel Companies Ltd* (Oxford: Blackwell, 1951); P. L. Payne, *Colvilles and the Scottish Steel Industry* (Oxford: Clarendon, 1979).

20 The BISF records are held at the University of Warwick's Modern Records Centre, in the collection MSS.365/BISF. The relevant SCOW records are RBA, CART/1/48/1–8.

21 WMR, MSS 365/ BISF 607, Extract from the Minutes of the Meeting of the Executive Committee held at Steel House, Tothill Street, London, 17 April 1951.

22 Burn, *The Steel Industry*, pp. 325–8.

23 World Bank, 'Appraisal of the MIFERMA Iron Ore Mining Project', 12 February 1960, pp. i–1.

24 R. J. Harrison Church, 'Problems and development of the dry zone of West Africa', *The Geographical Journal*, 127/2 (1961), 189.

25 WMR, MSS 365/BISF607, Memo, N. L. Goodchild (BISF) to R. M. Shone, 19 Nov 1952 'Mauretania'.

26 WMR, MSS 365/BISF608, Report on the Iron Ore Deposits of the Kédia D'Idjil (Fort Gouraud), French Mauretania (Afrique Occidentale Française) May–June, 1951, p. 22

27 R. Ranieri, 'Steel and the State in Italy and the UK. The Public Sector of the Steel Industry in Comparative Perspective', in W. Feldenkirchen and T. Gourvish (eds), *European Yearbook of Business History*, 2 (Ashgate: Society for European Business History, 1999), p. 139.

28 M. P. Guillén, *Models of Management: Work, Authority and Organization in a Comparative Perspective* (Chicago: University of Chicago Press, 1994), pp. 238–46.

29 See, for example, W. F. Cartwright, *Modern American Steelworks Practice* (Cardiff: South Wales Institute of Engineers, 1946); W. F. Cartwright, *The Design of Iron and Steel Works* (Cardiff: South Wales Institute of Engineers, 1950); W. F. Cartwright, 'Preliminary Planning of Margam and Abbey Works', in *A Technical Survey of Abbey, Margam, Trostre and Newport Plants of the Steel Company of Wales* (London: Industrial Newspapers, 1952), pp. 9–12.

30 Sir William Atkins, *Partners. Fifty Years of WSA & P* (Kent: Atkins Holdings Ltd, 1988), p. 27; 'He found his challenge in steel', *The New Scientist*, 21 May 1959, 1134–5; 'W. F. Cartwright – Deputy Chairman – British Steel Corporation', *Supplement on Industry, South Wales Magazine*, 1975.

31 Obituary of Sir Charles Wheeler, *The Times*, 26 November 1975.

32 A copy of the article can be found in RBA, CART1/48/2.

33 RBA, CART1/48/3, C. R. Wheeler to W. F. Cartwright, 2 February 1953.

34 RBA, CART1/48/3, W. F. Cartwright to Mike Wheeler, 22 July 1953.

35 J. L. N. Hernández, 'The Foreign Policy Administration of Franco's Spain. From Isolation to International Realignment (1945–1957)', in C. Leitz and D. J. Dunthorn (eds), *Spain in an International Context, 1936–1959* (Oxford: Berghahn, 1999), p. 280.

36 RBA, CART1/48/5, A. Choubersky to W. F. Cartwright, 10 July 1956.

37 'Railway Making Under Difficulties', *The Times*, 7 March 1938.

38 RBA, CART/1/48/5 W. F. Cartwright to Choubersky, 18 July 1956.

39 RBA, CART1/48/4, Report by W. F. Cartwright on visit to Paris office of MIFERMA to discuss the latest proposals for the development of the or deposit, 6 April 1959.

40 RBA, CART1/48/4, Report by W. F. Cartwright on visit to Paris office.

41 For details see J. Aylen and R. Ranieri (eds), *Ribbon of Fire: How Europe Adopted and Developed US Strip Mill Technology (1920–2000)* (Pendragon: Fondazione Ranieri di Sorbello, 2012).
42 In 1970 the output of crude steel in the UK and western Europe totalled 137,589 thousand metric tons, exceeding the US figure of 130,507 thousand metric tons for the first time. See *A Handbook of World Steel Statistics* (Brussels: International Iron and Steel Institute, 1978), p. 2.
43 J. Zeitlin and G. Herrigel (ed.), *Americanization and its Limits. Reworking US Technology and Management in Post-War Europe and Japan* (Oxford: Oxford University Press, 2000).
44 WMR, MSS365/BISF, MIFERMA Committee, draft minutes, 16 January 1957; 17 January 1957.
45 RBA, CART1/48/5, W. F. Cartwright, Brief Technical Report on Mauritanian Iron Ore project.
46 RBA, CART1/48/4, Copy of letter from A. Choubersky to W. MacGregor of George Wimpey and Co. Ltd, 6 February 1959.
47 K. Marshall, *The World Bank: From Reconstruction to Development to Equity* (Oxford and New York: Routledge, 2008), pp. 36–7.
48 A. M. M. Hoogvelt and A. M. Tinker, 'The role of colonial and post-colonial states in imperialism – a case-study of the Sierra Leone Development Company', *The Journal of Modern African Studies*, 16/1 (1976), 78.
49 S. Decker, 'Corporate legitimacy and advertising: British companies and the rhetoric of development in West Africa, 1950–1970', *Business History Review*, 81/1 (2007), 59.
50 *The Times*, 7 January 1959.
51 RBA, CART1/48/1, Report on Expedition Villa Cisneros – Fort Gouraud – Dakar, February 24 – March 12 1954, by W. F. Cartwright, Tuesday, 2 March 1954.
52 International Bank for Reconstruction and Development, 'Appraisal of the MIFERMA Iron Ore Mining project', 12 February 1960.
53 Decker, 'Corporate legitimacy', 61–2.
54 P. Bonté and B. Benson, 'Multinational companies and national development: Miferma and Mauretania', *Review of African Political Economy*, 2 (January–April 1975), 104.
55 Bennoune, 'Mauretania: formation of a neo-colonial society', 9.
56 G. Lanning with M. Mueller, *Africa Undermined: Mining Companies and the Underdevelopment of Africa* (Harmondsworth: Penguin, 1979), especially chapter 4.
57 K. Swindell, 'Iron ore mining in West Africa: some recent developments in Guinea, Sierra Leone and Liberia', *Economic Geography*, 43/4 (October 1967), 337–8.
58 *Iron and Steel Handbook*, 1963 (London: Norris Oakley Bros.), p. 277.
59 Bonté and Benson, 'Multinational companies', 98.

60 R. Craig, 'The Ports and Shipping', in G. Williams and A. H. John (eds), *Glamorgan County History. Volume V: Industrial Glamorgan* (Cardiff: Glamorgan County History Trust, 1980), p. 485.

61 See article on 'Cutting the Cargo Costs', *The Times*, 19 March 1970.

62 'Lack of Room in S. Wales Ore Ports Causes Concern', *The Times*, 26 June 1962.

63 S. Parry, 'A history of the steel industry in the Port Talbot area, 1900–1988' (unpublished PhD thesis, University of Leeds, 2011), pp. 175–6.

64 E. O. Smith, *Productivity Bargaining: A Case Study in the Steel Industry* (London: Pan Books Ltd, 1971), pp. 92–3.

65 W. K. V. Gale, *The British Iron and Steel Industry. A Technical History* (Newton Abbot: David and Charles, 1967), p. 157.

66 'An Age of Giants', *The Times*, 12 May 1970; Parry, 'A history of the steel industry in the Port Talbot area, 1900–1988', p. 177; J. Elliott and C. Deneen, 'Iron, Steel and Aluminium', in C. Williams and A. Croll (eds), *Gwent County History, Volume V: The Twentieth Century* (Cardiff: University of Wales Press, 2013), p. 68.

THE AGE OF FACTORIES
THE RISE AND FALL OF MANUFACTURING IN SOUTH WALES, 1945–1985

LEON GOOBERMAN AND BEN CURTIS

INTRODUCTION

AFTER the Second World War, central governments[1] used regulatory and incentive mechanisms to steer factories to south Wales to reduce unemployment and increase regional prosperity. Although central government intervention enabled manufacturing to attain a prominent role in south Wales, described by a contemporary observer in 1970 as 'probably the closest to a nationalised region that exist[s] in Britain',[2] the sector's status was short-lived and it declined from the mid-1970s. Despite manufacturing's importance to the economy of south Wales, its rise and fall has been little studied.[3] This chapter addresses this gap by profiling the sector, emphasising the state's role in attracting investment and illustrating the sector's trajectory through case studies of the British Nylon Spinners/Imperial Chemical Industries Fibres plant at Pontypool and the Enfield Cables/Dunlop Semtex factory at Brynmawr.

The chapter is based on archival data from the UK's National Archives and the Gwent Archives, oral history collected by Women's Archive Wales, as well as contemporary documentation including newspapers and official publications. It argues that the state intervened effectively to force the private sector to create large numbers of manufacturing jobs in south Wales. The new factories created thousands of jobs and helped create some regional prosperity. Most would not have located in south Wales without state intervention such as controls on industrial location and the provision of factories. However, many factories were 'branch plants', meaning that ownership and management control remained outside the region. South Wales depended on state intervention to attract new factories, while existing branch plants were vulnerable to external shocks. These weaknesses meant that the sector was unable to renew itself and was disproportionately impacted by UK-wide economic and political trends from the 1970s onwards. As a result, manufacturing's status as a leading sector in south Wales was short-lived, and state intervention was successful only over a relatively short period of time.

THE SCALE AND IMPACT OF MANUFACTURING

The industrial revolution transformed south Wales from a sparsely populated and largely agricultural region to one dominated by industry, as the population of Glamorgan and Monmouthshire grew from 116,527 in 1801 to 1,158,007 in 1901.[4] The region was heavily dependent on coal extraction and metal working, both with a largely male workforce. These two activities accounted for 49 per cent of the occupied male workforce in 1901,[5] while many of the remainder worked in linked activities such as transport or within the urban centres that sprang up to serve the new industries. However, the success of coal extraction and metal working did not encourage the development of a manufacturing base, but tended instead to crowd out other activity.

The lack of diversification did not matter when demand for basic goods was high, but a collapse in demand after the First World War led to a prolonged slump until the Second World War, which created an urgent requirement for manufacturing capacity. South Wales was an ideal location, given its supply of surplus labour and its distance from areas under the greatest threat of air raids. The advantages prompted central government to direct manufacturing to the region, and these new factories helped to virtually eliminate unemployment. After the war, central government's determination to ensure greater prosperity throughout the UK's regions and nations enabled a successful state-led drive to attract manufacturing to south Wales.

Figure 7.1: Manufacturing employees in south Wales, 1939–2000 (a, b)

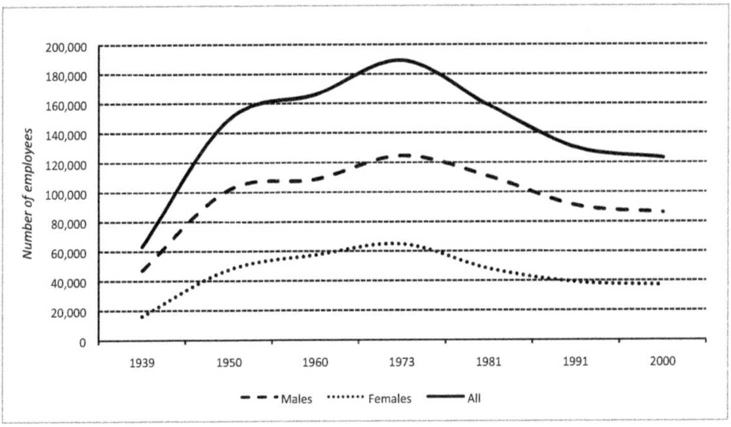

Notes:

(a) Data for 1939 include Carmarthenshire. Data for 1950, 1960 and 1973 include part of Carmarthenshire. Other data exclude Carmarthenshire.

(b) Excludes coal mining and the bulk of metal manufacture.

Sources: See endnotes.[6]

Figure 7.1 outlines trends in manufacturing employment in south Wales after 1939. Three phases are apparent: very rapid growth between the outbreak of war and the early 1950s; slower but continuous growth until the early 1970s; and rapid decline thereafter.

The first phase between 1939 and the early 1950s saw manufacturing employment almost double throughout south Wales.[7] Growth was driven by the war economy: for example, employment in the manufacture of chemicals, paints and oils throughout Wales between 1939 and 1944 increased from 4,000 to 69,000, and in engineering from 11,000 to 48,000 – most in industrial south Wales.[8] Manufacturing became even more diversified after the war, and in 1947 central government noted that new factories were producing 'dairy equipment, carpets, haberdashery, woven blouses, underwear, metal toys, cable sleeves, degreasing plant, brushes, nuts and bolts, tube-making machines, light-weight cycles, upholstery, toy motor cars, cartons, optical goods, piano actions, stud-welding plant, textile printing, springs for road vehicles, and paints'.[9]

The second phase, between the early 1950s and early 1970s, saw manufacturing employment assume a critical importance to south

Wales. It helped to offset the decline of the coal industry, within which employment in south Wales fell from 114,900 in 1945 to 40,300 in 1970.[10] By 1961, Wales was branded a 'land of modern light industry' as huge factories became part of the landscape.[11] As examples, South Wales Switchgear employed 2,000 people in Treforest and Blackwood, Aberdare Cables employed 3,000 people, and 1,500 people worked in the Rover gearbox factory in Cardiff.[12] The dominance of large factories was such that within the statistical sub-regions of 'industrial south Wales', the proportion of the manufacturing workforce employed in factories of more than 500 people stood at 64.8 per cent (west south Wales), 51 per cent (central and eastern valleys) and 51.7 per cent (coastal belt).[13] These large factories often paid relatively high wages, helping to create a more affluent society. By 1968 median manufacturing wages for full-time male workers in Wales stood at 105.4 per cent of the equivalent for Britain, while wages for full-time females stood at 97.4 per cent.[14]

One of the most striking transformations linked to manufacturing was the increased role of women in the workplace. Before the Second World War, women were often restricted to retail and domestic service occupations, but wartime necessity meant that they were needed to staff the new factories. While it was sometimes expected that their greater involvement in the workplace was to be temporary, with an official within central government's Board of Trade (BoT) assuming in 1943 that most women would 'wish to return to their normal peacetime occupation of housewives' after the war,[15] women retained their role. As a result, the number of women in insured occupations throughout Wales grew from 219,400 in 1944 to 269,000 in 1958.[16] While the expanding service sector was an important source of jobs, the new manufacturing industries provided opportunities – even if many jobs were low paid, part-time and semi-skilled. As a result of this growth, women comprised 28 per cent of the labour force in 1961 and 45 per cent by the mid-1970s.[17]

Another trend was the increasingly important role played by foreign direct investment from the 1960s. In 1959 some thirty foreign manufacturing firms existed in Wales, employing around 18,300 people; fifteen years later, 127 overseas firms operated 138 manufacturing units, employing nearly 53,000 employees.[18] Overseas investment was overwhelmingly located in industrial south Wales, and by 1976, three quarters of all foreign-owned employment in Wales was in Mid

Glamorgan, West Glamorgan and Gwent. The construction of the M4 from the 1960s helped to attract these investors, as locating by a motorway could enable easier accessibility for suppliers and employees, as well as to markets. As a result, seventy-eight of the 112 overseas manufacturing establishments in south Wales by 1976 were located within ten miles of the M4, with the motorway playing an important role in regional economic development.[19]

For the manufacturing sector in south Wales, the third phase covering the period after the mid-1970s was primarily characterised by deindustrialisation, but also by some reconstruction. Rapid growth in the first and second phases had been based on attracting subsidiaries of companies headquartered elsewhere. These 'branch plants' accounted for two thirds of the increase in manufacturing employment in Wales in the first half of the 1960s,[20] but such plants were more likely to be shut during downturns than those located closer to the company's headquarters and major domestic markets. The consequences of hosting so many branch plants became apparent in the early 1980s when recession proved disastrous, and the region lost more manufacturing jobs relative to its population than any other area in Britain.[21]

MANUFACTURING AS A STATE-LED DEVELOPMENTAL SOLUTION

Although central government made some efforts through its Commissioner for Special Areas to alleviate economic conditions in south Wales throughout the 1930s, these were small in scale and impact. However, the effectiveness of wartime intervention created a political consensus that central governments should intervene to increase regional prosperity. The drive for intervention was symbolised by Hugh Dalton, Chancellor of the Exchequer, after the Labour Party's 1945 general election victory. He famously promised in 1946 to 'find, with a song in my heart, whatever money is necessary to finance useful and practical proposals for developing these areas', to bring 'them to a condition which they never had in the past, a condition of full and efficient and diversified economic activity'.[22]

Central government intervened through 'regional policy'. Regional policy measures focused on spatial areas defined by central government as needing industrial diversification. These were found throughout the UK where there was a high dependence on heavy industry, with most of south Wales designated as a 'development area' in 1946. While the titles and coverage of these areas changed over time, much of south Wales was always prioritised for intervention. Regional policy measures had three components: regulatory instruments to control industrial location; constructing factories; and awarding financial support to investing companies. Intervention focused on creating the greatest number of jobs, as opposed to building integrated regional economies or stimulating entrepreneurship. While the degree to which regional policy was implemented varied, it was an important part of the postwar Keynesian consensus between the Labour and Conservative parties on economic management that lasted until the mid-1970s.

Regional policy's most important measure was controls over industrial location, with restrictions emerging by the end of the Second World War. Wartime controls were supplanted in 1947 by the BoT's industrial development certificate (IDC) system. All but the smallest industrial developments throughout the UK had to have a certificate before planning permission could be granted. Certificates were far easier to obtain in development areas than in locations such as London. As a result, industrialists planning to open new factories had little choice but to choose areas such as south Wales.

One of the most prominent examples was Hoover's washing machine factory. Having originally intended to locate in the south of England, central government pressure pushed the company to Merthyr Tydfil and it opened a new plant in March 1948. The importance of the large factory to the town and to broader society was recorded in a commemorative book given to the 450 attendees of the opening ceremony, including senior industrialists and politicians travelling from London on a chartered train. Speakers at the ceremony included central government's Minister of Labour and National Service, George Isaacs, who said: 'sunshine . . . will come into the homes and hearts of the people of this valley when they know that there is work and security instead of poverty and insecurity'. After the speeches, a stage production featured an illuminated image of the factory 'visualised as a beacon of promise in an area once dark and depressed', after which there was an evening of dancing.[23]

While the achievement of full employment throughout the 1950s led to some diminution in the application of regional policy, the election of an interventionist Labour government in 1964 led to intensification.

However, subsequent deindustrialisation reduced the effectiveness of the IDC regime. By the end of the 1970s, the number of large factories being opened throughout the UK had fallen from some 1,000 per year to 300, meaning that a 'surplus' of factory jobs in some parts of the UK that could be directed elsewhere did not exist.[24] As a result, the Labour government largely abandoned the use of IDCs in the late 1970s. The certificate system was then suspended by Margaret Thatcher's Conservative government in 1982, before being abolished.

Regional policy's second component was the construction of factories by central government. The war had endowed south Wales with a large stock of industrial floor space, while central government's Wales and Monmouthshire Industrial Estate Corporation (WMIE) embarked on a programme of converting wartime premises and factory construction, totalling 6.5 million sq. ft. (0.6 million sq. m.) across 224 projects by 1946.[25] The availability of modern floor space that could be rented or leased from the WMIE combined with the use of IDCs to enable an influx of industrial activity. While Treforest was the only state-owned industrial estate in south Wales before the war, by 1947 it had been joined by those at Hirwaun, Bridgend and Swansea, where some 7,000 people were employed.[26] By June 1948, 148 companies employing more than 24,000 people had established themselves in south Wales in either converted munitions factories or state-owned factories.[27] The IDC system also enabled a boom in the construction of privately financed factories, many of which were vast. By mid-1948, 152 privately financed factories, totalling 12.2 million sq. ft. (1.1 million sq. m.) of space, were approved for construction, compared to 168 state-financed factories, totalling 5.8 million sq. ft. (0.5 million sq. m.).[28] Factory construction largely ceased in the 1950s as central government believed that full employment removed the need for such activity, although some factories were built in the 1960s.

Regional policy's final component was financial support to investing companies. Although support was initially small in scale, the 1960s saw the creation of complex systems of spatially differentiated grants, loans and other incentives in development areas throughout the UK. By the later 1960s, virtually every manufacturing company in south Wales was receiving subsidies. This UK-wide system reached its peak after 1972's Industry Act, but this level of activity lasted only a few years. Budgetary problems faced by the Labour central government meant that resources were reduced sharply from 1976, while the election of Margaret Thatcher's government in 1979 saw further reductions as part of the new government's desire to reduce levels of state intervention across the economy.

Although central governments withdrew gradually from intervention from the mid-1970s, the creation of the Welsh Office[29] in 1964 enabled some intervention to continue. The most notable Welsh Office intervention was establishing the Welsh Development Agency in 1976.[30] The agency built large numbers of factories in the 1970s and 1980s and made strenuous and successful efforts to attract foreign direct investment to south Wales. Despite success, south Wales was eventually unable to compete with lowercost overseas locations and attracting manufacturing ceased to be a primary solution for south Wales's economic problems.[31]

BRITISH NYLON SPINNERS/ICI, PONTYPOOL

Nylon, an artificial fibre, was developed in the late 1930s by the American owned DuPont Company. By 1939 the patent was licensed to the giant British conglomerate, Imperial Chemical Industries (ICI). However, ICI had little experience in fibre production and needed a development partner. In 1939 it signed a joint venture with Courtaulds, a leading producer of textiles, and British Nylon Spinners (BNS) was established as a jointly owned subsidiary in January 1940.[32] Wartime circumstances made normal development impossible and the new company initially produced small quantities of parachute yarn at sites in Coventry and Suffolk. By 1943 the turning tide of war meant that postwar opportunities could be considered and plans were made for a factory that could manufacture some 7 million lb (3.2 million kg) of yarn, as opposed to the 300,000 lb (136,000 kg) produced in 1942.[33]

The initial plans were to construct the new factory in Oxfordshire and a site was bought in Banbury. However, central government's imposition of location controls stopped development and forced BNS to search for an alternative site. The BoT suggested sites in development areas including Lancashire and central Scotland, but BNS rejected these owing to inadequate road infrastructure or water availability. Others, such as a steeply angled site in Abercarn in the Ebbw valley, were unsuitable for a large development.[34] Finally, a large site at Mamhilad, near

Pontypool, was selected, as it was flat, had room for expansion, good road and rail links and a ready supply of water. While the Ministry of Agriculture would have preferred the factory to have been directed to a more built-up location rather than use agricultural land, the BoT noted that 'it was necessary to let the firm have the site upon which they have set their minds . . . we, as beggars, can't be choosers'.[35] Even at the height of central government intervention in the 1940s, the BoT knew that there was a limit to which it could direct the location of privately run factories. If the location was clearly unsuitable for a large factory, there was a risk that the company would refuse to proceed with any investment, as it was the company and not central government that would incur any financial losses arising from an unsuitable location.

The outcome was 'the biggest factory project in the whole Development Area [of south Wales] and probably in any of the areas [throughout the UK]'.[36] Construction of the 958,000 sq. ft. (89,001 sq. m.) plant commenced in 1945. As was always the case with large-scale projects, many construction jobs were created over the short term as the requirement for 5 million bricks necessitated the reopening of a disused brickworks adjacent to the site.[37] Hampered by shortages of raw materials and labour, as well as by bad weather, construction was delayed and full production was not reached until 1950. By this time, the impressive red-brick factory, with its large 'spinning tower' (see Figure 7.2), dominated the surrounding landscape and was a flagship for industrial regeneration. The factory's symbolic importance was reflected in the choice of its architect, Sir Percy Thomas, whose firm was responsible for many most prominent industrial and commercial buildings throughout Wales, including Swansea's Guildhall, Aberystwyth's university campus, and a complex of factories on the Treforest Industrial Estate.[38]

The 1950s and early 1960s were boom times for the factory, spurred by BNS's patent-protected domestic monopoly on Nylon production, with its uses including socks, hosiery, ropes and filters. As the consumer society expanded, so too did national and international demand for BNS's output, as synthetic fibres captured some 30 per cent of the western European textile market by the 1960s, compared to a negligible level in 1945.[39] By 1956 *The Economist* noted that BNS was 'only barely able to keep up with demand',[40] even though the company's production grew continuously throughout the 1950s and early 1960s,[41] while Pontypool was its largest manufacturing facility. Expansions at Pontypool

Figure 7.2: The 'spinning tower' at British Nylon Spinners, Pontypool, 1948

Source: National Monuments Record of Wales: © Crown Copyright: Percy Thomas Archive.

were frequent given the scale of demand, with the first occurring as early as 1951 when the BoT granted an IDC for a 176,320 sq. ft. (16,372 sq. m.) extension.[42]

The commercial success of BNS was reflected in the remarkable increase in employment at Pontypool. Even before full production was reached, some 2,000 people were employed by mid-1949.[43] Employment then trebled to exceed 6,000 by the early 1960s (see Figure 7.3) and the plant became the largest peacetime factory ever seen in Wales. While most employees were production operatives, many had higher level positions. These included managers as well as the 400 research staff in the plant's in-house research and development function.[44] Everything about the factory was on a huge scale, often creating direct and indirect employment across a range of services and supplies. This included employment linked to the 963,000 meals served each year in its canteen by 1962,[45] while its purpose-built staff club was of a sufficient size to host concerts from leading bands, and shifts competed to see which could host the most successful events. A former employee recalled 'six hundred or so in the clubhouse to watch the latest stars of the sixties – Lulu, Billy J Kramer, The Dave Clark Five, and Freddie and the Dreamers to mention but a few'.[46]

Figure 7.3: Numbers employed at BNS/ICI Pontypool, 1945–2000 (a)

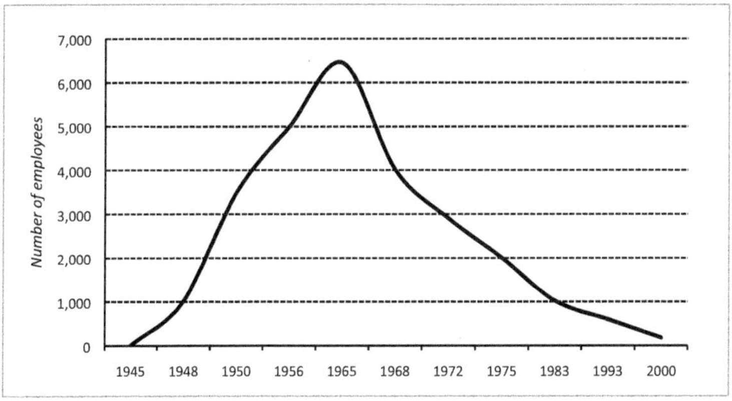

Note: (a) Includes the ICI activities transferred to DuPont in 1993.
Sources: See endnotes.[47]

As was often the case in postwar factories, many posts were filled by women, who accounted for one fifth of staff in the early 1950s.[48] While women may have been able to enter the industrial labour market in greater numbers, barriers remained. A former employee recalled that 'the majority of the people there' in the late 1950s and 1960s 'were men, on the actual factory floor. They didn't like women working shifts in those days. They didn't like women working nights.'[49] Prejudices were illustrated in 1958, when BNS managers told the local branch of the Transport and General Workers' Union that they intended to react to a fall in sales by deactivating some production areas, with reductions to hours worked only applying to women. The branch responded by passing a motion proposing that union policy on employment security be extended to 'single women, widows and married women with proven family responsibilities'.[50] However, wider opinion on the shop floor was strongly opposed, and complaints were made that the meeting at which this motion had been passed was unconstitutional due to a lack of notice. The complaint was upheld by branch officials and the motion was struck out. A new motion was passed instead, proposing that if hours needed to be reduced, management should immediately dismiss married women whose husbands worked before considering reductions elsewhere.[51] Fortunately for female employees, management refused, with this episode mirroring difficulties faced by women throughout the UK's manufacturing sector.[52]

While BNS was headquartered in Pontypool, it was still a branch factory, in that ownership and control lay elsewhere with the London-based boards of Courtaulds and ICI. By the mid-1960s, worsening relationships between the two firms caused Courtaulds to sell its holdings; BNS was renamed as ICI Fibres in 1965. The business was profitable and its future seemed assured. A further 750 jobs were created in the same year, while the plant was strengthened further by its production of a new geotextile called 'Terram', developed in-house at its research and development facility.[53] However, these developments marked the high-water mark of the factory, which now entered a decline even more dramatic than its rise.

Decline was caused by changes within the synthetic fibres market. Throughout much of the 1950s and 1960s, BNS had a monopoly position of the UK's production of nylon and was protected from overseas competition by import tariffs. Despite this seemingly secure position, ICI Fibres encountered difficulties from the late 1960s. First, its patents expired, enabling competitors, ironically including Courtaulds, to enter the market. Secondly, the UK's accession to the European Economic Community (EEC) in 1974 saw the gradual removal of tariffs within the EEC.[54] Finally, overseas competitors such as those from South Korea were increasingly active. The impact on the UK's synthetic textiles industry was devastating. While production of synthetic fibres in the UK grew throughout the 1950s and 1960s, output in the 1970s fell sharply and ICI Fibres became heavily loss making. Overall, employment in the UK's synthetic textiles industry collapsed by 77 per cent between 1975 and 1985, although new technology meant that productivity more than doubled.[55]

Employment at ICI Fibres's Pontypool plant followed a similar trajectory. Job losses were constant throughout the 1970s, and even where investment took place, it focused on productivity. For example, an investment programme and the loss of 600 jobs were announced simultaneously in 1972, with staff pointing out that 'very few jobs' would be created by the investment as new processes were 'highly capital intensive at the expense of labour'.[56] A former employee remarked that many redundancies were linked to 'automation. The shop floor got computerised and so it didn't need the extra person in the office looking after the books, or sample taking.'[57] Throughout the decade, the factory was gradually denuded of staffing and expertise with, for example, research and development being moved to Yorkshire in 1972. In 1977 *The Economist* noted that ICI Fibres had 'trimmed' almost a third of its workforce over the past two years while heavy financial losses were continuing.[58] Employees at Pontypool were by now expressing 'deep concern' as to job security and the future of the plant,[59] an understandable reaction given that employment in the factory had dropped by 65 per cent from its 1966 peak. The plant continued to shed jobs at an alarming rate, with 450 being lost in 1979, 260 in 1980 and 350 in 1981.[60] Symbolically but inevitably, the factory's famous social club was sold in 1983 and later demolished.

Difficulties continued after 1985 with, for example, company records from 1993 noting that the 'fibres business is suffering from very difficult trading conditions'.[61] Productivity gains continued, but competing with companies based in locations with far cheaper operating costs remained difficult. In 1992 DuPont, the original inventor of nylon, acquired ICI Fibres's nylon business and closed the Pontypool plant's production lines in the following year with the loss of 400 jobs, stating that 'despite the Pontypool Nylon Plant's impressive record of continuous improvement in quality and production . . . production can no longer be justified'. The immediate cause of closure was excess capacity within DuPont, with Pontypool being vulnerable as its capacity was less than half that of the company's main European plant in Germany.[62] The latter was more able to exploit economies of scale, while the UK's increasingly lax employment legislation meant that it was easier for DuPont to carry out redundancies in Pontypool than at factories elsewhere in Europe. After the end of nylon production, some 180 employees remained at the Pontypool complex. Most produced polyester for DuPont, with the remainder producing Terram for an eponymous company. However, another takeover, this time by the Turkish company Sabancı, led to all activity ceasing after 2000. By this time, the huge complex was mostly deserted, acting as a monument to industrial decline only forty years after its construction as a symbol of the new industry designed to secure the region's employment base.

ENFIELD CABLES/DUNLOP SEMTEX, BRYNMAWR

In 1945 Brynmawr was a small town of perhaps 6,000 inhabitants situated at a height of some 1,500 ft (457m), at the point where the uplands of the Brecon Beacons met the south Wales valleys. In common with its neighbours, the town was built to service the coal industry and became infamous during the interwar period for its high unemployment, with 74 per cent of insured males being unemployed in 1934.[63] Some relief efforts were made by the Society of Friends, whose organisation of outdoor public works and development of small-scale industries manufacturing tweed, boots and furniture created a limited number of jobs, known as the 'Brynmawr experiment'.[64] While these interwar attempts to generate employment created few jobs and could not solve the town's economic problems, they were to combine with central government's aim of increasing regional prosperity to create a bold attempt to inject large-scale manufacturing into the area: the Brynmawr rubber factory.

In May 1945 the managing director of London-based Enfield Cables announced at a meeting with the BoT in Cardiff that his company wanted to develop a rubber products factory in Brynmawr to 'alleviate the anticipated unemployment in the area'.[65] This was very unusual, in that companies did not normally choose to locate in such areas, with the entire apparatus of regional policy having to be deployed to force them to do. The reason behind Enfield Cables's keenness to locate in Brynmawr related to its director, Lord James Forrester. He had spent time in Brynmawr in the early 1930s as part of the 'Brynmawr experiment' and was a member of the Industrial Welfare Society, formed to encourage industrialists to improve working conditions. He became the director of Enfield Cables in 1939 and had little contact with Brynmawr throughout the war, but his idealism had been fired and he was determined to return. By 1945 his commercial experience combined with his interest in welfare, architecture and Brynmawr to enable an idea to germinate.

He was to locate a factory in the town, but commercial considerations were secondary. The factory would instead repair Brynmawr's social fabric by creating 1,000 jobs in a building that Lord Forrester intended to be an 'outstanding factory in an out-of-the way place'.[66]

No ordinary brick factory would suffice and Lord Forrester hired an untested team of young architects, with engineering support provided by Ove Arup, founder of the eponymous engineering consultancy. Unusually for factory construction at the time, engineering and architecture fused during the design process to create a distinctive building of some 275,000 sq. ft. (25,458 sq. m.) that was characterised by clean lines. Its nine large concrete domes pierced with circular windows created a spacious and bright working environment. Individual touches abounded, ranging from canteen facilities that were not grade-divided, to an unusual spiral staircase that accessed the boiler house. The staircase lacked a stabilising pillar, normally a vital structural component. It had been designed after Lord Forrester had seen a staircase in Switzerland apparently constructed without a pillar. He described it to Ove Arup who produced a design as instructed, although Lord Forrester later realised that the original staircase had, unsurprisingly, a stabilising pillar.[67] The company's philanthropic ideals and its pride in the new factory were apparent in 1949 when it organised a one-day tour for London-based industrialists. They were invited 'to study the establishment of new industry in a Development Area . . . to show something of what one industrial concern, coming from the more prosperous areas of Britain, is trying to do towards the rehabilitation of this forgotten corner of Wales'. [68]

While the press were delighted, with the *Architectural Review* noting that Enfield and the WMIE had created 'not only a good factory but an idea for a factory',[69] and a model of the factory was exhibited at the Festival of Britain in 1951, its construction exposed the shortcomings of Lord Forrester's idealistic approach. The WMIE's records are a litany of annoyance at the project's cost and complexity, noting in 1948 that 'this scheme is becoming more of a nightmare every day!' and bemoaning the 'incredible happenings'.[70] One such 'happening' was Lord Forrester's attempt to have the east elevation constructed from expensive glass bricks for what the WMIE diplomatically described as 'psychological and artistic reasons'.[71] He was eventually persuaded to accept large expanses of normal glazing, with a BoT official wearily arguing that 'windows are probably essential, but does he need such large windows?'[72] Enfield was given a long lease on the factory, whose cost was initially estimated as £455,000 but had doubled to £800,000 by the time of its completion, some three times the normal cost for a factory of its size.[73] The WMIE described this excess cost as 'social expenditure',[74] acceptable given central government's policy of using all measures to push manufacturing industries to locations where more jobs were most needed.

The factory opened in 1951 with 428 staff, 40 per cent of whom were female,[75] reflecting how the postwar influx of manufacturing created opportunities for women in an area where opportunities had been limited before the war. However, if the gap between what the BoT wryly described as Lord Forrester's 'fertile imagination'[76] and commercial reality was apparent during the construction process, it was even more obvious once the factory opened in autumn of 1951. It had been designed and equipped to produce rubber goods, but orders were in short supply. Philanthropic ideals had obscured commercial reality to the extent that the management of Enfield Cables had given little consideration as to what the factory was going to produce. The BoT noted retrospectively in 1952 that there was 'little evidence that the firm themselves had any clear ideas, apart from a general desire to produce rubber articles'.[77] The factory's chief production officer later remarked that 'no one knew anything about plastics and rubber, they didn't intend to make money . . . you had to use manpower – even if you designed a machine, it wasn't used'.[78] After a few months of operation, the factory's precarious finances were causing deep concern within the plant's parent company. While Lord Forrester was assiduously using his contact book to find work for the factory, financial losses could not be sustained by Enfield Cables. Its board of directors voted to cease subsidising its Brynmawr operation in May 1952, less than a year after production commenced.

However, having spent so much money on what the BoT recognised as a 'symbol of the Development Area policy',[79] the government was determined to find an alternative tenant. Discreet approaches were made to several firms before Dunlop Rubber Company's Semtex Division purchased the lease, with a relieved BoT noting that the new tenants were 'determined to go to town in a big way . . . we can all feel a good deal happier about the ultimate use of the factory than we did under its previous ownership'.[80] Dunlop Rubber Company specialised in tyre manufacture and it was firmly established as one of the UK's leading multinational companies. The factory's role now changed from a grand experiment in industrial welfare to a normal branch factory operation. While Enfield Cables had struggled to produce marketable goods, Dunlop was initially to have no such difficulties. The factory specialised in producing vinyl and rubber floor coverings (one of which was named Semtex), with demand created by the postwar expansion of the welfare state and new schools, hospitals and universities. Dunlop's Brynmawr factory expanded after 1957 and employment grew to 860. By 1964 demand for flooring products was 'booming',[81] spurring Dunlop to purchase the factory from the WMIE. The company funded and constructed an extension to the plant, and well over 1,000 people were employed on site by the mid-1960s.

Despite optimism, expansion coincided with a change in fortunes from the mid-1960s. New machinery enabled hard-wearing carpets to be produced, often overseas, at a cost equivalent to vinyl flooring. Buyers increasingly chose these warmer carpets over the somewhat utilitarian vinyl or rubber alternatives. The factory attempted to diversify, producing carpet underlay and patterned 'vinlay' floor tiles, but the decline in its main market proved impossible to offset and the plant was loss making by the late 1970s. At the same time, its parent company was imperilled by the near-collapse of car manufacturing in the UK and the inefficiency of its tyre plants relative to overseas competitors. As a result, the once mighty Dunlop Rubber Company was struggling to survive as its UK employment fell from 43,000 people in 1978 to 22,000 by the early 1980s.[82]

Dunlop's urgent need to stem losses throughout its operations coincided with depressed trading conditions, and 430 redundancies were announced at Brynmawr in 1980. In late 1981 a further round of redundancies was announced, followed by an industrial dispute accompanied by workforce demands for the job losses to be withdrawn. The dispute developed into a six-week occupation of the factory in December 1981 and January 1982, enlivened on Christmas Day by what the *Western Mail* described as 'dozens of Santa Clauses in civvies' bearing 'gifts of food and bottles of Christmas spirit' for the workers in occupation.[83] However, Christmas spirit was in short supply within Dunlop's central management, who noted in early January that the plant was losing £60,000 of turnover a day and that the remaining staff should not 'wait forever to make up their mind' about returning to work.[84] Within days, the management had lost patience and closed the plant with the loss of 600 jobs, arguing that 'recent events have undermined the whole basis of its Brynmawr operation and that [there was] no alternative but to close it completely'.[85] In reality, while the plant may have been able to continue, large-scale investment would have been needed to ensure competitiveness against overseas producers. In the end, the factory was overwhelmed by the urgent need of the parent company to immediately staunch losses to remain solvent.

Figure 7.4: Enfield Cables/Dunlop Semtex, Brynmawr.

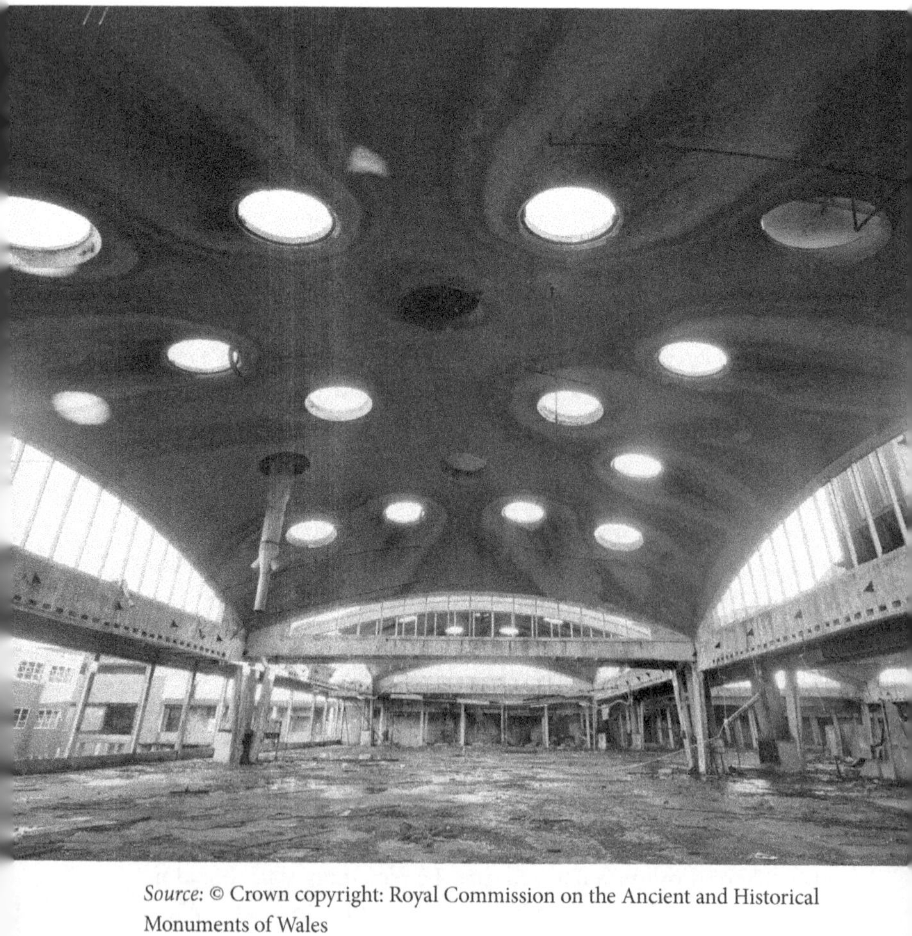

Source: © Crown copyright: Royal Commission on the Ancient and Historical Monuments of Wales

Although the factory's unique architecture (see figure 7.4) gifted it a strange and prolonged afterlife, being Grade II* listed in 1986, finding viable alternative uses for such a large and distinctive building proved impossible. The empty factory was eventually demolished after much controversy and its site is now occupied by a supermarket, although the boiler house remains, albeit in a state of advanced dereliction.

CONCLUSION

While the trajectories of BNS/ICI Fibres and Dunlop Semtex have their unique elements, they illustrate trends that characterised the rise and fall of manufacturing in south Wales throughout the postwar era. First, they provided large volumes of relatively well-paid employment, including new opportunities for women to join the waged workforce. Secondly, the role of government was crucial. Even in the case of the Brynmawr factory whose initial owner, Enfield Cables, was unusually keen to locate in one of the most economically underperforming areas of south Wales, the government played an important role.

Construction costs for the Brynmawr factory to be leased by Enfield Cables were met by central government's WMIE, while the BoT played a key role in attracting Dunlop to purchase the lease after Enfield's failure. State intervention was also apparent with BNS as regional policy instruments forced them to invest in a development area, while their factory was also built by the WMIE. The extent to which the trauma of the 1930s was still a recent memory meant that the cost to the state of building factories was little questioned by contemporaries, given the scale of the employment benefits obtained by the local workforce. Thirdly, both factories reflected the extent to which the industrial economy of south Wales was integrated into that of the UK. Ownership and ultimate control rested outside of Wales, as did the economic determinants of their rise and decline. Finally, their presence was short-lived. Enfield Cables/Dunlop Semtex only lasted some thirty years, and although BNS/ICI Fibres reached its fiftieth anniversary in 1996, it was a fraction of its former size, with the decline of both factories mirroring broader trends of deindustrialisation in south Wales and the UK.

The determination of postwar central governments to restructure the industrial economy of south Wales was executed successfully, but only over the short-term. State intervention helped to offset the impact of declining employment within the coal industry, but a relative overdependence on coal was replaced with a similar emphasis on manufacturing branch plants. While this did not matter when the UK's manufacturing sector was growing, its presence in south Wales was overwhelmed by rapid deindustrialisation from the 1960s, even if the sector did not disappear as did the deep coal-mining industry.

Given the short-lived nature of some manufacturing plants, it is tempting to conclude that the policy was mistaken and that governments should have instead attempted to build up indigenous momentum. However, the reality is more nuanced. Historic overdependence on the coal industry, limited levels of commercial entrepreneurship and the rapid rundown of wartime industries combined to create a requirement for large numbers of jobs to be created quickly. The only realistic source of such jobs was manufacturing attracted from elsewhere. If central government had focused instead on indigenous development, then the full employment of the 1950s and 1960s would almost certainly not have happened. Creating greater volumes of home-grown business through state action was, and remains, very difficult. Finally, deindustrialisation was on a scale that few observers predicted, as demonstrated by the investment plans pursued by both BNS and Dunlop Semtex in the mid-1960s.

While regional policy was effective over the short-term, it did little to secure a long-term economic base for south Wales. In many respects, it simply swapped one type of dependence on externally focused economic investment for another, perpetuating the inability of the economy to renew itself without large-scale assistance. The cycle of ebbing and flowing waves of external investment that had long characterised the economy of south Wales continued in the 1970s and beyond, eventually leading to dislocation and disappointment.

NOTES

1 'Central government' in this chapter refers to the UK-wide government based in London.

2 G. Humphreys, *Industrial Britain - South Wales* (Newton Abbott: David and Charles, 1973), p. 64.

3 For contemporary studies of manufacturing, see Humphreys, *Industrial Britain – South Wales*, and B. Thomas (ed), *The Welsh Economy: Studies in Expansion* (Cardiff: University of Wales Press, 1962).

4 L. J. Williams, *Digest of Welsh Historical Statistics*, vol. 1 (Cardiff: Welsh Office, 1985), pp. 17, 20.

5 Williams, *Digest of Welsh Historical Statistics*, vol. 1, pp. 113, 115.

6 Fully consistent sectoral labour market time series data are not available at sub-Wales level. Graphed data are not strictly comparable over time given methodological variation. They are primarily derived from: **1939**, D. A. Thomas, 'War and the Economy: The South Wales Experience', in C. Baber and L. J. Williams (eds), *Modern South Wales: Essays in Economic History* (Cardiff: University of Wales Press, 1986), pp. 251–77 (pp. 270–1); **1950, 1960**, Humphreys, *Industrial Britain – South Wales*, p. 44; **1973**, Welsh Office, *Welsh Economic Trends No. 2*, **1975** (Cardiff: Welsh Office, 1975), p. 14; **1981**, *Welsh Office, Welsh Economic Trends No. 10*, **1986** (Cardiff: Welsh Office, 1986), p. 19; **1991**, Welsh Office, Welsh Economic Trends No. 16, **1995** (Cardiff: Welsh Office, 1995), pp. 104, 106, 108, 109; **2001**, StatsWales (online) *https://statswales.gov.wales/Catalogue* (accessed 23 April 2017).

7 Thomas, 'War and the Economy', p. 271. Carmarthenshire included in these data; Humphreys, *Industrial Britain - South Wales*, p. 44.

8 Thomas (ed.), *The Welsh Economy*, p. 31.

9 *Wales and Monmouthshire, Report of Government Action for the Year Ended 30th June 1949* (Cmd 7820) (London: Her Majesty's Stationery Office, 1949), p. 17.

10 Williams, *Digest of Welsh Historical Statistics*, vol. 1, p. 308.

11 Development Corporation of Wales, *Wales: Land of Industrial Opportunity* (Cardiff: Development Corporation of Wales, 1962), p. 5.

12 Humphreys, *Industrial Britain - South Wales*, pp. 131, 133.

13 *Welsh Economic Trends No. 2*, 1975, p. 36.

14 Department of Employment and Productivity, *New Earnings Survey, 1968* (London: Her Majesty's Stationery Office, 1968), pp. 42, 44, 100.

15 The National Archives [hereafter TNA], BT 64/3129, *Note by Board of Trade*, 3 August 1943.

16 Thomas (ed.), *The Welsh Economy*, p. 42.

17 J. Davies, 'Wales in the nineteen sixties', *Llafur*, 4/4 (1987), 79.

18 G. Davies and I. Thomas, *Overseas Investment in Wales: The Welcome Invasion* (Swansea: C. Davies, 1976), pp. 10, 21, 23.

19 Davies and Thomas, *Overseas Investment*, pp. 11, 53; M. Johnes, 'M4 to Wales – and prosper! The history of a motorway', *Historical Research*, 87/237 (2014), 556–73 (561).

20 Commission on the Constitution, *Research Paper 8, Survey of the Welsh Economy* (London: Her Majesty's Stationery Office, 1975), p. 56.

21 J. England, *The Wales TUC: Devolution and Industrial Politics* (Cardiff: University of Wales Press, 2004), p. 83.

22 Hansard, HC Deb, 9 April 1946, vol. 421, *c.*1808.

23 *The Official Opening of the Hoover Factory at Pentrebach, Merthyr Tydfil*, 12 October 1948 (Hoover, 1948), pp. 41, 56, 58.

24 P. Balchin, *Regional Policy in Britain: The North-South Divide* (London: Chapman, 1987), p. 67.

25 G. Percival, *The Government's Industrial Estates in Wales 1936–1975* (Treforest: Welsh Development Agency, 1978), p. 55.

26 Percival, *The Government's Industrial Estates in Wales*, appendix.

27 *Statement on the Distribution of Industry in Relation to Development Areas* (Cmd 7540) (London: Her Majesty's Stationery Office, 1948), appendix 8.

28 *Wales and Monmouthshire, Report of Government Action for the Year Ended 30th June 1948* (Cmd 7532) (London: Her Majesty's Stationery Office, 1948), p. 17.

29 An administratively devolved department of central government responsible for some aspects of government activity in Wales. Based in Cardiff and headed by a cabinet-level Secretary of State for Wales, its initial responsibilities were modest but gradually expanded over time.

30 See below, chapter 8: L. Gooberman and T. Boyns, 'The Welsh Development Agency: Activities and Impact, 1976–2006'.

31 Gooberman and Boyns, 'The Welsh Development Agency'.

32 W. J. Reader, *Imperial Chemical Industries. Volume Two: The First Quarter-Century 1926–1952* (Oxford: Oxford University Press, 1975), pp. 372–4.

33 D. C. Coleman, *Courtaulds, An Economic and Social History: Vol. III – Crisis and Change, 1940–1965* (Oxford: Clarendon Press, 1980), p. 78.

34 A. Elliott, *History of British Nylon Spinners* (Abertillery: Old Bakehouse Publications, 2010), p. 8.

35 TNA, HLG 79/1488, *BoT Note*, 10 April 1945.

36 Monmouthshire County Council, *Industrial Monmouthshire: Official County Guide, 4th edition* (London: Monmouthshire County Council, n.d. [after 1952 and before 1955]), p. 34.

37 Elliott, *History of British Nylon Spinners*, p. 15.

38 E. Davey and H. Thomas, ' "Chief creator of modern Wales": the neglected legacy of Percy Thomas', *North American Journal of Welsh Studies*, 9 (2014), 54–70.

39 R. Shaw and P. Simpson, 'Synthetic Fibres', in Peter Johnson (ed.), *The Structure of British Industry* (London: Unwin Hyman, 1988), pp. 119–39 (p. 120).

40 'Nylon's Strength', *The Economist*, 22 December 1956.

41 Coleman, *Courtaulds, An Economic and Social History*, pp. 79, 179.
42 TNA, HLG 79/1488, *BoT Note*, 3 December 1951.
43 *Government Action, 1949* (Cmd 7820) (London: Her Majesty's Stationery Office, 1949), p. 18
44 Elliott, *History of British Nylon Spinners*, p. 102.
45 Elliott, *History of British Nylon Spinners*, p. 120.
46 *The Pontypool Site, 1948–1998, The First Fifty Years* (Pontypool: DuPont, 1998), p. 11.
47 Consistent time-series not available. These derived from: **1948, 1950**, TNA, HLG 79/1488, *BoT Note* (undated); 1956, Elliott, *History of British Nylon Spinners*, p. 33. **1964, 1965**, *Pontypool Site, The First Fifty Years*, pp. 9, 12. **1966**, Welsh Office, *Wales*, 1966 (Cardiff: Welsh Office, 1966), p. 14; **1968**, *The Times*, 1 March 1968; **1972**, following redundancies referenced in Hansard, 27 July 1971, and *The Times*, 7 November 1972; **1975**, *The Times*, 10 March 1975; **1983**, Gwent Archives (hereafter GA), D4211/2/2, Weekly Staff Numbers; **1993**, GA, D4211/2/4, Weekly Staff Numbers; **2000**, following earlier closure of nylon production with loss of 400 jobs.
48 TNA, HLG 79/1488, *BoT (Wales) Note*, undated.
49 Women's Archive Wales, 'Voices from the Factory Floor', interview with Sheila Hughes, 29 November 2013, p. 6, *http://www.factorywomensvoices.wales/uploads/VSE009.2.pdf* (accessed 5 September 2016).
50 GA, D4211/1/2: *Branch 4/162 T&GWU Minutes*, 11 April 1959, pp. 65–7.
51 GA, D4211/1/2, *Branch 4/162 T&GWU Minutes*, 23 April 1959, pp. 74–5.
52 S. Boston, *Women Workers and the Trade Unions* (London: Lawrence and Wishart, 2015), pp. 246–65.
53 *Pontypool Site, The First Fifty Years*, p. 12.
54 Shaw and Simpson, 'Synthetic Fibres', p. 123.
55 Shaw and Simpson, 'Synthetic Fibres', pp. 134–5.
56 'ICI Fibres Plan at Pontypool', *The Times*, 7 November 1972.
57 Women's Archive Wales, 'Voices from the Factory Floor', interview with Audrey Grey, 22 April 2014, p. 14, *http://www.factorywomensvoices.wales/uploads/VSE050.2.pdf* (accessed 5 September 2016).
58 'Heading for Losses of $900 million', *The Economist*, 12 March 1977.
59 GA, D4211.2.2, *Works Committee Minutes*, 21 September 1977.
60 House of Commons, *The Impact of Regional Industrial Policy on Wales. Report of House of Commons Committee on Welsh Affairs* (appendices) (London: Her Majesty's Stationery Office, 1983–4), p. 230.
61 GA, D4211.2.4, *Works Committee Minutes*, March 1993.
62 GA, D4211.5.3, *Closure of Nylon Operations, Pontypool*, October 1993.
63 'The Plight of South Wales', *The Economist*, 19 December 1936.
64 Some sixty jobs had been created by 1931. See P. Mannaseh, 'Brynmawr experiment 1928–1940: Quaker values and Arts and Crafts principles' (unpublished PhD thesis, University of Plymouth, 2009), p. 217.

65 V. Perry, *Built for a Better Future: The Brynmawr Rubber Factory* (Oxford: White Cockade Publishing, 1995), p. 21.
66 'Brynmawr', *The Architectural Review*, May 1952.
67 Perry, *Built for a Better Future*, p. 51.
68 TNA, BT 177/ *Limited Requests the Honour of Your Company in South Wales*, 19 July 1949.
69 'Brynmawr', *The Architectural Review*, May 1952.
70 TNA BT 177/1136, *Wales and Monmouthshire Industrial Estates (WMIE) to BoT*, 5 October 1948, 21 June 1948.
71 TNA, 177/1138, *WMIE to BoT*, 15 August 1949.
72 TNA, 177/1138, *Letter from BoT to WMIE*, 30 August 1949.
73 Perry, *Built for a Better Future*, pp. 47–8; TNA, BT 177/1133, *BoT Internal Memorandum*, 20 May 1952.
74 TNA, BT 177/1133, *BoT Internal Memorandum*, 20 May 1952.
75 TNA, BT 177/1133, *BoT Note*, 20 May 1952.
76 TNA, BT 177/1133, *BoT Wales to Board of Trade London*, undated.
77 TNA, BT 177/1133, *BoT Internal Memorandum*, 15 May 1952.
78 Perry, *Built for a Better Future*, p. 56.
79 TNA, BT 177/1133, *BoT Internal Memorandum*, 20 May 1952.
80 TNA, BT 177/1133, *Letter from WMIE to BoT*, 26 February 1955.
81 'Expansion Plans by Dunlop Semtex', *The Times*, 14 September 1964.
82 J. McMillan, *The Dunlop Story* (London: Wiedenfield and Nicholson, 1989), p. 176.
83 'Santa Bounce for Dunlop Sit-In', *Western Mail*, 28 December 1981.
84 'Dunlop Hold Sit-In Talks', *Western Mail*, 5 January 1981.
85 Hansard, HC Deb, 28 January 1982, vol. 16, *c*.402W.

THE WELSH DEVELOPMENT AGENCY
ACTIVITIES AND IMPACT, 1976–2006

LEON GOOBERMAN AND TREVOR BOYNS

INTRODUCTION

IN THE 1970s and 1980s, echoing events elsewhere but to a much larger extent, unemployment in Wales surged to levels not previously seen in the postwar era as the traditional industries of coal and metal manufacture declined rapidly. The postwar decline of the coal industry had previously been offset by central governments'[1] deployment of regional policies to boost manufacturing by constructing factories, awarding grants to companies investing in priority areas, and using regulatory instruments to direct industry to these areas.[2] However, economic turbulence throughout the UK meant that resources for regional policy were increasingly absent by the mid-1970s. From 1979 the government of Margaret Thatcher further downgraded regional policy, given her ideological emphasis on reducing the level of state intervention. The lessening application of regional policy coincided with worsening economic conditions in Wales, where employment in the steel, coal and manufacturing industries fell by 124,000 people between 1979 and 1983.[3]

Despite central government's changing priorities, the existence of an administratively devolved Welsh Office[4] allowed some regional assistance to continue. The primary vehicle for Welsh Office intervention from 1976 was the Welsh Development Agency (WDA). The agency's role was set out by the eponymous Act of 1975 and included: promoting Wales as a location for industrial development; providing finance to industry; promoting or assisting 'the establishment, growth, modernisation or development of an industry'; providing and managing industrial sites and premises; and reclaiming derelict land.[5] A Development Board for Rural Wales was also established to exercise similar functions in mid-Wales.

The WDA was established as a statutory body with its own board because it was required to work closely with industry, a task that required different skills from those typically found in the civil service. According to John Morris, Secretary of State for Wales in the 1974–9 Labour government, there was a need to 'go outside and bring in industry . . . set up bodies which were arm's length from the government and the civil service'.[6] The WDA was a relatively small organisation, employing between 400 and 500 people at any one time between 1976 and 1999. However, it subsequently doubled in size to 996 people by 2003–4,[7] due to changing priorities and the increased resources available after political devolution. The agency was funded by the Welsh Office (and the Welsh Government[8] after 1999), supplemented by rental and sales income from its property portfolio. Annual expenditure generally rose above inflation, reaching £61.3 million in 1979–80, £93.8 million in 1987–8, and £140 million in 1998–9 before more than doubling in the early years of devolution to £312.3 million by 2004–5.[9]

Crucially, the agency retained political support from most Secretaries of State for Wales until 1999, as they favoured the WDA's activities given the economic difficulties facing Wales.[10] The exception was the mid-1990s when the less interventionist John Redwood was in post and the agency was suffering from reputational damage caused by criticism of its management culture.[11] After 1999 the Welsh Government was determined to address economic issues, setting ambitious growth targets and vastly increasing the WDA's resources. Despite such ambitions, economic performance remained mixed, contributing to disappointment with the agency and its merger with the Welsh Government's civil service in April 2006.

The WDA deserves study for two reasons. One is that despite the agency's scale and profile, an assessment of its activities and impact over the entirety of its thirty-year lifespan is not present in the literature.[12]

The other is that the decision by the Welsh Government to merge the WDA remains controversial. Calls are occasionally made by politicians and commentators for its reinstatement, meaning that a review of the agency's achievements is timely.

This chapter asks: what impact did the agency's activities have on economic and social development in Wales during its thirty-year existence, and what legacy did it leave for the future? It draws on the WDA's board papers as available from the UK's National Archives; contemporary documentation including newspapers and official publications; and interviews with former agency staff and politicians, to argue that the picture is somewhat mixed. The WDA's initial interventions did generate some success and create employment through encouraging foreign inward investment, establishing industrial premises and trading estates, and encouraging business start-ups and fostering their longer term development. In particular, the WDA managed a comprehensive programme of land reclamation and the regeneration of many cities, towns and villages, transforming the environment for much of the population. However, the agency was less successful in encouraging a shift away from reliance on manufacturing towards the service sector, and its overall effectiveness declined from the mid-1990s.

INDUSTRIAL PROPERTY

Economic regeneration policies of central government throughout the postwar era prioritised the construction of factories on new industrial estates. By 1976 the state-owned Welsh Industrial Estates Corporation and its predecessors had constructed some 1.4 million sq. m. of floor space across seven industrial estates and 168 other sites.[13] The largest estates were at Treforest, Hirwaun, Waterton (Bridgend), Swansea and Wrexham. All were transferred to the WDA in 1976 and the agency initiated a large-scale construction effort. Between the start of 1977 and March 1979, seven construction programmes were announced involving 499 factories covering some 0.2 million sq. m. These buildings were known as 'advance factories' as they were constructed without confirmed tenants before being marketed to potential occupiers. Factories were developed throughout Wales, although sixty-eight were located in Ebbw Vale and south Cardiff, both affected by the closure or part-closure of steel plants.[14] Due to the lack of space in the congested valleys, large estates were constructed in the unlikely locations of Rassau and Tafarnaubach, bleak and windswept sites high above Ebbw Vale.[15] By 1979, 58,900 people were employed on industrial estates or factories owned by the agency across 1.47 million sq. m. of floor space.[16]

Activity increased again after the election of Margaret Thatcher in 1979 as the WDA desperately sought to create jobs against the backdrop of deep industrial recession and the brutal rationalisation of the steel industry in Wales and elsewhere. While the construction of advance factories was common throughout many parts of the UK, the influence of the Welsh Office enabled more factories to be built in Wales than was the case in English regions.[17] Between December 1979 and March 1980 the WDA announced the construction of 356 factories, comprising some 0.2 million sq. m. of floor space. The scale of construction meant that sixty-four factories were completed over one two-month period in mid-1982,[18] but many were impossible to let, given that manufacturing throughout the UK was struggling to an unexpected extent. High vacancy levels spurred a change in emphasis and the agency's first corporate plan in 1984 marked 'the end of the period when the majority of the agency's resources were devoted to providing factories in advance of need'.[19]

The volume of factories built then dropped drastically, from *c.*230,000 sq. m. in 1981–2 to *c.*28,000 sq. m. by 1984–5 (see Figure 8.1), although increasing levels of overseas investment led to subsequent growth as factories were built to attract and house those investors. Also, factories tended to be built in locations more attractive to investors, which meant a shift in focus from the south Wales valleys in favour of sites closer to good transport links, such as the M4 in south Wales and the A55 in north Wales. By 1989–90 total floor space in WDA factories stood at over 1.8 million sq. m.

Economic trends apparent throughout the UK in the mid-1980s and beyond impacted on the factory programme in Wales. Manufacturing became increasingly focused on technology as opposed to traditional assembly-type operations, spurring the construction of high-specification technology and innovation centres. Four were constructed by 1985–6, totalling 19,000 sq. m. of floor space, including one on the Deeside Industrial Estate. Other efforts to foster high technology included a science park at Newport and a medical technology centre in Cardiff.[20] Crucially, the UK's economy was shifting from manufacturing towards services, with correspondingly fewer investors willing to locate factories

Figure 8.1: WDA property activity, 1976–7 to 1989–90 (a)

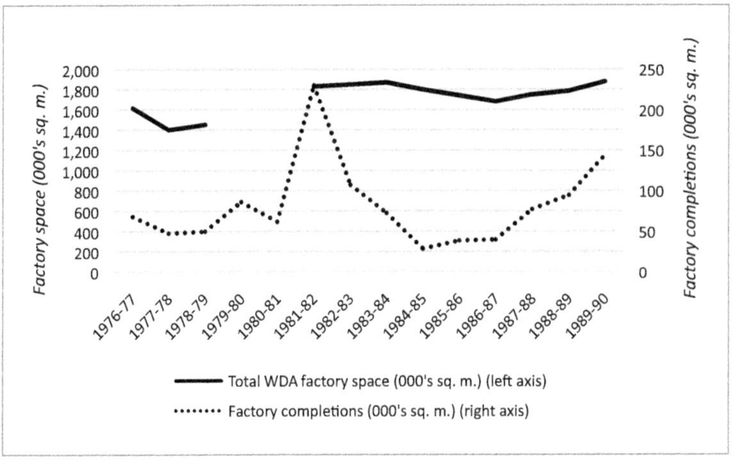

Note: (a) Factory space data not available for 1979–80 and 1980–1.
Source: WDA annual reports, various editions.

in Wales. However, limited effort was made to increase the supply of offices and other types of property more suitable for service sector occupiers. As a result, the agency's portfolio overwhelmingly comprised standard factories, later labelled by Jim Driscoll, the Secretary of State's industrial advisor, as 'diarrhoea coloured boxes'.[21]

By the 1990s the agency was moving away from direct intervention in the property market, with this change symbolised by the absence of such data in its annual reports from 1991–2. At the same time, political developments within the Welsh Office caused the agency's estate to be broken up. While all previous Secretaries of State had been strong supporters of the WDA, this changed after the appointment of John Redwood in 1993. His free market ideology meant that he was opposed to large-scale interventions and the agency was instructed to sell its portfolio. As a result, the agency's tangible assets reduced from £274 million in 1993–4 to £89 million in 1997–8.[22] The disposal programme was predicated on the basis that private sector developers would construct premises, but they were often reluctant to do so. By the end of the 1990s the WDA's former estate was largely in private hands. The agency's large-scale construction programmes ceased, although it still constructed bespoke premises for inward investors. The years following devolution in 1999 saw the agency construct 'technium' facilities such as those at Swansea and Bangor. These were designed to support high-technology activities but created few jobs and the programme was eventually cancelled.[23]

Four periods can be identified in assessing the WDA's construction programmes, with the agency's effectiveness gradually decreasing over time. First, the late 1970s saw the agency continue with an approach rooted in postwar regional policy, effective given the continuing importance of manufacturing. Secondly, during the early 1980s recession, the construction of advance factories and their subsequent occupation by manufacturing investors enabled jobs to be created quickly. Crucially, interventions during both periods delivered additional outputs as factories were constructed in locations where the private sector was reluctant to invest. However, during the third period of the late 1980s and 1990s, the agency did not shift its approach from manufacturing towards services and its impact dissipated. This was due to a reluctance to move away from its 'glory days' of constructing advance factories and bespoke units for overseas investors; the difficulty of intervening in the service sector where investors, influenced by poor perceptions as to skills and infrastructure, were often reluctant to locate in Wales, even when suitable properties were available; and the temporary refocusing of Welsh Office policies in the mid-1990s away from intervention. During the final period after political devolution, some property activity continued but at a relatively low level and met with mixed success.

LAND RECLAMATION AND URBAN REGENERATION

While the economic impacts of structural change spurred the agency to intervene through factory construction, such change also left a physical legacy of land made derelict by resource-based industry such as mineral extraction and metal manufacturing. Central and local government paid little attention to dereliction until the Aberfan disaster of 1966, when a coal tip avalanched into a primary school and surrounding area, killing 116 children and twenty-eight adults. Large-scale land clearance programmes funded by the Welsh Office soon followed, with the scale of the problem illustrated by a 1975 survey that identified 2,685 derelict sites throughout Wales.[24] Forty-six per cent of these were disused spoil heaps linked to the mining of minerals such as slate, copper and coal, with the balance made up of disused mineral excavations, derelict buildings or partially derelict sites where commercial activity was continuing.

In 1976 the WDA inherited land clearance responsibility from the Welsh Office's derelict land unit. The new agency planned for reclamation to be its second-most resourced activity (after factory construction) between 1976–7 and 1981–2, and such activity accounted for some 20 per cent of its total allocations by 1983–4.[25] Although the WDA did not generally carry out reclamation projects itself and instead provided grants to local authorities, it was responsible for the management, control and funding of the entire programme. When assessing sites proposed for clearance, the legacy of Aberfan meant that the WDA prioritised those with safety, flooding or contamination issues, followed by sites with potential to be reused as locations for factories or housing and, finally, those with potential for leisure usage or environmental enhancement.[26] Annual clearance totals varied (see Table 8.1), as a

Table 8.1: Derelict land clearance funded by the WDA, 1978–9 to 2005–6 (a)

Year	Land reclaimed (hectares)	Year	Land reclaimed (hectares)
1978–9	168	1992–3	452
1979–80	580	1993–4	–
1980–1	378	1994–5	544
1981–2	345	1995–6	400
1982–3	134	1996–7	401
1984–4	197	1997–8	202
1984–5	79	1998–9	391
1985–6	263	1999–00	189
1986–7	275	2000–1	81
1987–8	86	2001–2	248
1988–9	416	2002–3	88
1989–90	709	2003–4	132
1990–1	401	2004–5	121
1991–2	752	2005–6	281

Note: (a) Data not available for 1993–4.
Source: WDA annual reports, various editions.

result of one or two large sites being completed in a particular year, but between 1978–9 and 2005–6, more than 8,300 hectares were reclaimed across hundreds of sites.

The varied nature and scale of derelict land was reflected in the types of projects carried out. In north Wales, large areas of slate tips were cleared, while mine workings related to lead, silver and copper were also reclaimed. Figures 8.2 and 8.3 show the results of a typical clearance scheme at a site leaching lead waste into rivers.[27]

Figure 8.2: Parc Mine, Llanrwst, before reclamation

Source: WDA.

Figure 8.3: Parc Mine, Llanrwst, after reclamation, 1978

Source: WDA.

In south-west Wales, former military installations such as ammunition depots and airfields were cleared, while some of the most dramatic transformations took place in the south Wales valleys. Projects included the removal of a 120m high spoil tip at Bargoed,[28] as well as the clearance of a 73-hectare site at Blaina, incorporating a former colliery, brickworks and tinworks. Much of the waste removed from sites was used for construction or road building, with, for example, coal waste spoil used to stabilise an extension to the Treforest Industrial Estate in 1982.[29]

The scale of reclamation was such that the WDA declared in 1992 that it could 'see the beginning of the end of dereliction in Wales and particularly in the Valleys'.[30] As a result, the reclamation of large sites gave way to urban regeneration where reclamation was combined with the provision of housing, retail, infrastructure and leisure facilities. According to the agency, urban regeneration went 'beyond environment and urban face-lifts to the very heart of the Welsh economy. It is about modernisation of towns, once the blight of dereliction has been removed'.[31] Urban joint ventures launched in the 1990s included those in the Cynon valley, Merthyr Tydfil, Rhyl and Holyhead. In Holyhead, the agency worked with local authorities to develop 'an action programme of industrial and retail development, tourism, road and drainage infrastructure'.[32] By 1991–2, thirty joint ventures existed and the agency's expenditure on urban regeneration more than doubled from £11.2 million in 1991–2 to £25.8 million in 1993–4.[33] By 1996 the agency claimed that its £120 million of urban schemes had levered in private sector investment of £200 million, creating or safeguarding 5,000 jobs.[34] Urban regeneration, such as initiatives in the Gwynedd Slate Valleys and an Urban Village at Llandarcy continued as an important element of agency activity until 2006.

Overall, the WDA's land reclamation activities changed the face of much of Wales for the better, with few sites being recognisable as former industrial locations. Improvements were dramatic, especially once sites had been transformed into parkland or afforested areas, and many schemes had a positive impact on the quality of life experienced by local residents. However, economic impact was more nuanced. Many reclaimed sites were in isolated areas with limited economic activity. Also, many sloped steeply and were unsuitable for development, meaning that less than 20 per cent of land reclaimed up to 1993 was developed. The WDA's urban programmes improved many townscapes left shabby by relative economic decline, although regeneration by itself was never a panacea for deep-seated economic issues.

Importantly, the agency's activities across both land reclamation and urban regeneration led to a gradual, if unquantifiable, attitudinal change in the views of those outside the country of Wales's qualities as an investment location and tourist destination. While Nicholas Edwards, Secretary of State for Wales, could in 1985 rail against an 'extraordinary gulf of perception' leading investors to 'dismiss any venture in Wales, on the general assumption that [it] is a bad place . . . there is nothing to be seen but decaying coal mines, run-down steelworks and slagheaps',[35] by 2006 dramatic examples of dereliction barely existed.

FOREIGN DIRECT INVESTMENT

As well as constructing property to be occupied by commercial investors, the WDA marketed Wales to such investors, the attraction of which had long been a priority in Wales.[36] In the late 1970s the agency worked with and part-funded the Development Corporation for Wales, a small semi-state marketing organisation active since 1957. In 1983 the corporation merged with the WDA to form the agency's WINvest (Wales investment location) division. It ran overseas offices in North America, continental Europe and the far east from which agency representatives marketed Wales to potential investors. Two trends were apparent within the agency's foreign direct investment (FDI) activity. The first was its focus on manufacturing, which the WDA was well placed to attract given that companies were looking for locations with the attributes offered by Wales: access to European markets; low-cost labour; ready availability of sites and factories; good road and rail communications; and grants. The other trend was that while service sector activities such as software or financial services were important in terms of job creation, attracting these was difficult, in part due to poor perceptions of the skills base in Wales, subsumed in investors' broader impressions of economic backwardness.

The volume of investors seeking access to European markets combined with the effectiveness of agency operations to enable the capture of between 12 per cent and 18 per cent of all UK FDI projects in the mid to late 1980s.[37] Secretaries of State for Wales intervened enthusiastically

Figure 8.4: Foreign direct investment in Wales, 1984–5 to 2005–6 (a)

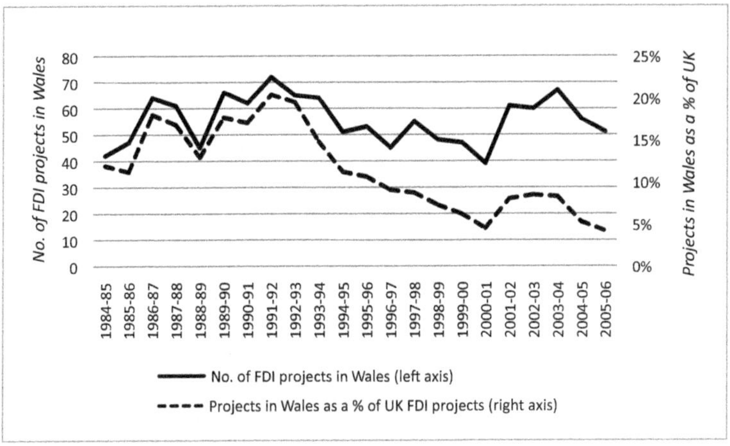

Note: (a) Data prior to 1984–5 not available.
Source: UK Trade and Investment.

to ensure that local authorities and trade unions worked with the WDA to offer a united service to potential investors, an approach known as 'Team Wales'. By the start of the 1990s Wales was capturing up to 20 per cent of all UK FDI projects (see Figure 8.4) including globally significant companies such as Sony, Aiwa, Toyota, Brother and Sharp. Confidence was such that by 1993 the agency was discussing how an 'appropriate target for the years ahead' could be that Wales would become 'the leading region within the European Community for inward investment'.[38]

However, success was short-lived. Wales dropped from attracting 14.8 per cent of UK projects in 1993–4 to 7 per cent in 1998–9, while its regional ranking dropped from first in 1990–1 to sixth in 1996–7. Manufacturing investors were increasingly likely to choose low-tax locations in Ireland or low-wage locations in eastern Europe, both of which also offered tariff-free access to European markets. As well as this, FDI projects attracted to the UK were becoming increasingly concentrated within service sector activity, but Wales was struggling to attract such investment. When choosing locations, service sector investors emphasised skilled labour of a volume and type often not available in areas previously dominated by heavy industry or in sparsely populated rural districts. While locations such as Cardiff were able to attract this type of investment, other areas struggled. As a result, 73 per cent of FDI projects in Wales were in manufacturing in 1998, compared to 49 per cent throughout the UK.

Ironically, at the same time as manufacturing FDI was declining, it reached its symbolic peak with the 1996 announcement of the Lucky Goldstar (LG) project in Newport. LG was a South Korean electronics conglomerate that planned to construct a semiconductor plant and a consumer electronics factory, forecast to create more than 6,000 jobs.[39] It was hailed as a crowning achievement and was awarded a large package of financial support, but the semiconductor plant failed to open and the consumer electronics plant had closed by 2006 when remaining production was transferred to Poland.[40] The high-profile failure of LG acted to discredit FDI as a solution for problems facing the Welsh economy with, for example, First Minister Rhodri Morgan describing the failure as a 'classic example of [the WDA] putting too many eggs in one basket'.[41]

Contemporary political criticism of FDI's impact focused on four issues. First, the degree to which such investment was sufficient to fill the jobs gap created by deindustrialisation was queried, given the small totals of jobs created when compared to the number of unemployed. While FDI created or safeguarded an annual average of 7,363 jobs between 1984–5 and 1994–5, average annual unemployment stood at 127,918 people.[42] Secondly, the specialisation of many factories in assembly-type activities meant that higher skilled and better-paid jobs, such as research and development, were often absent. Thirdly, many of the new jobs were part-time posts geared towards females, meaning that those who had lost their jobs in the male-dominated coal and steel industries were not necessarily being re-employed. Finally, data quoted as evidence of success referred to announcements of estimated future employment, as per central government guidelines. No data exist as to the numbers of people actually employed by announced projects.

Despite such criticism, the investment attracted by the WDA was highly beneficial to Wales and factories operated by well-established multinationals did bring large-scale benefits, both in terms of local employment and supply chain impact. Crucially, foreign firms in Wales tended to be larger, more productive and higher paying than domestic firms.[43] The position of Wales as a leading FDI location was a significant achievement, something that was in no small part due to the effectiveness of the WDA, though the agency did overprioritise manufacturing FDI and was too slow to respond to its decline. This in part reflected difficulty in attracting service sector investment, with workforce skills often biased towards resource-based or manufacturing activity.

INDUSTRIAL INVESTMENT

The provision of loan and equity finance to companies was a priority throughout the UK in the 1970s, as evidenced by central government's establishment of a National Enterprise Board in 1975. The WDA was tasked with providing such support in Wales and it aimed to fill what had long been considered to be a gap: the perceived reluctance of banks and other finance providers to lend to viable businesses. The agency was granted powers to invest in companies, including those within areas covered by the Development Board for Rural Wales, and saw its role as supporting 'smaller and medium sized enterprises, particularly in high risk situations'.[44] By 1978–9 the WDA's investment portfolio comprised £7.6 million across eighty companies.[45] Investments were almost always in traditional manufacturing operations, with the largest being a £2 million transaction with P. Leiner and Sons, a gelatine manufacturer in Treforest.[46]

However, while identifying investment opportunities overlooked by the private sector was simple in theory, it was far more difficult in practice. The WDA expected its overall portfolio to be profitable and in 1978 the Welsh Office instructed that the agency should achieve a specified rate of return on its investment capital.[47] Aspirations soon collided with reality and overall losses were recorded instead. Leiner's collapse in 1980 caused further difficulties, especially given that the agency's commercial director at the time of the decision to invest subsequently joined the company as a director.[48] The agency's reputation was tarnished, with the Welsh Office subsequently insisting on signing off all investments over £1 million and resources were redirected to factory construction. As a result, WDA investments dropped from £8.6 million in 1978–9 to £0.9 million in 1980–1.[49]

The mid-1980s did see an upturn in investment levels, in part due to the agency's chief executive, David Waterstone. He felt that there was insufficient private sector capital to support business, often due to the City of London perceiving Wales as backward.[50]

By mid-1985 the agency was portraying itself as a 'leading source of venture capital' and was striving to attract investment from London-based venture capital funds. It supported 300 companies between 1981–2 and 1984–5, providing finance totalling some £24 million.[51] Other companies were also assisted to pitch ideas to commercial funders, with sixty-seven being helped to obtain funding in 1981–2.[52] High levels of investment were maintained and, by 1991, the agency had an investment portfolio of £31.5 million across 1,021 companies.[53] The focus remained on manufacturing, although investment in the service sector did grow from just 5.1 per cent of investments in 1980–1 to 16.2 per cent in 1986–7 and 23.9 per cent in 1992–3.[54]

Despite optimism, difficulties continued. In 1981 the Welsh Office set targets of achieving a return at least equivalent to the cost of central government borrowing over a rolling five-year period. However, the WDA failed to meet this target between 1983–4 and 1989–90. Rates of return were negative between 1983–4 and 1988–9, while nineteen businesses in receipt of investment failed in 1984–5, incurring losses to the agency of £1.76 million.[55] By 1986–7 the target was downgraded to breaking even but even this proved impossible. The difficulty of identifying viable projects was symbolised by the agency's Cardiff Consortium project, which aimed to market funds from a variety of commercial providers. After its 1986 launch, 844 enquiries for information were received and 144 proposals were submitted. Of these, only 10 per cent were judged as having potential, but none obtained funding and the agency noted that their quality was 'too low'.[56]

At the end of the 1980s the agency took a 'new, more commercially orientated approach to investing' rather than 'operating as the lender of last resort',[57] accepting that it was 'difficult, if not impossible' to invest in start-up or early-stage businesses and 'make a positive return'. Its investments reduced in scale and the agency made an overall profit 'for the first time ever' in 1989–90.[58] Despite this partial change in fortunes, difficulties continued and activity began to decrease in the early 1990s. The agency finally withdrew from investment activity in 1994–5, spurred by the difficulties of identifying successful investments, as well as John Redwood's ideologically driven desire to scale back all forms of state intervention.

However, devolution led to a policy reversal and a new body, Finance Wales, was established in 2001 as an agency subsidiary. Finance Wales's chief executive described its role as bridging the 'sometimes narrow' gap between what new and small firms need to start or to expand and what was currently available from conventional funding sources.[59] It also provided management support, particularly that which enabled business to grow, while managing a Wales spin-out fund designed to support companies emerging from academia.[60] By 2005–6 Finance Wales had invested some £26 million in over ninety companies and although it was recording successes with individual investments, limited data availability meant that the extent to which it was succeeding in its overall mission was unclear.

While the WDA's investments did increase commercial activity, they were financially unsuccessful in overall terms. If neither commercial providers nor the WDA could find enough viable projects, it is likely that they did not exist in any volume. Also, the failure of investments such as Leiner highlighted the difficulties faced by the agency. It acted as a lender of last resort, making losses to the public purse inevitable but these were politically unacceptable by the 1980s, during an era of downward pressure on public expenditure. Despite this, the volume of activity meant that some investments did effectively support successful businesses, although the extent of this cannot be quantified. Crucially, the WDA saw its investments as not only supporting businesses but also building confidence, and so it was prepared to absorb losses to increase 'levels of commercial spirit' and employment.[61]

BUSINESS SUPPORT

The provision of advisory services to businesses, eventually to become the WDA's primary focus, had modest beginnings. In the late 1970s advisors from its small business advisory unit visited companies and provided advice across advertising, exporting and financial support. In 1978–9 the unit expanded, taking over central government's counselling service and annually providing 2,000 business counselling sessions and visiting more than 5,000 small business by 1981–2 (see Table 8.2). Activities included the identification of contracting opportunities offered by public sector bodies.[62]

Table 8.2: WDA business support, 1977–8 to 1989–90

Year	Advisory visits	Business counselling sessions (a)
1977–8	2,750	–
1978–9	2,981	–
1979–80	3,910	485
1980–1	4,605	736
1981–2	5,250	2,006
1982–3	5,142	3,170
1983–4	4,890	3,661
1984–5	6,024	5,395
1985–6	7,091	6,689
1986–7	7,746	7,698
1987–8	9,765	8,365
1988–9	11,994	8,831
1989–90	13,327	10,042

Note: (a) Activity did not commence until 1979–80.
Source: WDA annual reports, 1977–8 to 1989–90.

The WDA's business support activities grew throughout the 1980s as the dangers of overdependence on manufacturing and extractive industries became apparent. Encouraging indigenous businesses was seen as way of offsetting this over-dependence, and the agency encouraged unemployed people to start their own businesses. The agency also educated those about to enter the workforce as to the benefits of running their own business, with activities including a young initiative programme presented to 315 groups in 1988–9. Finally, the WDA wanted to create greater numbers of high-technology businesses, launching its Wales investment and technology (WINtech) division in 1984. WINtech encouraged businesses to profit from new technology, stimulated links between industry and academia and promoted the growth of high-technology companies.[63] Activities included a product development service to connect investors with companies in need of funding and the creation of higher education research centres. However, WINtech struggled to achieve measurable impact and a 1986 review noted its inability to 'stamp its presence firmly on the Welsh scene'.[64]

Business support intensified further in the 1990s, with the agency's chief executive arguing in 1990 that while inward investment was 'welcome . . . the engine of recovery in Wales in fact lies in the resurgence and diversification of the small and medium business sector'.[65] By 1991–2 the business development unit had merged with WINtech to form the business support division, the agency's largest division. Increased resources led to expansion in the volume and nature of activities, now characterised by a complex, project-driven approach. By the early 1990s support was provided across: European issues; technology; supplier development; and skills development. Within European issues, projects included centres providing information on tendering opportunities, grant programmes and European legislation. Technology activities included the 'Competitive Strategy Review' project, which aimed to assist companies to access advanced production technologies. Supplier development programmes included Source Wales, which identified supply opportunities within overseas-owned plants that could be serviced by Welsh-based companies. By 1993–4 some £80 million of supply opportunities had been identified, while ten supply company associations had been formed to spread best practice.[66] Skills development programmes included management training and a range of other conferences and courses.

While the WDA had previously tended to concentrate on industrial areas, a Rural Prosperity Programme was launched in 1991–2 to broaden the agency's foci of activity. Projects included the creation of local development agencies in areas such as south Pembrokeshire, while a Welsh food promotions company was established as an agency subsidiary in 1992. The remainder of the 1990s saw growth across the scale and complexity of business support. Much of this was attributable to the increasing volume of European funding with, for example, Wales receiving £146.5 million in 1993.[67] This encouraged complexity, given that such funding was delivered through hundreds of projects loosely grouped into thematic programmes used by the European Commission to prioritise business support. Attempts were made to knit these strands together, most notably in 1996 by a regional technology plan that drew on responses from 600 organisations to 'develop a consensus . . . on a strategy to improve the innovation and technology performance of the Welsh economy'.[68] The WDA incorporated the plan's contents into its programmes, although the mechanisms by which this took place and their effectiveness are unclear.

The early years of the twenty-first century saw further increases in business support. Attempts to move towards a more knowledge-based economy were common, including 'Know-How' Wales, an initiative that sought to commercialise research by introducing businesses to academic partners. By 2003–4 the agency was claiming to have facilitated some 770 collaborations between industry and academia.[69] Advisory services were also overhauled, with the WDA being tasked in 2003 to introduce and manage the Business Eye service, which was responding to some 25,000 enquiries per year by 2005–6.[70] A greater focus on entrepreneurship was also apparent, most notably through the delivery of activities under the entrepreneurship action plan.

Between 1976 and 2006 business support moved from being a relatively marginal priority to the agency's central activity. Despite this, Garel Rhys, a WDA board member in the 1990s, stated that 'we never found the silver bullet, we never even found a bronze bullet to engage the SMEs in what was happening or to really increase the numbers'.[71] Overall, the intangible nature of some agency activities such as providing advice and information to companies means that measuring their impact is difficult – problems mirrored across the UK.

ASSESSING IMPACT

Assessing the impact of historic activities within economic development is challenging. While it is often assumed that official data enable such activities and their impacts to be quantified and evaluated, this is often not the case. Problems arise due to the lack of comparable and reliable data sets necessary for such assessments, and the difficulty of retrospectively reassembling such data sets. In theory, four methodologies are available to measure impact. These are: contemporary evaluations; agency output data; economic convergence or divergence; and informal assessment based in part on contemporary opinion. This section examines the availability and reliability of data on the agency's performance and outlines how the lack of such data largely precludes the use of the first three methodologies. It then uses the fourth method, informal assessment, based in part on contemporary opinion, to provide an assessment of the WDA's impact.

The first methodology (contemporary evaluations) would summarise agency studies that fully assessed the economic and employment impact of its activities.[72] However, the bulk of agency activity was not subjected to such analysis, which was not adopted widely by the UK's public sector until after 2000. Some evaluations were commissioned in the mid-1990s of activities such as urban regeneration but used varying methodologies and are not generally present in the archives. All suffered from what the WDA referred to as a 'paucity of monitoring and output information',[73] reflecting poor management. The lack of evaluations was noted in 1991 by central government's National Audit Office, which reported that the programmes carried out by agencies including the WDA 'had resulted in substantial numbers of new jobs being created' but that the agencies stated that they 'cannot assess the extent to which these initiatives have influenced . . . the labour market'. This inability to evaluate impact was caused by the Welsh economy being 'subject to many influences outside their responsibility'. The National Audit Office concluded that it was 'therefore very difficult to evaluate the full success of these initiatives'.[74]

The second approach focuses on data published by the WDA. From 1990–1 it published figures for the number of jobs claimed as being created or safeguarded by its activities, while data on inward investment, private capital investment and business secured for Welsh companies are available from the mid-1990s. At first glance, data on jobs created or safeguarded are impressive, especially during the early years of the twenty-first century, with a remarkable 52,900 jobs being recorded in 2003–4 (see Figure 8.5).

Despite these data, there is no guarantee that these outcomes either took place, or if they did, that they were a direct result of WDA activity. At the same time, the passage of time and the complexity and scale of the agency's activities precludes any realistic retrospective allocation. Also, some jobs were double-counted by different agency departments. For example, the WDA may have reclaimed a site and built a factory, before attracting an overseas investor. Different departments undertook these activities, each of which could count jobs created. These management problems were later summarised by Brian Morgan, the agency's chief economist in the 1990s, in the following words: 'the monitoring of jobs was so haphazard . . . property was counting jobs, inward investment was counting jobs, so jobs created and safeguarded, were just almost meaningless numbers by the mid-90s'.[75]

Figure 8.5: Jobs claimed as created or safeguarded by WDA activities, 1990–1 to 2005–6

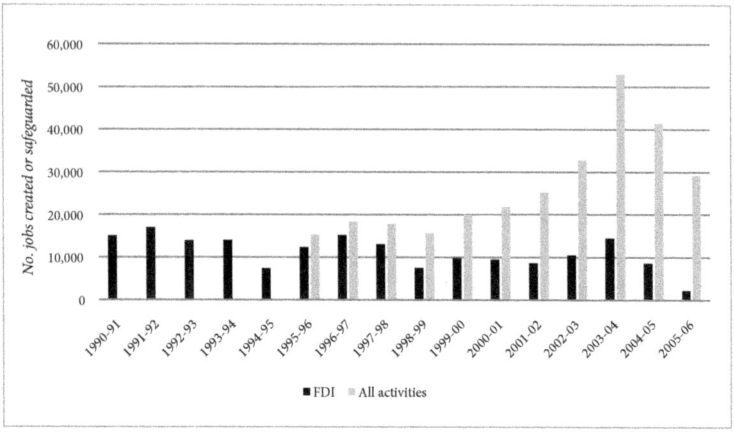

Source: WDA annual reports, 1990–1 to 2005–6.

The third approach, that of convergence or divergence, proposes that if interventions were successful, then the economic indicators for Wales would gradually converge with those of the UK. This approach was often used by politicians as it offered simplicity and the ability to choose data to suit different agendas, with the WDA's chief executive stating in 1990 that 'almost anything can be proved with statistics, often by using the very simple device of changing the start date of a series'.[76] As a result, different measures can be used to draw contrasting conclusions. A positive argument for some years could be based on measures such as FDI and manufacturing productivity, while a negative case could focus on how unemployment was usually higher than the UK average, while economic output per head remained relatively low. A second disadvantage is additionality. If performance is converging, this may be due to reasons aside from intervention such as a favourable resource endowment or an existing concentration in growth sectors. Conversely, if a region is diverging, it can be argued that such trends would have been worse without intervention.

The difficulties of applying the first three methodologies imply that the complexities of evaluation are such that an accurate quantification of the WDA's economic impact is impossible. As a result, this chapter uses the final methodology of informal assessment based in part on contemporary opinion. A starting point is the retrospective views of senior opposition politicians on the WDA's performance before political devolution in 1999. Importantly, the opposition status of these politicians meant that they had no vested interests in praising the WDA. As an example, Rhodri Morgan, Labour MP for Cardiff West from 1987, frontbench spokesman for Wales in the early 1990s and the Welsh Government's First Minister between 2000 and 2009, strongly criticised the WDA's management throughout the 1990s and in 2004 took the decision to disband the agency.

Despite their opposition status, three senior politicians were able to point to some successes, although their assessments were balanced by criticism. Ron Davies, Labour MP for Caerphilly from 1983 and Shadow Secretary of State in the 1990s, surmised that 'we would be in a worse state had we not had these [interventions]. But at the same time [as attracting FDI] we should have been saying either, how can we grow our own industry, our own indigenous industry?' Rhodri Morgan argued that 'I thought it [the WDA in the 1980s] was very effective in a short-term sense. You want branch factories to act as a patch to staunch the rise in unemployment . . . but a vision of where Wales would be in fifteen or twenty or twenty-five years . . . it wasn't there'. Finally, Dafydd Wigley, Plaid Cymru MP for Caernarfon from 1974 and party president (1980–4, 1991–2000), suggested that 'the successes must be in terms of the bringing in overseas investment [but] perhaps not enough was done to attack the needs of industry and commerce, and . . . the element of entrepreneurship'.[77]

As for informally assessing activity by type, factory construction helped to attract large volumes of manufacturing, with much activity being additional given that the private sector was often unwilling to construct factories. However, manufacturing investment was decreasing by the 1990s and insufficient attention was paid to the role of property in stimulating service sector investment. Land reclamation was hugely successful, not just in terms of improving the environment, but also in changing the public face of much of Wales as an investment location and tourist destination, while urban regeneration had a positive impact on many townscapes. Such activity would not have taken place without the WDA's financial support, although direct economic impact was limited. Inward investment was also successful as

Wales needed large numbers of jobs quickly and FDI presented an obvious opportunity. Despite successes, FDI was never going to be attracted in sufficient volume to entirely offset deindustrialisation. At the same time, much of Wales's success as an investment location was due to a short-lived combination of circumstances, although the WDA expertly exploited these.

However, other interventions were less successful. Industrial investment met with mixed results. The agency struggled to identify profitable opportunities, although this reflects a relative lack of such opportunities rather than failings on the agency's part. Finally, assessing the impact of the business support activities is virtually impossible, given the lack of contemporary evaluations and the difficulty of measuring the impact of intangible activities such as advisory services given to thousands of individual companies. It is likely that such services assisted some companies to grow but these impacts cannot be quantified.

In conclusion, the WDA successfully created some positive economic impacts. It was effective within manufacturing but struggled to achieve impact within the service sector. Overall, it is probable that if the agency had not intervened, the Welsh economy would have been in a significantly worse state. The agency was effective over its first two decades,[78] as it could respond to market demand and focus on tangible outputs. As a result, the WDA often played an important role in securing some economic modernisation.[79] However, once the focus of intervention shifted to services by necessity, the agency found it difficult to achieve measurable impact. While some of this difficulty was attributable to how Wales had always struggled to develop a more services-based economy, the agency could have made greater efforts to adapt its activities earlier and develop a stronger approach to long-term planning. As well as this, governance problems in the early 1990s also impacted on the agency's reputation and subsequent effectiveness.

Despite these difficulties, it is important not to be overly critical. Many service sector activities were more responsive to interventions in areas such as skills and technological infrastructure than was the case for manufacturing, but the agency had little influence in such areas. At the same time, public sector organisations throughout the UK and elsewhere struggled with how greater levels of indigenous business could be created. The agency's effectiveness dissipated as economic change continued throughout the 1990s and beyond, while the dramatic increases in funding after 1999 created a bloated organisation lacking in focus. This ultimately contributed to political disappointment and the dissolution of the agency in April 2006 as the over-ambitious economic aims of the Welsh Government proved difficult to deliver.

NOTES

1 'Central government' in this chapter refers to the UK-wide government based in London.

2 See the previous chapter in this volume, Leon Gooberman and Ben Curtis, 'The Age of Factories: The Rise and Fall of Manufacturing in South Wales, 1945–1985'.

3 L. J. Williams (ed.), *Digest of Welsh Historical Statistics, 1974–1996* (Cardiff: Welsh Office, 1998), p. 138.

4 The Welsh Office was an administratively devolved department of central government responsible for some aspects of government activity in Wales between 1964 and 1999. Based in Cardiff and headed by a cabinet level Secretary of State for Wales, its initial responsibilities were modest but gradually expanded over time.

5 Welsh Development Agency Act 1975. Section 1(3): *http://www.legislation.gov.uk/ukpga/1975/70/pdfs/ukpga_19750070_en.pdf* (accessed 12 May 2016).

6 Interview with Lord Morris, Labour MP for Aberavon (1951–2001), Secretary of State for Wales (1974–9), 21 March 2012.

7 *WDA Financial Report and Accounts 2003–04*, p. 27.

8 The Welsh Government is the politically devolved government of Wales, formed from members of the democratically elected National Assembly for Wales. It was established in 1999 and inherited the Welsh Office's responsibilities. During the early years of devolution, there was no separation between the executive, the legislature and the civil service, all of whom were known as the National Assembly for Wales. The term 'Welsh Assembly Government' was introduced in 2002 to cover the executive and the civil service, before being subsequently shortened to 'Welsh Government' from 2007.

9 *WDA Annual Report, 1979–80*, p. 1; *WDA Annual Report, 1987–88*, p. 4; *WDA Accounts, 1998–99*, p. 8.

10 For analysis of the political economy of economic development, see L. Gooberman, 'Welsh Office exceptionalism, economic development and devolution, 1979 to 1997', *Contemporary British History*, 30/4 (2016), 563–83.

11 House of Commons Public Accounts Committee, *Welsh Development Agency Accounts 1991–92* (London: HMSO, 1993).

12 For contemporary assessments of the agency, see K. Morgan and D. Henderson, 'The Fallible Servant: Evaluating the Welsh Development Agency', in H. Thomas and R. Macdonald (eds), *Nationality and Planning in Scotland and Wales* (Cardiff: University of Wales Press, 1997), pp. 77–98; K. Morgan, 'The regional animateur: taking stock of the Welsh Development Agency', *Regional & Federal Studies*, 7/2 (1997), 70–94. Studies of individual activities over time include: M. Munday, 'Foreign Direct Investment in Wales: Lifeline or Leash?', in J. Bryan and C. Jones (eds), *Wales in the 21st Century* (Basingstoke: Macmillan, 2000), pp. 37–54; M. Munday, *Japanese Manufacturing Investment in Wales* (Cardiff: University of Wales Press, 1990); L. Gooberman, 'Moving mountains: derelict land reclamation in post-war Wales', *Welsh History Review*, 27/3 (2015), 521–58. For economic development in general, see L. Gooberman, *From Depression to Devolution: Economy and Government in Wales, 1936–2006* (Cardiff: University of Wales Press, 2017).

13 G. Percival, *The Government's Industrial Estates in Wales 1936–1975* (Treforest: Welsh Development Agency, 1978), pp. 1–2.

14 *WDA–The First Five Years* (Pontypridd: WDA, 1981), p. 6.

15 Interview with Gwyn Griffiths: WDA Executive Director, Land Reclamation (1980s–1990s), 10 November 2011.

16 Williams (ed.), *Digest of Welsh Historical Statistics, 1974–1996*, p. 99.

17 Gooberman, 'Welsh Office exceptionalism', 569.

18 The National Archives (hereafter TNA), WA 8/79, *WDA Board Papers*, 21 September 1982.

19 WDA, *Wales Ahead–the Newspaper of the WDA, No. 30*, October 1984, p. 2.

20 TNA, WA 8/166, WDA Board Papers, May 1990.

21 Interview with Dr Jim Driscoll: Advisor to Nicholas Edwards, Under-Secretary at Welsh Office Industry Department (1982–5), 1 March 2012.

22 *WDA Annual Report, 1997–98*, p. 46.

23 DTZ, *Evaluation of the Technium Programme* (Cardiff: DTZ, 2008).

24 Welsh Office, *The Derelict Land Survey of Wales 1971–72* (Cardiff: Welsh Office, 1975), p. 5.

25 *WDA Annual Report, 1984–85*, p. 7; TNA, WA 8/13, *WDA Board Papers*, December 1976.

26 TNA, WA 8/101, *WDA Board Papers*, 16 July 1984.

27 G. Griffiths and S. Smith, 'Risk Assessment and Management Strategies', in R. E. Hester and R. M. Harrison (eds), *Contaminated Land and its Reclamation* (Cambridge: Royal Society of Chemistry), pp. 103–20 (p. 107).

28 *WDA Annual Report, 1994–95*, p. 18.

29 *WDA Annual Report, 1981–82*, p. 26.

30 *WDA Annual Report, 1991–92*, p. 22.

31 *WDA Annual Report, 1991–92*, p. 22.

32 *WDA Annual Report, 1990–91*, p. 26.

33 *WDA Accounts, 1992–93*, p. 4; *WDA Accounts 1994–95*, p. 6.
34 WDA, *20: 1976–1996 – 20 years of working for Wales* (Treforest: Welsh Development Agency, 1996), inside front cover.
35 National Library of Wales, Crickhowell Papers 2/9. *Speech by Nicholas Edwards to Cardiff Business Club* (March 1985).
36 See the previous chapter in this volume: Gooberman and Curtis, 'The Age of Factories'.
37 UK Trade and Investment, *FDI Project Announcements Database.*
38 I. Rooks, 'Prospects and Policies', *Welsh Economic Review*, 6/2 (1993), 46–7 (47).
39 Wales Audit Office, *Protecting Public Money in the LG Projects* (Cardiff: Wales Audit Office, 2007).
40 L. Gooberman, 'Business failure during an age of globalisation: interpreting the rise and fall of the LG project in South Wales, 1995–2006', *Business History*. Published online 26 January 2018: *https://doi.org/10.1080/00076791.2018.1426748* (accessed 9 August 2018).
41 *BBC News*, 'Doomed LG Plant-Inquiry Call', 23 May 2003: *http://news.bbc.co.uk/1/hi/wales/2930852.stm* (accessed 9 August 2017).
42 Office for National Statistics (claimant count); UK Trade and Investment.
43 Munday, 'Foreign Direct Investment in Wales', p. 40.
44 *WDA Annual Report, 1976–77*, p. 9.
45 Welsh Office, *Welsh Economic Trends* (hereafter *WET*), no. 6, 1979, p. 57.
46 TNA, WA 8/50, *WDA Board Papers*, February 1980.
47 TNA, WA 8/33, *WDA Board Papers*, September 1978.
48 TNA, WA 8/40, *WDA Board Papers*, 23 April 1979.
49 *WDA–The First Five Years*, p. 14.
50 Interview with David Waterstone: chief executive (1983–1990), 6 January 2012.
51 Hansard, HC, 17 June 1985, vol. 81, *c.*11.
52 *WDA Annual Report, 1981–82*, p. 18.
53 *WET, 13*, 1992, p. 89.
54 *WET, 8, 1982–83*, p. 59; *WET, 11, 1987*, p. 82; *WET, 14, 1993*, p. 85.
55 *WDA Annual Report*, 1984–85, p. 15.
56 TNA, WA 8/126, *WDA Board Papers*, 17 November 1986.
57 *WDA Annual Report, 1988–89*, p. 12.
58 TNA, WA 8/166, *WDA Board Papers*, May 1990; TNA, WA 8/189, *WDA Board Papers*, 27 May 1991.
59 *WDA Annual Report, 1999–2000*, p. 12.
60 G. Jones, *The Third Mission* (Cardiff: Institute of Welsh Affairs, 2002), p. 25.
61 Interview with David Waterstone, 6 January 2012.
62 *Wales Ahead, No. 14*, October 1980, p. 1.
63 TNA, WA 8/126, *WDA Board Papers*, 17 November 1986.
64 *1986 Review* (Cardiff: Welsh Office, 1987), p. 76.

65 D. Waterstone, 'The Incomer's View', in D. Cole (ed.), *The New Wales* (Cardiff: University of Wales Press, 1990), pp. 233–40 (p. 239).
66 *WDA Annual Report, 1993–94*, p. 9.
67 *WET No. 16, 1995*, p. 83.
68 *Wales Regional Technology Plan* (Treforest: Welsh Development Agency, 1996).
69 *WDA Annual Report, 2003–04*, p. 6.
70 *WDA Annual Report, 2005–06*, p. 14.
71 Interview with Garel Rhys: WDA board member (1994–8), 5 November 2012.
72 For example, an evaluation of an industrial estate's construction would establish the amount of financial support granted towards construction, the aims in terms of floor space and jobs creation, and any gaps between aims and outputs. A survey would identify whether each company occupying space on the finished estate would have created jobs had the agency not intervened (additionality) and whether employment had been at the expense of locations elsewhere (displacement). Data would then be collated to estimate the additional direct impact of intervention, with indirect impacts calculated through multipliers derived from economic modelling.
73 TNA, WA 96/239, *WDA Board Papers*, 2 October 1996.
74 National Audit Office, *Creating and Safeguarding Jobs in Wales* (London: National Audit Office, 1991), p. 4.
75 Interview with Brian Morgan, WDA chief economist (1991–7), 1 December 2011.
76 Waterstone, 'The Incomer's View', p. 238.
77 Interviews with: Rhodri Morgan: industrial development officer, South Glamorgan County Council (1974–80), head of the European Community's office in Wales (1980–7), then MP for Cardiff West (1987–2001), Frontbench Spokesman on Welsh Affairs (1992–7), subsequently First Minister (2001–9), 13 December 2011; Ron Davies: Labour MP for Caerphilly (1983–2001), Secretary of State for Wales (1997–9), Labour AM for Caerphilly (1999–2003), 7 March 2011; Dafydd Wigley: Plaid Cymru MP for Caernarfon (1974–2001), Plaid Cymru president (1980–94, 1991–2000), 11 August 2012.
78 As argued in Morgan, 'The regional animateur', 90.
79 Morgan and Henderson, 'The Fallible Servant', pp. 77–98.

BIBLIOGRAPHY

The following is a list of the published academic works cited. For primary sources, see individual chapter endnotes.

BOOKS AND BOOK CHAPTERS

Abel-Smith, B., A *History of the Nursing Profession* (London: Heinemann Educational Books Ltd, 1970).

Abrams, L., *Oral History Theory* (Abingdon: Routledge, 2010).

Abromeit, H., *British Steel: An Industry between the State and the Private Sector* (Berg: Leamington Spa, 1986).

Andrews, P. W. S., and E. Brunner, *Capital Development in Steel: A Study of the United Steel Companies Ltd* (Oxford: Blackwell, 1951).

Ashton, T. S., *Iron and Steel in the Industrial Revolution* (Manchester: Manchester University Press, 1924).

Atkinson, M., and C. Baber, *The Growth and Decline of the South Wales Iron Industry, 1720–1880: An Industrial History* (Cardiff: University of Wales Press, 1987).

Aylen, J., and R. Ranieri (eds), *Ribbon of Fire: How Europe Adopted and Developed US Strip Mill Technology (1920–2000)* (Pendragon: Fondazione Ranieri di Sorbello, 2012).

Baber, C., and J. Dessant, 'Modern Glamorgan: Economic Development after 1945', in G. Williams and A. H. John (eds), *Glamorgan County History. Volume V: Industrial Glamorgan* (Cardiff: Glamorgan County History Trust, 1980), pp. 581–658.

Baber, C., and L. J. Williams (eds), *Modern South Wales: Essays in Economic History* (Cardiff: University of Wales Press, 1986).

Balchin, P., *Regional Policy in Britain: The North-South Divide* (London: Chapman, 1987).

Bartrip, P. W. J., and S. Burman, *The Wounded Soldiers of Industry: Industrial Compensation Policy, 1833–1897* (Oxford: Oxford University Press, 1983).

Beetham, M., 'Domestic Servants as Poachers of Print: Reading, Authority and Resistance in Late Victorian Britain', in L. Delap et al., *The Politics of Domestic Authority in Britain since 1800* (London: Palgrave Macmillan, 2009), pp. 185–203.

Berg, T., and P. Berg (eds), *R. R. Angerstein's Illustrated Travel Diary, 1753-1755: Industry in England and Wales from a Swedish Perspective* (London: Science Museum, 2001).

Berger, S., A. Croll, and N. LaPorte (eds), T*owards a Comparative History of Coalfield Societies* (Aldershot: Ashgate, 2005).

Blanchard, I., *Russia's 'Age of Silver': Precious Metal Production and Economic Growth in the Eighteenth Century* (London: Routledge, 1989).

Bolitho, H., *Alfred Mond, First Lord Melchett* (London: Martin Secker, 1933).

Bornat, J., 'Reminiscence and Oral History: Parallel Universes or Shared Endeavour?', in R. Perks and A. Thomson (eds), *The Oral History Reader*, 2nd edn (Abingdon: Routledge, 2006), pp. 219–41.

Boston, S., *Women Workers and the Trade Unions* (London: Lawrence and Wishart, 2015).

Bowen, H. V., (ed.), *Wales and the British Overseas Empire: Interactions and Influences, 1650–1830* (Manchester: Manchester University Press, 2011).

Bowen, P., *Social Control in Industrial Organisations, Industrial Relations and Industrial Sociology: A Strategic and Occupational Study of British Steelmaking* (London: Routledge & Kegan Paul, 1976).

Boyns, T., and C. Baber, 'The Supply of Labour', in G. Williams and A. H. John (eds), *Glamorgan County History. Volume V: Industrial Glamorgan from 1700 to 1970* (Cardiff: Glamorgan County History Trust, 1980), pp. 311–62.

Brandes, S. D., *American Welfare Capitalism, 1880–1940* (Chicago: University of Chicago Press, 1976).

Braybon, G., *Women Workers in the First World War* (London: Routledge, 1989).

Bromley, R., and G. Humphrys (eds), *Dealing with Dereliction: The Redevelopment of the Lower Swansea Valley* (Swansea: University College Swansea, 1979).

Bryant, K. M., *The Health of a Nation: The History and Background of the National Health Service with Thoughts on its Future* (Farncombe: Kenneth M. Bryant, 1998).

Burn, D. L., *The Steel Industry, 1939–1959: A Study in Competition and Planning* (Cambridge: Cambridge University Press, 1961).

Burt, R., et al., *Mining in Cornwall and Devon: Mines and Men* (Exeter: University of Exeter Press, 2014).

Campbell, G. L., *Miners' Insurance Funds: Their Origin and Extent* (London: Waterlow & Sons, 1880).

Carr, E. H., *What is History?* (Harmondsworth: Penguin, 1964).

Carr, J. C., and W. Taplin, *History of the British Steel Industry* (Oxford: Blackwell, 1962).

Cartwright, W. F., *Modern American Steelworks Practice* (Cardiff: South Wales Institute of Engineers, 1946).

——, *The Design of Iron and Steel Works* (Cardiff: South Wales Institute of Engineers, 1950).

——, 'Preliminary Planning of Margam and Abbey Works', in *A Technical Survey of Abbey, Margam, Trostre and Newport Plants of the Steel Company of Wales* (London: Industrial Newspapers, 1952), pp. 9–12.

Church, R. A., *The History of the British Coal Industry, Vol. 3: 1830–1913 Victorian Pre-eminence* (Oxford: Clarendon Press, 1986).

Clegg, H. A., A. Fox and A. F. Thomson, *A History of British Trade Unions since 1889, Volume 1: 1889–1910* (Oxford: Clarendon Press, 1964).

Cole, D., (ed.), *The New Wales* (Cardiff: University of Wales Press, 1990).

Cole, W. A., 'Economic history as a social science', inaugural lecture, University College of Swansea, 24 October 1967.

Coleman, D. C., *Courtaulds, An Economic and Social History: Vol. III – Crisis and Change, 1940–1965* (Oxford: Clarendon Press, 1980).

Cook, C., *The Routledge Companion to Britain in the Nineteenth Century, 1815–1914* (Abingdon: Routledge, 2005).

Cooke, P., 'Inter-regional Class Relations and the Redevelopment Process', *Papers in Planning Research* (Cardiff: University of Wales Institute of Science and Technology, 1981).

Cooper, J., and C. R. Elrington, 'Modern Colchester: Economic Development', *A History of the County of Essex: Volume 9: The Borough of Colchester* (London: Victoria County History, 1994).

Cowman, D., *The Making and Breaking of a Mining Community: The Copper Coast, County Waterford 1825–1875* (Dublin: Mining History Trust of Ireland, 2006).

Craig, R., 'The Ports and Shipping', in G. Williams and A. H. John (eds), *Glamorgan County History. Volume V: Industrial Glamorgan* (Cardiff: Glamorgan County History Trust, 1980), pp. 465–518.

Craig, R. S., R. Protheroe Jones and M. V. Symons, *The Industrial and Maritime History of Llanelli and Burry Port 1750–2000* (Carmarthen: Carmarthenshire County Council, 2002).

Curtis, B., *The South Wales Miners, 1964–1985* (Cardiff: University of Wales Press, 2013).

Davidoff, L., and C. Hall, *Family Fortunes: Men and Women of the English Middle-Class 1780–1850* (London: Hutchinson Education, 1987).

Davies, G., and I. Thomas, *Overseas Investment in Wales: The Welcome Invasion* (Swansea: C. Davies, 1976).

Davies, M., 'Balanced costs: inland copper smelting location and fuel in South Australia 1848–76: were they so naive?', University of Western Australia, Department of Economics, working paper 05-25 (2005).

Dawes, F. V., *Not in Front of the Servants: A True Portrait of Upstairs, Downstairs Life* (London: Century in Association with the National Trust, 1973).

Deane, P., and W. A. Cole, *British Economic Growth, 1688–1959: Trends and Structure* (Cambridge: Cambridge University Press, 1962).

Delap, L., *Knowing their Place: Domestic Servants in Twentieth-Century Britain* (Oxford: Oxford University Press, 2011).

Dodd, A. H., *The Industrial Revolution in North Wales* (Cardiff: University of Wales Press Board, 1933).

Ebery, M., and Preston, B., *Geographical Papers: Domestic Service in Late Victorian and Edwardian England, 1871–1914* (Reading: University of Reading, 1976).

Edwards, N., *The Industrial Revolution in South Wales* (London: Labour Publishing Company, 1924).

Egan, D., Pobl, *Protest a Gwleidyddiaeth: Mudiadau Poblogaidd yng Nghymru'r Bedwaredd Ganrif ar Bymtheg* (Llandysul: Gomer, 1988).

Elliott, A., *History of British Nylon Spinners* (Abertillery: Old Bakehouse Publications, 2010).

Elliott, J., 'The Iron and Steel Industry', in C. Williams and S. R. Williams (eds), *The Gwent County History, Volume IV: Industrial Monmouthshire, 1780–1914* (Cardiff: University of Wales Press, 2011), pp. 73–86.

——, and C. Deneen, 'Iron, Steel and Aluminium', in C. Williams and A. Croll (eds), *Gwent County History, Volume V: The Twentieth Century* (Cardiff: University of Wales Press, 2013), pp. 59–74.

England, J., *The Wales TUC: Devolution and Industrial Politics* (Cardiff: University of Wales Press, 2004).

Evans, D. G., *A History of Wales 1815–1906* (Cardiff: University of Wales Press, 1989).

Evans, E. W., *The Miners of South Wales* (Cardiff: University of Wales Press, 1961).

Evans, N., 'Two Paths to Economic Development: Wales and the North-east of England', in P. Hudson (ed.), *Regions and Industries: A Perspective on the Industrial Revolution in Britain* (Cambridge: Cambridge University Press, 1989), pp. 201–27.

Fevre, R., *Wales is Closed: The Quiet Privatisation of British Steel* (Nottingham: Spokesman, 1989).

Fitzgerald, R., *British Labour Management and Industrial Welfare 1846–1939* (London: Croom Helm, 1988).

Flanders, J., *The Victorian House* (London: Harper Perennial, 2004).

Francis, H., *History on our Side: Wales and the 1984–85 Miners' Strike* (London: Lawrence and Wishart, 2015).

——, and D. Smith, *The Fed: A History of the South Wales Miners in the Twentieth Century* (London: Lawrence and Wishart, 1980).

——, and S. F. Williams, *Do Miners Read Dickens? Origins and Progress of the South Wales Miners Library, 1973–2013* (Cardigan: Parthian, 2013).

Franko, L. G., *The European Multinationals. A Renewed Challenge to American and British Big Business* (London: Harper and Row, 1976).

Gale, W. K. V., *The British Iron and Steel Industry: A Technical History* (Newton Abbot: David and Charles, 1967).

Geary, D., 'The Myth of the Radical Miner', in S. Berger, A. Croll and N. Laporte (eds), *Towards a Comparative History of Coalfield Societies* (Aldershot: Ashgate, 2005), pp. 43–64.

George, K. D., and L. Mainwaring (eds), *The Welsh Economy* (Cardiff: University of Wales Press, 1988).

Gibson, F. A., *A Compilation of Statistics (Technological, Commercial, and General) of the Coal Mining Industry of the United Kingdom, the Various Coalfields Thereof, and the Principal Foreign Countries of the World* (Cardiff: Western Mail Ltd, 1922).

Gilbert, D., 'Strikes in Postwar Britain', in C. Wrigley (ed.), *A History of British Industrial Relations, 1939–1979* (Cheltenham: Edward Elgar, 1996).

Gildart, K., (ed.), *Coal in Victorian Britain, Part II: Coal in Victorian Society, Volume 6, Industrial Relations and Trade Unionism* (London: Pickering & Chatto, 2012).

Gillingham, J., *Coal, Steel, and the Rebirth of Europe, 1945–1955. The Germans and French from Ruhr Conflict to Economic Community* (Cambridge: Cambridge University Press, 1991).

Goldman, L., 'The First Students in the Workers' Educational Association: Individual Enlightenment and Collective Advance', in S. K. Roberts (ed.), *A Ministry of Enthusiasm: Centenary Essays on the Workers' Educational Association* (London: Pluto Press, 2003), pp. 41–58.

Goldthorpe, J. H., D. Lockwood, F. Bechhofer and J. Platt, *The Affluent Worker in the Class Structure* (Cambridge: Cambridge University Press, 1969).

Gooberman, L., *From Depression to Devolution: Economy and Government in Wales, 1934–2006* (Cardiff: University of Wales Press, 2017).

Goodman, J., *The Mond Legacy: A Family Saga* (London: Weidenfeld and Nicolson, 1982).

Griffiths, G., and S. Smith, 'Risk Assessment and Management Strategies', in R. E. Hester and R. M. Harrison (eds), *Contaminated*

Land and its Reclamation (Cambridge: Royal Society of Chemistry, 1997), pp. 103–24.

Griffiths, R., *The Entrepreneurial Society of the Rhondda Valleys, 1840–1920: Power and Influence in the Porth-Pontypridd Region* (Cardiff: University of Wales Press, 2010).

Griffiths, R. A., 'William Rees and the Modern Study of Medieval Wales', in R. A. Griffiths and P. R. Schofield (eds), *Wales and the Welsh in the Middle Ages* (Cardiff: University of Wales Press, 2011), pp. 203–20.

Guillén, M. P., *Models of Management: Work, Authority and Organization in a Comparative Perspective* (Chicago: University of Chicago Press, 1994).

Hamilton, H., *The British Brass and Copper Industry to 1800* (London: Longmans,1926).

Harris, J. R., *The Copper King: A Biography of Thomas Williams of Llanidan* (Liverpool: Liverpool University Press, 1964).

Harte, N., 'The Economic History Society, 1926–2001', *http://www.history.ac.uk/makinghistory/resources/articles/EHS.html* (accessed 13 August 2018).

Heaton, H., *The Yorkshire Woollen and Worsted Industries: From the Earliest Times up to the Industrial Revolution* (Oxford: Oxford University Press, 1920).

Hernández, J. L. N., 'The Foreign Policy Administration of Franco's Spain. From Isolation to International Realignment (1945–1957)', in C. Leitz and D. J. Dunthorn (eds), *Spain in an International Context, 1936–1959* (Oxford: Berghahn, 1999), pp. 277–98.

Higgs, M., *Tracing your Servant Ancestors: A Guide for Family Historians* (Barnsley: Pen and Sword Books Ltd, 2012).

Hilton, K. J., *The Lower Swansea Valley Project* (London: Longmans, 1967).

Hirzel, T., and N. Kim (eds), *Metals, Monies, and Markets in Early Modern Societies: East Asian and Global Perspectives* (Berlin: LIT Verlag, 2008).

Hobsbawm, E., *The Age of Revolution: Europe, 1789–1848* (London: Abacus, 1977).

Hoggart, R., *The Uses of Literacy: Aspects of Working-Class Life with Special Reference to Publications and Entertainments* (Harmondsworth: Penguin Books Ltd, 1958).

Horn, P., *The Rise and Fall of the Victorian Servant* (Dublin: Gill and Macmillan Ltd, 1975).
——, *Life Below Stairs in the 20th Century* (London: Sutton Publishing Ltd, 2001).
——, *Pleasures and Pastimes in Victorian Britain* (Stroud: Amberley Publishing, 2011).
Hudson, P., 'Economic History in Britain. The "First Industrial Nation"', in F. Boldizzoni and P. Hudson (eds), *Routledge Handbook of Global Economic History* (Routledge: New York, 2016), pp. 17–34.
Hughes, S., Copperopolis: *Landscapes of the Early Industrial Period in Swansea* (Aberystwyth: Royal Commission on the Ancient and Historical Monuments of Wales, 2000).
Humphreys, G., *Industrial Britain – South Wales* (Newton Abbott: David and Charles, 1973).
Hyde, C. K., *Copper for America: The United States Copper Industry from Colonial Times to the 1990s* (Tucson: University of Arizona Press, 1998).
Jenkins, P., *A History of Modern Wales, 1536–1990* (London: Longman, 1992).
Jenkins, G. H., *A Concise History of Wales* (Cambridge: Cambridge University Press, 2007).
John, A. H., *The Industrial Development of South Wales, 1750–1850: An Essay* (1st edn, Cardiff: University of Wales Press, 1950; 2nd edn, Cardiff: University of Wales Press, 1995).
John, A. V., *The Actors' Crucible: Port Talbot and the Making of Burton, Hopkins, Sheen and all the Others* (Cardigan: Parthian, 2015).
——, (ed.), *Our Mother's Land: Chapters in Welsh Women's History* (Cardiff: University of Wales Press, 1991).
Johnes, M., *Wales Since 1939* (Manchester: Manchester University Press, 2012).
Jones, D., 'Counting the Cost of Coal: Women's Lives in the Rhondda, 1881–1911', in A. V. John (ed.), *Our Mother's Land: Chapters in Welsh Women's History, 1830–1839* (Cardiff: University of Wales Press, 1991), pp. 109–33.
Jones, D. J. V., *Before Rebecca: Popular Protests in Wales, 1793–1835* (London: Allen Lane, 1973).
——, *The Last Rising: The Newport Insurrection of 1839* (Oxford: Clarendon, 1985).

Jones, E., *A History of GKN Volume 1: Innovation and Enterprise, 1759–1918* (Basingstoke: Macmillan, 1987).
Jones, E. D., 'Rees, Sir James Frederick (1883–1967), Principal of the University College at Cardiff', *Dictionary of Welsh Biography*, *http://yba.llgc.org.uk/en/s2-REES-FRE-1883.html* (accessed 2 August 2018).
Jones, E. J., *Some Contributions to the Economic History of Wales* (London: P. S. King and Son Ltd, 1928).
Jones, G., *The Third Mission* (Cardiff: Institute of Welsh Affairs, 2002).
Jones, I. G., *Communities: Essays in the Social History of Victorian Wales* (Llandysul: Gomer Press, 1987).
Jones, O., *The Early Days of Sirhowy and Tredegar* (Newport: Starling Press, 1972).
Jones, R. M., *The North Wales Quarrymen, 1874–1922* (Cardiff: University of Wales Press, 1981).
Lanning, G., with M. Mueller, *Africa Undermined: Mining Companies and the Underdevelopment of Africa* (Harmondsworth: Penguin, 1979).
Lethbridge, L., *Servants: A Downstairs View of Twentieth-Century Britain* (London: Bloomsbury, 2013).
Lewis, E. D., *The Rhondda Valleys: A Study in Industrial Development, 1800 to the Present Day* (London: Phoenix House, 1959).
Le Play, F., *Description des procédés métallurgiques employés dans le Pays de Galles pour la fabrication du cuivre* (Paris: Carilian-Goeury et Von Dalmont, 1848).
Lieven, M., *Senghennydd: Universal Pit Village, 1890–1930* (Llandysul: Gomer, 1994).
Lodwick, J., and V. Lodwick, *The Story of Carmarthen* (Carmarthen: St. Peter's Press, 1995).
Lyons, J. S., L. P. Cain and S. H. Williamson (eds), *Reflections on the Cliometrics Revolution: Conversations with Economic Historians* (Oxford: Routledge, 2008).
McBride, T., *The Domestic Revolution: The Modernisation of Household Service in England and France 1820–1920* (London: Croom Helm Ltd, 1976).
McCusker, J. J., 'The Business of Distilling in the Old World and the New World during the Seventeenth and Eighteenth Centuries:

the Rise of a New Enterprise and its Connection with Colonial America', in J. J. McCusker and K. Morgan (eds), *The Early Modern Atlantic Economy* (Cambridge: Cambridge University Press, 2000), pp. 186–224.

McKibbin, R., *The Ideologies of Class: Social Relations in Britain 1880–1950* (Oxford: Oxford University Press, 1994).

McMillan, J., *The Dunlop Story* (London: Wiedenfield and Nicholson, 1989).

Mantoux, P., *The Industrial Revolution in the Eighteenth Century: An Outline of the Beginnings of the Modern Factory System in England* (New York: Harcourt, Brace & Co., 1928).

Marshall, K., *The World Bank: From Reconstruction to Development to Equity* (Oxford and New York: Routledge, 2008).

Martello, R., *Midnight Ride, Industrial Dawn, Paul Revere and the Growth of Industrial Enterprise* (Baltimore: Johns Hopkins University Press, 2010).

Martin, A., and J. P. Lewis, *Welsh Economic Statistics: A Handbook of Sources* (Cardiff: University College of South Wales and Monmouthshire, 1953).

Minchinton, W. E., (ed.), *Industrial South Wales, 1750–1914. Essays in Welsh Economic History* (London: Frank Cass, 1969).

Miskell, L. (ed.), *The Origins of an Industrial Region: Robert Morris and the First Swansea Copper Works* (Newport: South Wales Record Society, 2010).

Mitchell, B. R., *Economic Development of the British Coal Industry 1800-1914* (Cambridge: Cambridge University Press, 1984).

——, and P. Deane, *Abstract of British Historical Statistics* (Cambridge: Cambridge University Press, 1962).

——, and H. G. Jones, *Second Abstract of British Historical Statistics* (Cambridge: Cambridge University Press, 1971).

Melling, J., 'Employers, Industrial Welfare, and the Struggle for Work-place Control in British Industry, 1880–1920', in H. F. Gospel and C. R. Littler (eds), *Managerial Strategies and Industrial Relations: An Historical and Comparative Study* (London: Heinemann Educational, 1983), pp. 55–81.

——, 'Employers, Workplace Culture and Workers' Politics: British Industry and Workers' Welfare Programmes, 1870–1920', in J. Melling and J. Barry (eds), *Culture in History: Production,*

Consumption and Values in Historical Perspective (Exeter: University of Exeter Press, 1992), pp. 109–36.

Mond, A., *Industry and Politics* (London: MacMillan & Co., 1927).

Morgan, K., and D. Henderson, 'The Fallible Servant: Evaluating the Welsh Development Agency', in H. Thomas and R. Macdonald (eds), *Nationality and Planning in Scotland and Wales* (Cardiff: University of Wales Press, 1997), pp. 77–97.

Morgan, K. O., 'Consensus and Conflict in Welsh History', in D. W. Howell and K. O. Morgan (eds), *Crime, Protest and Police in Modern British Society* (Cardiff: University of Wales Press, 1999), pp. 16–41.

——, *Wales in British Politics 1868–1922* (Cardiff: University of Wales Press, 1963).

——, *Rebirth of a Nation: Wales 1880–1980* (Oxford: Oxford University Press; Cardiff: University of Wales Press, 1981).

——, *Modern Wales: Politics, Places and People* (Cardiff: University of Wales Press, 1995).

——, *Michael Foot: A Life* (London: Harper Press, 2007).

Morris J. H., and L. J. Williams, T*he South Wales Coal Industry, 1841–1875* (Cardiff: University of Wales Press, 1958).

Munday, M., *Japanese Manufacturing Investment in Wales* (Cardiff: University of Wales Press, 1990).

——, 'Foreign Direct Investment in Wales: Lifeline or Leash?', in J. Bryan and C. Jones (eds), *Wales in the 21st Century* (Basingstoke: Macmillan, 2000), pp. 37–54.

Musson, J., *Up and Down Stairs: The History of the Country House Servant* (London: John Murray, 2009).

Nevin, E. T., *The Social Accounts of the Welsh Economy* (Aberystwyth: University of Wales Press, 1957).

Payne, P. L., *Colvilles and the Scottish Steel Industry* (Oxford: Clarendon, 1979).

Paz, D. G., 'Tremenheere, Hugh Seymour (1804–1893)', *Oxford Dictionary of National Biography* (Oxford: Oxford University Press, 2004; online edn, January 2008), *http://www.oxforddnb.com/view/article/27695* (accessed 5 November 2012).

Percival, G., *The Government's Industrial Estates in Wales 1936–1975* (Treforest: Welsh Development Agency, 1978).

Percy, J., Metallurgy: *The Art of Extracting Metals from their Ores, and Adapting them to Various Purposes of Manufacture* (London: John Murray, 1861).

Perry, V., *Built for a Better Future: The Brynmawr Rubber Factory* (Oxford: White Cockade Publishing, 1995).

Peters, E. D., *The Practice of Copper Smelting* (New York and London: McGraw-Hill Book Co., 1911).

Phillips, E., *A History of the Pioneers of the Welsh Coalfield* (Cardiff: Western Mail, 1925).

Randall, H. J., *Bridgend: The Story of a Market Town* (Newport: R. H. Johns Ltd, 1955).

Ranieri, R., 'Steel and the State in Italy and the UK. The Public Sector of the Steel Industry in Comparative Perspective', in W. Feldenkirchen and T. Gourvish (eds), *European Yearbook of Business History*, 2 (Ashgate: Society for European Business History, 1999), pp. 125–54.

——, and J. Aylen, 'Technological Trajectories. The Wide Strip Mill for Steel in Europe (1920 to the Present)', in C. Barthel, I. Kharaba and P. Mioche (eds), *The Transformation of the World Steel Industry from the XXth Century to the Present* (Brussels: Peter Lang, 2014), pp. 363–80.

Reader, W. J., *Imperial Chemical Industries. Volume Two: The First Quarter-Century 1926–1952* (Oxford: Oxford University Press, 1975).

Rees, W., *Industry before the Industrial Revolution, Volume 1* (Cardiff: University of Wales Press, 1968).

Roberts, R. O., 'The Smelting of Non-ferrous Metals since 1750', in G. Williams and A. H. John (eds), *Glamorgan County History. Volume V: Industrial Glamorgan from 1700 to 1970* (Cardiff: Glamorgan County History Trust, 1980), pp. 47–95.

Rosser, C., and C. C. Harris, *The Family and Social Change: A Study of Family and Kinship in a South Wales Town* (London: Routledge and Kegan Paul, 1965).

Sambrook, P., *Keeping their Place: Domestic Service in the Country House 1700–1920* (Stroud: Sutton Publishing, 2005).

Scadden, R., *No Job for a Little Girl: Voices from Domestic Service* (Llandysul: Gomer Press, 2013).

Schmitz, C. J., *World Non-Ferrous Metal Production and Prices, 1700–1976* (London: Frank Cass, 1979).

Shaw, R., and P. Simpson, 'Synthetic Fibres', in Peter Johnson (ed.), *The Structure of British Industry* (London: Unwin Hyman, 1988), pp. 119–39.

Shute, J., Henry Ayers: *The Man who Became a Rock* (London: I. B. Tauris, 2010).

Smith, E. O., *Productivity Bargaining: A Case Study in the Steel Industry* (London: Pan Books Ltd, 1971).

Smith, M. S., *The Emergence of Modern Business Enterprise in France, 1800-1930* (Cambridge, MA: Harvard University Press, 2006).

Snowden Piggot, A., *The Chemistry and Metallurgy of Copper, Including a Description of the Principal Copper Mines of the United States and other Countries* (Philadelphia: Lindsay & Blakiston, 1858).

Spurrell, W., *A Guide to Carmarthen and its Neighbourhood* (Carmarthen: W. Spurrell, 1882).

Sturney, A. C., *The Story of Mond Nickel* (Plaistow: Curwen Press, 1951).

Taylor, R., 'The Rise and Disintegration of the Working-classes', in P. Addison and H. Jones (eds), *A Companion to Contemporary Britain, 1939–2000* (London: Blackwell, 2007), pp. 371–88.

Thomas, B., (ed.), *The Welsh Economy: Studies in Expansion* (Cardiff: University of Wales Press, 1962).

Thomas, D., and D. Jones, *Welsh Economy and Society Post-1945: A Database of Statistical and Documentary Material* (Cardiff: University of Wales Press, 1996).

Thomas, D. A., 'War and the Economy: The South Wales Experience', in C. Baber and L. J. Williams (eds), *Modern South Wales: Essays in Economic History* (Cardiff: University of Wales Press, 1986), pp. 251–77.

Todd, S., *The People: The Rise and Fall of the Working Class, 1910–2010* (John Murray: London, 2014).

Tolliday, S., 'Steel and Rationalization Policies, 1918–1950', in B. Elbaum and W. Lazonick (eds), *The Decline of the British Economy* (Oxford: Oxford University Press, 1986), pp. 82–108.

Tone, A., *The Business of Benevolence: Industrial Paternalism in Progressive America* (London: Cornell University Press, 1997).

Turner, D. M. and D. Blackie, *Disability in the Industrial Revolution: Physical Impairment in British Coalmining, 1780–1880* (Manchester: Manchester University Press, 2018).

——, et al., 'Disability and industrial society 1780–1948: a comparative cultural history of British coalfields: statistical compendium' (data set), Zenodo: *http://doi.org/10.5281/zenodo.183686* (accessed 30 August 2018).

Turner E. S., *What the Butler Saw: Two Hundred and Fifty Years of the Servant Problem* (London: Penguin Publishers, 2001).

Vincent, J. E., *John Nixon: Pioneer of the Steam Coal Trade in South Wales – A Memoir* (London: John Murray, 1900).

Vivian, H. Hussey, *Notes of a Tour in America* (London: Edward Stanton, 1878).

Wadsworth, A. P., and J. de Lacy Mann, T*he Cotton Trade and Industrial Lancashire, 1600–1780* (Manchester: Manchester University Press, 1931).

Walters, R. H., *The Economic and Business History of the South Wales Steam Coal Industry* (New York: Arno Press, 1977).

Waterstone, D., 'The Incomer's View', in D. Cole (ed.), *The New Wales* (Cardiff: University of Wales Press, 1990), pp. 233–40.

Watson, R., *Rhondda Coal, Cardiff Gold – The Insoles of Llandaff: Coal Owners and Shippers* (Cardiff: Merton Priory Press, 1997).

Webb, S., and B. Webb, *Industrial Democracy* (London: Longmans & Co., 1920 edn).

Williams, A., *A Detested Occupation? A History of Domestic Servants in North Wales 1800–1930* (Llanrwst: Gwasg Carreg Gwalch, 2016).

Williams, C., *Capitalism, Community and Conflict: The South Wales Coalfield, 1898–1947* (Cardiff: University of Wales Press, 1998).

——, and S. R. Williams (eds), *Gwent County History Volume IV: Industrial Monmouthshire, 1780–1914* (Cardiff: University of Wales Press, 2011).

——, and A. Croll (eds), *Gwent County History Volume V: The Twentieth Century* (Cardiff: University of Wales Press, 2013).

Williams, D., *A History of Modern Wales* (London: John Murray, 1950).

——, *John Frost: A Study in Chartism* (Cardiff: University of Wales Press, 1939).

——, *The Rebecca Riots: A Study in Agrarian Discontent* (Cardiff: University of Wales Press, 1955).

Williams, G., and A. H. John (eds), *Glamorgan County History. Volume V: Industrial Glamorgan* (Cardiff: Glamorgan County History Trust, 1980).

Williams, G. A., *Merthyr Politics: The Making of a Working-class Tradition* (Cardiff: University of Wales Press, 1966).
——, *Artisans and Sans-culottes: Popular Movements in France and Britain during the French Revolution* (London: Edward Arnold, 1968).
——, *The Merthyr Rising* (London: Croom Helm, 1978).
——, *When Was Wales? A History of the Welsh* (Harmondsworth: Penguin, 1985).
Williams, L. J., 'The Coalowners', in D. Smith (ed.), *A People and a Proletariat: Essays in the History of Wales 1780–1980* (London: Pluto Press, 1980), pp. 94–113.
——, *Digest of Welsh Historical Statistics*, vols 1 and 2 (Cardiff: Welsh Office, 1985).
——, *Digest of Welsh Historical Statistics, 1974–1996* (Cardiff: Welsh Office, 1998).
——, *Was Wales Industrialised? Essays in Modern Welsh History* (Llandysul: Gomer, 1995).
Williams, M. A., *A Forgotten Army: Female Munitions Workers of South Wales, 1939–1945* (Cardiff: University of Wales Press, 2002).
Williams, R. A., *The Berehaven Mines* (Kenmare: A. B. O'Connor, 1993).
Wilson, J. R., *Memorializing History: Public Sculpture in Industrial South Wales* (Aberystwyth: Centre for Advanced Welsh and Celtic Studies, 1996).
Winstanley, M. J., *The Shopkeeper's World 1830–1914* (Manchester: Manchester University Press, 1983).
Wrigley, E. A., *Continuity, Chance and Change: The Character of the Industrial Revolution in England* (Cambridge: Cambridge University Press, 1990).
Young, M. D., and P. Willmott, *Family and Kinship in East London* (London: Routledge and Kegan Paul, 1957).
Zahedieh, N., 'Technique or demand? The revival of the English copper industry ca 1680–1730', in P. R. Rössner (ed.), *Cities-Coins-Commerce: Essays presented to Ian Blanchard on the Occasion of his Seventieth Birthday* (Stuttgart: Franz Steiner Verlag, 2012), pp. 167–73.
Zeitlin, J., and G. Herrigel (eds), *Americanization and its Limits. Reworking US Technology and Management in Post-War Europe and Japan* (Oxford: Oxford University Press, 2000).
Zweig, F., *The British Worker* (Harmondsworth: Penguin, 1952).

JOURNAL ARTICLES

Asteris, M. 'The rise and decline of south Wales coal exports, 1870–1930', *Welsh History Review*, 13/1 (1986), 24-43.

Bennoune, M., 'Mauretania: formation of a neo-colonial society', *Middle East Research and Information Project Report*, 54 (February 1977), 3–13.

Benson, J., 'Coalminers, coalowners and collaboration: the miners' permanent relief fund movement in England, 1860–1895', *Labour History Review*, 68/2 (2003), 181–94.

Bonté P., and B. Benson, 'Multinational companies and national development: Miferma and Mauretania', *Review of African Political Economy*, 2 (January–April 1975), 89–109.

Boyns, T., 'The Welsh economy – historical myth or modern reality?', *Llafur*, 9/2 (2005), 84–94.

——, and S. Gray, 'Welsh coal and the informal empire in South America, 1850–1913', *Atlantic Studies: Literary, Cultural and Historical Perspectives*, 13/1 (2016), 53–77.

Burge, A., 'Exorcising demonologies: coal companies and colliery communities in south Wales', *Llafur*, 9/4 (2007), 101–9.

Coleman, D. C., et al., 'What is economic history?', *History Today*, 35/2 (February 1985), 35–43.

Couche, M., 'Sur l'emploi de la houille maigre du Pays de Galles dans les machines locomotives', *Annales des Mines*, 5th series, XV (1859), 575-82.

Croll, A., 'People's remembrancers in a post-modern age: contemplating the non-crisis of Welsh labour history', *Llafur*, 8/1 (2000), 5–17.

Crouzet, F., 'British coal in France in the nineteenth century', in F. Crouzet, *Britain Ascendant: Comparative Studies in France-British Economic History* (Cambridge: Cambridge University Press, 1990), pp. 414-41.

Daunton, M. J., 'The Dowlais Iron Company in the iron Industry, 1800–1850', *Welsh History Review*, 6/1 (January 1972), 16–45.

Davey, E., and H. Thomas, ' "Chief creator of modern Wales": the neglected legacy of Percy Thomas', *North American Journal of Welsh Studies*, 9 (2014), 54–70.

Davies, J., 'Wales in the nineteen sixties', *Llafur*, 4/4 (1987), 78–88.

Decker, S., 'Corporate legitimacy and advertising: British companies and the rhetoric of development in West Africa, 1950–1970', *Business History Review*, 81/1 (2007), 59–86.

Delap, L., 'Kitchen sink laughter: domestic service humour in twentieth-century Britain', *Journal of British Studies*, 49 (2010), 623–54.

Evans, C., 'Global commerce and industrial organization in an eighteenth-century Welsh enterprise: the Melingriffith Company', *Welsh History Review*, 20/3 (2001), 413–34.

——, 'El Cobre: Cuban ore and the globalization of Swansea copper, 1830–70', *Welsh History Review*, 27/1 (2014), 112–31.

——, and O. Saunders, 'A world of copper: globalizing the industrial revolution, 1830–70', *Journal of Global History*, 10/1 (2015), 3–26.

Evans, N., 'Cardiff's labour tradition', *Llafur*, 4/2 (1985), 77–90.

——, 'Writing the social history of modern Wales: approaches, achievements and problems', *Social History*, 17/3 (1992), 479–92.

Friedelbaum, S. H., 'The British iron and steel industry: 1929–9', The *Journal of Business of the University of Chicago*, 23/1 (1950), 117–32.

Gildart, K., 'Labour Politics', in K. Gildart (ed.), *Coal in Victorian Britain, Part II: Coal in Victorian Society, Volume 6, Industrial Relations and Trade Unionism* (London: Pickering & Chatto, 2012), pp. 385–94.

Godfrey, A., '"We would rather starve idle than starve while working hard": the Swansea copperworkers' strike of 1843', *Llafur*, 11/4 (2015), 5–25.

Gooberman, L., 'Moving mountains: derelict land reclamation in post-war Wales', *Welsh History Review*, 27/3 (2015), 521–58.

——, 'Welsh Office exceptionalism, economic development and devolution, 1979 to 1997', *Contemporary British History*, 30/4 (2016), 563–83.

——, 'Business failure during an age of globalisation: interpreting the rise and fall of the LG project in South Wales, 1995–2006', *Business History*. Published online 26 January 2018: *https://doi.org/10.1080/00076791.2018.1426748* (accessed 9 August 2017).

Gospel, H. F., 'Employers' labour policy: a study of the Mond-Turner talks 1927–33', *Business History*, 21/2 (1979), 180–97.

Hamilton, P., and B. W. Higman, 'Servants of empire: the British training of domestics for Australia, 1926–31', *Social History*, 28 (2003), 67–82.

Harris, J. R., 'Copper and shipping in the eighteenth century', *Economic History Review*, 19/3 (1966), 550–68.

Harrison Church, R. J., 'Problems and development of the dry zone of West Africa', *The Geographical Journal*, 127/2 (1961), 187–99.

Harvey, C., and P. Taylor, 'Mineral wealth and economic development: foreign direct investment in Spain, 1851–1913', *Economic History Review*, 40/2 (1987), 190.

Hobsbawm, E. J., 'The forward march of Labour halted', *Marxism Today*, 22 (September 1978), 279–86.

Hoogvelt, A. M. M., and A. M.Tinker, 'The role of colonial and post-colonial states in imperialism – a case-study of the Sierra Leone Development Company', *The Journal of Modern African Studies*, 16/1 (1976), 67–79.

Howard, S., 'Servants in early modern Wales: co-operation, conflict and survival', *Llafur*, 9/1 (2004), 33–43.

Humphrys, G., 'Mining activity in Labrador Ungava', *Transactions of the Institute of British Geographers*, 29 (1961), 187–99.

James, L., 'War and industry: a study of the industrial relations in the mining regions of south Wales and the Ruhr during the Great War, 1914–1918', *Labour History Review*, 68/2 (2003), 195–215.

Jenkins, B., 'Women's professional employment in Wales during the First World War', *Welsh History Review*, 28/4 (2017), 646–75.

Jenkins, G. H., 'Clio and Wales: Welsh remembrancers and historical writing, 1751–2001', *Transactions of the Honourable Society of Cymmrodorion*, 8 (2001), 119–36.

——, 'Reading history: modern Wales', *History Today*, 37/2 (1987), 49–53.

Johnes, M., ' "For Class and Nation": dominant trends in the historiography of twentieth-century Wales', *History Compass*, 8/11 (2010), 1257–74.

——, 'M4 to Wales – and prosper! The history of a motorway', *Historical Research*, 87/237 (2014), 556–73.

Jones, D. J. V., 'The Scotch Cattle and their black domain', *Welsh History Review*, 5/3 (1971), 220–49.

Jones, R. M., 'Beyond identity? The reconstruction of the Welsh', *Journal of British Studies*, 31 (1992), 330–57.

Jones, W. D., 'Labour migration and cross-cultural encounters: Welsh copper workers in Chile in the nineteenth century', *Welsh History Review*, 27/1 (2014), 132–54.

Kinzley, W. D., Japan in the world of welfare capitalism: imperial railroad experiments with welfare work', *Labor History*, 47/2 (2006), 189–212.

Lewis, A., 'The story of Merthyr General Hospital', *Merthyr Historian*, 4 (1989), 104–30.

Light, J., 'Manufacturing the past – the representation of mining communities in history, literature and heritage: '... Fantasies of a world that never was'?, *Llafur*, 8/1 (2000), 19–31.

McCreary, E. C., 'Social welfare and business: the Krupp welfare program, 1860–1914', *Business History Review*, 42/1 (1968), 24–49.

Matthews, M. D., 'Coal communities: aspects of the economic and social impact of coastal shipping in south-west Wales, *c.*1700–1820', *Maritime Wales*, 25 (2004), 56–71.

Melling, J., 'Industrial strife and business welfare philosophy: the case of the South Metropolitan Gas Company from the 1880s to the war', *Business History*, 11/2 (1979), 163–79.

Miskell, L., 'From Copperopolis to Coquimbo: international knowledge networks in the copper industry of the 1820s', *Welsh History Review*, 27/1 (2014), 92–111.

——, 'Doing it for themselves: the Steel Company of Wales and the study of American industrial productivity, *c.*1945–1955', *Enterprise and Society*, 18/1 (2017), 184–213.

Moore-Colyer, R. J., 'Horse and equine improvement in the economy of modern Wales', *Agricultural History Review*, 39/2 (1991), 122–42.

Morgan, K., 'The regional animateur: taking stock of the Welsh Development Agency', *Regional & Federal Studies*, 7/2 (1997), 70–94.

Muller, C. R., 'Saint-Malo – Saint-Servan: un port charbonnier', *Annales de Géographie*, 31 (1922), 49-456.

Newell, E., ' "Copperopolis": the rise and fall of the copper industry in the Swansea district, 1826–1921', *Business History*, 32/3 (1990), 75–97.

Pollard, S., 'Economic history: a science of society', *Past & Present*, 30 (April 1965), 3–22.

Rees, J. F., and W. Rees, 'A select bibliography of the economic history of Wales', *Economic History Review*, 2/2 (1930), 320–6.
Richardson, F., 'Women farmers of Snowdonia, 1750–1900', *Rural History*, 25/2 (2014), 161–81.
Roberts, R. O., 'The development and decline of copper and other non-ferrous metal industries in south Wales', *Transactions of the Honourable Society of Cymmrodorion* (1956), 78–115.
——, 'Financial crisis and the Swansea "branch bank" of England, 1826', *National Library of Wales Journal*, 11/1 (1959), 76–85.
——, 'Enterprise and capital for non-ferrous metal smelting in Glamorgan, 1694–1924', *Morgannwg*, 23 (1979), 48–82.
——, 'Copper and economic growth in Britain, 1729–84', *National Library of Wales Journal*, 10/1 (1957), 65–74.
Roldán de Montaud, I., 'El ciclo cubano del cobre en el siglo XIX, 1830–1868', *Bolétin Geológico y Minero*, 119/3 (2008), 361–82.
Rooks, I., 'Prospects and Policies', *Welsh Economic Review*, 6/2 (1993), 46–7.
Shone, R. M., 'The sources and nature of statistical information in special fields of statistics: statistics relating to the UK iron and steel industry', *Journal of the Royal Statistical Society*, series A, 113/4 (1950), 464–86.
Stevens, M. F., 'Women brewers in fourteenth-century Ruthin', *Transactions of the Denbighshire Historical Society*, 54 (2005/6), 15–31.
Swindell, K., 'Iron ore mining in West Africa: some recent developments in Guinea, Sierra Leone and Liberia', *Economic Geography*, 43/4 (October 1967), 333–46.
Thomas, B., 'Wales and the Atlantic economy', *Scottish Journal of Political Economy*, VI (November 1959), 169–92.
——, 'A cauldron of rebirth: population and the Welsh language in the nineteenth century', *Welsh History Review*, 13/4 (1987), 418–37.
——, 'The migration of labour into the Glamorganshire coalfield (1861–1911)', *Economica*, 30 (November 1930), 275–94.
Thomas, D. A., 'The growth and direction of our foreign trade in coal during the last half century', *Journal of the Royal Statistical Society*, 66 (1903), 439-533.

Thompson, S., 'To relieve the sufferings of humanity, irrespective of party, politics or creed: conflict, consensus and voluntary hospital provision in Edwardian south Wales', *Social History of Medicine*, 16/2 (2003), 247–62.

——, 'The friendly and welfare provision of British trade unions: a case study of the South Wales Miners' Federation', *Labour History Review*, 77/2 (2012), 189–210.

Valenzuela, L., 'The Chilean copper-smelting industry in the mid-nineteenth century: phases of expansion and stagnation, 1834–1858', *Journal of Latin American Studies*, 24/3 (1992), 507–50.

Vogel, H. Ulrich, 'Chinese central monetary policy, 1644–1800', *Late Imperial China*, 8/2 (1987), 1–52.

Watts, D. G., 'Changes of location of the south Wales iron and steel industry', *Geography*, 53/3 (1968), 294–307.

Williams, C., 'Going underground? The future of coalfield history revisited', *Morgannwg*, 42 (1998), 41–58.

Williams, M. A., 'The new London Welsh: domestic servants 1918–1939', *Transactions of the Honourable Society of Cymmrodorion*, 9 (2003), 135–51.

Zahedieh, N., 'Colonies, copper and the market for inventive activity in England and Wales, 1680–1730', *Economic History Review*, 66/3 (2013), 805–25.

UNPUBLISHED THESES

Howells, C., 'Sales assistants, shops and the development of Cardiff's retail sector, 1850–1920' (unpublished MA thesis, Swansea University, 2010).

——, 'Wales's hidden industry: domestic service in South Wales, 1871–1921' (unpublished PhD thesis, Swansea University, 2014).

Light, J., ' "Of inestimable value to the town and district?" A study of the urban middle classes in south Wales with particular reference to Pontypool, Bridgend and Penarth *c.*1850–1890' (unpublished PhD thesis, Swansea University, 2003).

Lins, H. N., 'Changes in production and employment decline in the south Wales steel industry' (unpublished MSc Econ. thesis, University College Swansea, 1982).

Mannaseh, P., 'Brynmawr experiment 1928–1940: Quaker values and Arts and Crafts principles' (unpublished PhD thesis, University of Plymouth, 2009).

Milburn, A., 'Female employment in nineteenth-century ironworking districts: Merthyr Tydfil and the Shropshire coalfield, 1841–1881' (unpublished PhD thesis, Swansea University, 2013).

Morel du Boil, A., 'The closure of East Moors steelworks: a 1970s of decline and calamity, possibility and calm' (unpublished MA dissertation, Swansea University, 2015).

Morton, J., 'The rise of the modern copper and brass industry in Britain 1690–1750' (unpublished PhD thesis, University of Birmingham, 1985).

Newell, E., 'The British copper ore trade in the nineteenth century, with particular reference to Cornwall and Swansea' (unpublished DPhil thesis, University of Oxford, 1988).

Parry, S., 'History of the steel industry in the Port Talbot area, 1900–1988' (unpublished PhD thesis, University of Leeds, 2011).

Penny, B., 'Class, work and community: Port Talbot's steelworkers, 1951–1988' (unpublished PhD thesis, Swansea University, 2016).

Smith, G. P., 'Social control and industrial relations at the Dowlais Iron Company *c.*1850–1890' (unpublished MSc Econ. thesis, University of Wales, Aberystwyth 1981).

Symons, J. C., 'The mining and smelting of copper in England and Wales 1760–1820' (unpublished MPhil thesis, Coventry University, 2003).

Thomason, G. F., 'An analysis of the effects of industrial change upon selected communities in south Wales' (unpublished PhD thesis, University College of Wales, Cardiff, 1963).

Toomey, R. R., 'Vivian and Sons, 1809–1924: a study of the firm in the copper and related industries' (unpublished PhD thesis, University College Swansea, 1979).

INDEX